Narrative Environments and Experience Design

This book argues that narrative people and place are inseparable and pursues the consequences of this insight through the design of narrative environments.

This is a new and distinct area of practice that weaves together and extends narrative theory, spatial theory and design theory. Examples of narrative spaces, such as exhibitions, brand experiences, urban design and socially engaged participatory interventions in the public realm, are explored to show how space acts as a medium of communication through a synthesis of materials, structures and technologies, and how particular social behaviours are reproduced or critiqued through spatial narratives.

This book will be of interest to scholars in design studies, urban studies, architecture, new materialism and design practitioners in the creative industries.

Tricia Austin is Director of the MA in Narrative Environments at Central Saint Martins, University of the Arts London, UK.

Cover image adapted from a photograph of Making Beauty by Elpida Hadzi-Vasileva at the Djanogly Gallery, Nottingham University 2016. Photo and adaption: Tricia Austin.

Routledge Research in Design Studies

Routledge Research in Design Studies is a new series focusing on the study of design and its effects using analytical and practical methods of inquiry. Proposals for monographs and edited collections on this topic are welcomed.

For more information about this series, please visit: https://www.routledge.com/Routledge-Research-in-Design-Studies/book-series/RRDS

Narrative Environments and Experience Design

Space as a Medium of Communication

Tricia Austin

Routledge
Taylor & Francis Group

NEW YORK AND LONDON

First published 2020
by Routledge
52 Vanderbilt Avenue, New York, NY 10017

and by Routledge
2 Park Square, Milton Park, Abingdon, Oxon, OX14 4RN

Routledge is an imprint of the Taylor & Francis Group, an informa business

© 2020 Taylor & Francis

Library of Congress Cataloging-in-Publication Data
Names: Austin, Tricia, 1954- author.
Title: Narrative environments and experience design: space as a medium of communication/Tricia Austin.
Description: New York, NY: Routledge, 2020. | Includes bibliographical references and index.
Identifiers: LCCN 2019057599 (print) | LCCN 2019057600 (ebook) | ISBN 9780367138042 (hbk) | ISBN 9780367138073 (ebk)
Subjects: LCSH: Communication in architecture. | Space (Architecture)–Psychological aspects.
Classification: LCC NA2584 .A97 2020 (print) | LCC NA2584 (ebook) | DDC 720.1/03–dc23
LC record available at https://lccn.loc.gov/2019057599
LC ebook record available at https://lccn.loc.gov/2019057600

ISBN: 978-0-367-13804-2 (hbk)
ISBN: 978-0-367-13807-3 (ebk)

Typeset in Sabon
by Deanta Global Publishing Services, Chennai, India

To Natalie and Claudie

Contents

Figures

Plates

Acknowledgements

There are many people to whom I am indebted in the writing of this book. I owe a special debt to my present and former colleagues from MA Narrative Environments, in the Spatial Practices Programme at Central Saint Martins, University of the Arts London, who have contributed so much to the development of the design of environments. I am particularly grateful to Tom Butler, Sarah Featherstone, Kevin Flude, Claire Healy, Ingrid Hu, Stuart Jones, Xavier Llarch Font, Joel Lewis, Andrea Lioy, Dr. Jona Piehl and Bethany Shepherd. I am also very grateful to my PhD students who have each pursued an aspect of narrative environments in depth and helped to inform the practice. They are Clare Brown, Dr. Brian Dixon, Dr. Silvia Grimaldi, Valerie Mace, Matt Haycocks, Julia Pitts, Olga Surawska and Ryo Terui. I would also like to thank our MA Narrative Environments graduates for their inspiring interpretation of the practice and particularly those whose remarkable innovations are featured in the book. They are the Decorators, Nele Vos, Chloe Morris, Melissa Mongiat, Kelsey Snook, Julie Howell, Hannes Palsson and Zishu Zhou. I must also mention the inspirational industry figures who have kindly spent time being interviewed, and many of whom have contributed images to the book. They are Mouna Andreos, Andy Bass, Ruedi Baur, Julien de Casabianca, Dosfotos, Tim Gardom, Alison Grey, Usman Haque, Peter Higgins, Mass Design, Noel McCauley, Brendan McGetrick, Robin McNicholas, Dr. Noah Raford, David Rich, Polly Richards, Ronald Rietveld, Adam Scott, Thomas Sevcik, Teil Silverstein, Katherine Skellon, Anna Strongman and Sam Willis. I would also like to thank Central Saint Martins for an award that gave me the time to develop and write the book. Finally, special thanks go to Bethany Shepherd who designed the diagrams and to Allan Parsons who edited the draft text and without whom it would not have been possible to complete the book. I am also very grateful to Katie Armstrong at Routledge for her support in editing the book.

Introduction

This book formalises the research and knowledge that have emerged from the MA in Narrative Environments at Central Saint Martins, University of the Arts London, a postgraduate degree instigated in 2003 at the behest of leading design practitioners in the UK. In the early 2000s, the creative industries were living through a post-millennial boom in the demand for novel visitor experiences to cultural centres, brand experiences and leisure and urban environments. In this diverse, expanding, international market, companies and organisations were seeking open-minded creative practitioners who could transcend their own disciplines and collaborate across architecture, communication design, interaction design, scenography and curation. The MA programme drew these disciplines into a multidisciplinary, team-based practice, challenging individualism, traditional educational specialisation and entrenched professional hierarchies, all of which can stifle momentum in advancing design practice.

In 2003, urban planning, architecture and design were very different kinds of educational programmes, with distinctive vocabularies and methods, discouraging collaboration. Overcoming this lack of collaboration is important because, in practice, it is planners and architects who conventionally take the first step in reinventing our lived environment. In this regime, the functionality of the physical space usually takes precedence over the experience of the space. Content developers, spatial designers, communication designers and interaction designers typically enter the fray only at a later stage, by which time they are often limited by the physical structures that have already been signed off. Problems can then arise. For example, city planners may leave insufficient space for diverse civic life; corporate master planners may prioritise efficiency and maximum return on investment, creating bland, uninviting swathes of city; architects may prioritise aesthetics and impressive feats of engineering above the social dynamics of neighbourhood, producing landmark architecture which may play little role in urban vitality. Cultural institutions may be designed with dramatic, light-filled architectural forms but, when in use, these often require additional complex and costly internal structures to exhibit artefacts, stage performances or hold social gatherings. In short, hierarchical regimes can lead to urban forms and public spaces that are not fit for purpose. Consequently, these spaces may fail in social and economic terms. To address some of the problems arising from such hierarchical processes, MA Narrative Environments has consistently advocated and practised a collaborative, multidisciplinary approach whereby content and design are considered together from the start and the experience of the future inhabitant or visitor is researched, envisaged and incorporated as part of the planning. This strategy has led to a new, expanded, holistic area of practice: the 'design of narrative environments'.

The thesis of MA Narrative Environments is that space and built environment not only embody our culture and traditions, they actively shape our feelings, aspirations and actions. Space speaks to us. We interpret our socio-spatial environments similarly to the way we follow literary stories. In other words, we 'read' space by collating the cues and experiencing events in the environment as we move around it, and we proceed to form the elements we encounter into stories. We use narrative to make sense of the world around us. However, unlike literary stories, we 'read' and interpret worldly spatio-temporal situations with our whole bodies, not just our eyes. The design of narrative environments, therefore, involves a deliberate and coordinated three-part sequence of movement: the progression of *content*, through *space* and over *time*, in order to tell a story and communicate a message or messages to particular audiences. In narrative environments, stories are not just overlain on a space; they are embedded *in* and expressed *through* form and materiality. While architectural structures and materials evoke histories, identities and meanings, in narrative environments they are complemented by environmental graphics, projections, sound design, performance, mobile, social, locative media or augmented reality. The tangible and experiential dimensions of the built environment interact with existing regulatory systems and cultures of inhabitation, forming explicit and implicit communications. In the design of narrative environments such communications are used oftentimes to question the normativity of those systems and cultures.

Narrative environments are very diverse in form and purpose. They are not defined by medium or scale. They can be as large and diverse as a city and as small and cohesive as a single room. Because they are stories, they are capable of great complexity. They can be resolved or open-ended. They can be deliberately created to deceive and manipulate or to inform and empower. The research and explorations pursued through the MA programme have positioned the design of narrative environments as a contributor to critical, cultural, commercial and community practices. Critical narrative environments, such as provocative urban interventions, aim to question the ways in which space is conceived, constructed and lived. They provide commentaries, probe dominant histories and seek ways to enhance the agency of individuals and groups in civil society. Cultural narrative environments, such as museums, heritage sites and historic trails, provoke curiosity and provide information and enable both didactic and experiential learning. Commercial narrative environments, such as brand experiences, hospitality and event design, communicate brand messages in innovative and engaging ways, while also contributing to a positive financial return on investment. Placemaking and city narratives are included in this last category because, although they may offer cultural activities, their underlying goal is to attract inward investment and enhance the prosperity of a city or city quarter. Community-based and civic narrative environments, designed for parks, libraries and public squares, for example, aim to stir the public imagination, address social inequities and empower individuals and groups to take actions that create a more just and cohesive society.

Growing populations and global mobility mean that many cities across the world are densifying while undergoing economic regeneration, challenging them to accommodate a panoply of communities. This is visible in public spaces where separate groups of people simultaneously engage in different activities, such as exercising, socialising, working, celebrating, sleeping, buying and selling goods and so on. Well-designed and well-managed public spaces can accommodate this multiplicity. Densification, the economic forces of regeneration, urban decay and marginalisation may disrupt this coexistence, bringing to the fore contested histories, identities and meanings of spaces. It is in this context that narrative environments can make important contributions to the negotiation of spatial practices, by focusing on the way we discuss, shape, use and, most importantly, share our public spaces, while also developing new understandings of our lived environment as it continues to become ever more complex.

The MA Narrative Environments programme is particularly concerned to find practical ways of designing and implementing meaningful and inclusive narrative spaces that produce significant socio-economic legacies. When the programme was launched, the theory to support this new methodological approach was dispersed and unintegrated. The past 16 years have been a voyage of exploration, discovery and creativity. Staff and students have applied and tested the reciprocities between narratives and environments while developing a particular understanding of the interweaving of theory and practice in this field. The programme has developed principles, procedures and methods which, it is proposed, will contribute to the development of transmedial narrative theory and also to the design of more vivid, meaningful and sustainable human environments and experiences.

Theoretical Principles

One of the theoretical anchors of narrative environments is spatial theory, one major strand of which derives from the work of phenomenologist Maurice Merleau-Ponty (1962), who provides a theory of embodied perception. He argues that our understanding of the world is gathered sensorily as our moving bodies encounter each other and the everyday environment around us, to which we respond intellectually and emotionally. We think, feel and narrate through our bodies in relation to our surrounding physical environment, an environment that is already infused with sense and meaning. A second major strand is the work of Henri Lefebvre, particularly his conception of the politics of space. Lefebvre (1984) saw space not just as a physical and material phenomenon but also as social, constructed and contested, replete with vested and conflicting interests. The design of narrative environments sees such conflicts as the starting point for narratives. Geographer Doreen Massey (2004) provides a third major strand. She introduces the important idea that location is created in the cross-cutting trajectories of people and infrastructures as well as finance, media and other flows. In interrogating the politics of space, she argues that space can be conceived as a series of causally related events. The MA programme interprets such chains of events as narratives which constitute specific socio-economic, political and spatial identities over time.

In order to create a theoretical framework for the design of narrative environments, events as part of environment, on the one hand, and events as part of narrative discourse, on the other hand, are brought together into a networked relationship with a third element: 'people'. Without this triangulation, 'narrative', 'environment' and 'people' would remain three distinct, unrelated spheres, with narrative studied through narratology, under the aegis of literary studies; environment studied through spatial theory, under the aegis of architecture and the natural and ecological sciences; and people studied through the social sciences, under the aegis of economics, psychology, sociology and anthropology. In the design of narrative environments, however, narrative, environment and people are interrelated to form a top-level tripartite, interdependent network. Through this network social practices, as concrete, spatio-temporal situated practices, can be seen to emerge and be studied (Figure 0.1).

The narrative environments tripartite network can be understood by starting at any one of its nodes, treated as portals. For example, starting from the people node, and employing insights from the psychoanalytic theory of Jacques Lacan (1968, 1977), the human subject partakes, discovers and reflects upon the world, as interrelated networks, through the situated, embodied, socialised narratives in which they find themselves. The narratives unfold through embodied human psychic investment in spatialised, spoken

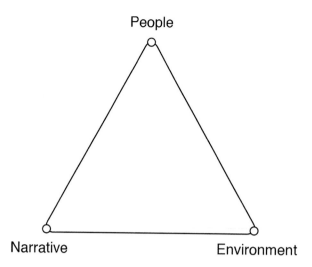

People

Narrative   Environment

Figure 0.1 The tripartite network model of narrative environments.

and written discourse in specific situations. The environment emerges through the spatialised, embodied human interactions organised in narrativised, socialised situated events and their material structures.

This is a brief demonstration of how the whole narrative environment acts, as a site of action and interaction among people, narratives and places. This scheme is, in part, a development of Actor Network Theory (ANT) (Latour 2005), which describes a system of human and non-human actors and their interdependence. In ANT, non-human objects and technologies are treated as having agency, or the ability to act. The design of narrative environments seeks to create critical and reflective experiences for people, enabling them to understand how they are implicated and entangled as responsible agents in the networked world. This gives substance to Latour's proposal that the world is not simply constituted by matters of fact, identifiable through the social and natural sciences, but also by matters of concern, which implies human practical, ethical and political engagement in the world, not just scientific, aesthetic or critical observation.

The design of narrative environments bears some relationship to ontological design, a practice which emerged in the early 2000s, in as far as "ontological designing is a way of characterising the relation between human beings and lifeworlds" Willis (2006: 80). For ontological design, far from being aesthetic packaging, design is knowing-in-action and reflection-in-action and relies on unstated or tacit knowledge. The design of narrative environments, through its tripartite network model, similarly assumes a kind of material semiotic, relational ontology (Maturana and Varela 1987), which performs a critique of the Cartesian dualistic ontology of mind (*res cogitans*) and matter (*res extensa*). It also takes heed of Jacques Derrida's (1973) Heidegger-inspired (1972) warning that one may fall, without continued vigilance, into a religious or metaphysical understanding of ontology in terms of a fundamental substance aligned to foundational theories of absolute origin and transcendental endings, so-called onto-theology. The design of narrative environments concerns ontology in that it is a conversation about possibilities. It is about the making of worlds and knowledges constructed on the basis of different ontological commitments. In this way, it brings to attention quite explicitly the politics of design.

Thus, the design of narrative environments, through its networked tripartite model, shows that subjective and objective knowledge are brought into existence and inter-related through material, social practices which are therefore open to change through design. In terms of the social practice of dwelling, for example, although a house may be understood in a conventional dualistic ontology to be constructed from materials and therefore be an object in a common-sense understanding, more importantly, in a net-worked ontology, all of the material and environmental aspects of the house form part of the inhabitant's self-understanding and self-narration. It is not just a house, which is an abstract concept, nor is it just the house on the left, for example, an empirical, practical concept, but it is also *my* house, *your* house or *their* house, a significant loca-tion in the spatialisation of my narrative being, its social relations and its history. A 'house' becomes a 'home', a place of belonging and possession, and a home gives rise to 'homeliness', an embodied, emotional, practised response. The house, as home, is a place of departure and return over a period of time. It gives durability, and narratability, to my sense of self. These psychodynamic senses of dwelling and belonging are ratified as ownership through rights, laws and statutes, confirming 'myself' as the legal owner, the home-owner, as well as the imaginary dweller.

Narrative environments bring people to an awareness of the regularities, embodied and enacted in social practices, enabling people to question their inevitability, natu-ralness, or their moral, ethical and political decision-making frameworks, and, from a different direction, may bring people to an awareness of the consequences of fall-ing outside of those categories, such as homelessness and statelessness. The design of narrative environments can also bring to awareness the temporal and spatial scale of attachment to place and to particular worlds, for example, by extending the narrative from my home to my neighbourhood to my city to my country, each of which territories could be breached by those who appear to have no right to be there. The psychodynamic associations from one scale can be exploited at other scales, for example, when a home and a country, as nation state, are treated as having the same existential status, a process through which people's narrative identity can be drawn from personal selfhood to col-lective nationhood.

By engaging with the network effects of scale, narrative environments are capable of conceiving and acting on some of the major issues affecting contemporary societies across the world. For example, in relation to the Anthropocene (Lewis and Maslin 2015), the current era in which human activity has become a significant factor in the planet's ecological balance, narrative environments can translate between scientific and abstract concepts and concrete experiential situations, materialising and enacting urgent global questions, such as unsettlement and displacement, the climate emergency and the impact of ongoing digitisation. In this way, the design of narrative environments might be seen to respond to the call for stories issued by Thom van Dooren (2014), who sees, "story-telling as a dynamic act of 'storying' the world, utterly inseparable from lived experi-ence and a vital contributor to the emergence of 'what is'". Van Dooren follows Donna Haraway (2016) in asserting the inter-relationship of storying and worlding, in a context where a "radical restorying" is needed to dispel the philosophical and cultural imaginary inherited from Descartes and Kant and the socio-juridical order that it maintains (Grear 2013). Alternatively, the design of narrative environments might be seen to respond to George Monbiot's (2017) insight that those who tell the most compelling stories run the world. This is because, as much as strong leaders or parties, it is powerful political nar-ratives that dominate politics. Therefore, Monbiot argues, "Political renewal depends on a new political story". Such a story will need to address the global crisis of liberal democracy which concerns the conflicting worldviews of the world's diverse citizenry, increasing economic inequality and the social heterogeneity of nation states' populations (Mounk 2018). Once a powerful story has taken hold in people's imaginations, such as that of neoliberalism, the simple presentations of facts will not dislodge their belief in the story. There is an urgent need for new stories to address the problems inherent in accepted stories that order our worlds.

Related Literature

In terms of narrative theory and narratology, narrative environments draw inspiration from the writing of transmedial narrative theorist Marie Laure Ryan (2004), who argues narratology needs to be seen as applicable beyond text and as separate from writing, that is, beyond conventional media such as literature and broadcast mass media. The book Ryan co-wrote with geographers Kenneth Foote and Moaz Azaryahu, *Narrating Space/Spatializing Narrative* (2016), looks at narrative and maps, space, narrative and digital media, street names as story and history, and landscape narratives and museum narratives. The discussion constructs an important bridge between narratology and geography, building on the 'spatial turn' (Jameson 1991) in the late twentieth century and also on the earlier 'narrative turn' in the humanities in the 1980s, which saw narrative theory applied in distinct areas such as law, medicine, education, the natural sciences and music. In the concluding chapter of *Narrating Space/Spatializing Narrative*, the writers identify research opportunities and questions that might elucidate the relationship of geography and narrative and the definition of territories that are not occupied by either narratology or geography. This is a place where the design narrative environments already practise and can lay claim to specific epistemological and ontological insights.

This book responds in many ways to Ryan et al., who call for the development of a larger range of case studies on toponymical, landscape and museum narratives. They suggest exploring how the spoken word is used to narrate in space by tour guides and re-enactors in scripted and unscripted tours. They recommend investigating the choice of symbolic locations for protest. Like this book, Ryan et al. also raise the issue of authorship in place-based narratives, pointing out that such places often have multiple and uncredited authors. This book follows Ryan et al. in making a plea for a clearer use of narrative in other disciplines where the word can be used quite loosely and, in the process, take on different meanings. In design, the word narrative is used, for example, to mean vision, identity, explanation, theory or proposal, whereas here it is argued its meaning is quite specifically about story and telling. Finally, Ryan, Foote and Azaryahu highlight the importance of researching how digital media change the way people explore and experience space through, for example, locative media and geo-tagging. As part of the process of defining the scope of the design of narrative environments, this book addresses the emergence of hybrid physical/digital space in order to understand its potential in designed narrative experiences.

A number of design writers have published useful books for students and professional designers about narrative and design. Matthew Purington and Jamie Potteiger's book *Landscape Narratives* (1998), for example, sets out a theory of narrative landscape. It very clearly and eloquently describes narrative design tropes such as revealing and concealing, provides in-depth analysis of case studies and shows the application of spatialised narrative in the social and political context of the USA in the 1990s. Ellen Lupton's (2017) book *Design is Storytelling* lays out some basic methods for applying narrative, particularly in graphic design. Frank den Oudsten's (2011) book *Space.time.narrative: The Exhibition as Post-spectacular Stage* is an important European contribution to theorising narrative environments in exhibition design and its relationship to scenography, urban installation and rural space. Den Oudsten examines the exhibition as a cultural practice, placing exhibition-making within a broad range of philosophical, museological, linguistic and media-theoretical practices.

Given its concern with relationships among people, place and story, the design of narrative environments is particularly associated with principles developed in user experience design (UX). UX designers collect data to map customer journeys in order to capture the whole ecology of the user's relationship with a brand or service. Experience maps show moments and locations of difficulties that people may experience in the journey. These are known as pain points. The identification of such pain points then allows for inventive thinking to develop novel ways to avoid or mitigate the pain. UX grew out of studies of website navigation, user interface design (UI), in the 1990s and users' interactions with products (Jordon 2000). UX has now spread to the development of models of consumer experiences on and offline, customer experience design (CX). The business dimension of experience design was highlighted by Joseph Pine and James Gilmore (1999) in their book *The Experience Economy*. They use the example of the journey and changing value of a coffee bean to explain their idea. The newly harvested bean is a raw material, a natural product. Once it is ground, it becomes a good that is more valuable in economic terms. When the ground good is packaged, it becomes a more valuable commercial product, retailed across the world. It can, however, also be made into a drink sold in a café, a place which offers additional services, such as opportunities to sit, meet others, read and relax. The staging of the coffee making, serving and drinking is not just a convenient and efficient service but also an engaging field of performances that creates a strong memory, thereby further increasing the economic value. Pine and Gilmore argue that good services offer time well saved, an efficiency criterion, whereas good experiences offer time well spent, with positive feelings gained from being associated with the brand's status. They suggest that the highest level of value is achieved when the customer experience is transformative and that this transformation is what companies might charge for. They may, for example, offer coffee for free but make the café a members-only space that charges for membership. Membership transforms the consumers' sense of themselves into a high-status individual. The transformed consumer, in this view of commercial transaction, is the ultimate product. Pine and Gilmour's ideas have had a huge impact and led to the establishment of research centres such as the European Centre for the Experience Economy. While the logic of their arguments cannot be denied, more critical theories of experience in social practice, beyond the domain of marketing, are also needed if the intention is to address pressing issues such as environmental, cultural, social or political sustainability.

The Structure of the Book

The book starts by providing the core theoretical scaffold, the tripartite network model, into which different theoretical contributions can be grafted in order to develop design at an increasingly granular level. It goes onto describe the educational context which shows how the design of narrative environments relates to, but also differs from, other design studies. This is followed by a review of historical precursors of narrative environments. Although not an exhaustive survey it demonstrates the variety of narrative environments, pointing to fertile ground for further investigation. A discussion of methods of current practice explores the importance of identifying and applying dramatic conflicts to produce moving and thought-provoking experiences. The process of story content development for narrative environments is investigated across commercial and cultural sectors and ways of storytelling show how content can be folded into space to create linear and non-linear narrative environments. The book then turns to investigate audience experience, discussing engagement, meaningful interaction and the benefits and challenges of full body immersion in narrative environments. A discussion of reframing shows how fixity can be dissolved to create poetic and critical experiences which can be made more provocative and powerful by the transgression of story boundaries. The book concludes with an examination of the challenges to sole authorship by co-creation and participatory design in narrative environments. Each chapter expands the theoretical base while demonstrating the relevance of the theory through case studies. The case studies are based on observations and interviews with creative teams from across the world. Numerous voices are heard, representing many different, and sometimes conflicting, perspectives. The intention is that the book will appeal to both theorists and practitioners, providing numerous connections between theory and practice while inspiring fresh approaches in the design industry and in academia.

References

den Oudsten, F. (2011) *Space.time.narrative: The Exhibition as Post-spectacular Stage*. Farnham: Ashgate Publishing.

Derrida, J. (1973) *Speech and Phenomena and Other Essays on Husserl's Theory of Signs*. Evanston, IL: Northwestern University Press.

Grear, A. (2013). Towards a new horizon: In search of a renewing socio-juridical imaginary. *Oñati Socio-Legal Series*, 3(5), 966–990.

Haraway, D. (2016). *Staying with the Trouble: Making Kin in the Chthulucene*. Durham, NC: Duke University Press.

Heidegger, M. (1972). *On Time and Being*. New York, NY: Harper Torchbooks.

Jameson, F. (1991) *Postmodernism: Or, the Cultural Logic of Late Capitalism*. London: Verso.

Jordon, P. (2000) *Designing Pleasurable Products: An Introduction to the New Human Factors*. New York, NY: Taylor & Francis.

Lacan, J. (1968) *The Language of the Self: The Function of Language in Psychoanalysis*. New York, NY: Dell Publishing.

Lacan, J. (1977) *Ecrits: As Selection*. London: Tavistock Publications.

Latour, B. (2005) *Reassembling the Social: An Introduction to Actor-Network-Theory*. Oxford, UK: Oxford University Press.

Lefebvre, H. (1984) *The Production of Space*. Oxford, UK: Blackwell.

Lewis, S. L. and Maslin, M. A. (2015) Defining the Anthropocene. *Nature*, 519 (7542), 171–180.

Lupton, E. (2017) *Design is Storytelling*. New York, NY: Cooper Hewitt, Smithsonian Design Museum.

Massey, D. (2004) *For Space*. London: Sage.

Maturana, H.and Varela, F. (1987). *The Tree of Knowledge: The Biological Roots of Human Understanding*. Berkeley, CA: Shambhala.

Merleau-Ponty, M. (1962) *The Phenomenology of Perception*. Trans. Colin Smith. London: Routledge Classics.

Monbiot, G. (2017). How do we get out of this mess? *Guardian*, 9 September. Online. Available HTTP: https://www.theguardian.com/books/2017/sep/09/george-monbiot-how-de-we-get-out-of-this-mess Accessed 9 September 2017.

Mounk, Y. (2018) *The People Versus Democracy: Why Our Freedom Is in Danger and How to Save It*. Cambridge, MA: Harvard University Press.

Pine, J. and Gilmour, J. (1999) *The Experience Economy*. Boston, MA: Harvard Business Review Press.

Purington, M, and Potteiger, J. (1998) *Landscape Narrative*. New York, NY; Chichester: John Wiley.

Ryan, M.-L. (2004) *Narrative across Media: The Languages of Storytelling*. (Frontiers of Narrative). Lincoln: University of Nebraska Press.

Ryan, M.-L., Foote, K. and Azaryahu, M. (2016) *Narrating Space/Spatializing Narrative: Where Narrative Theory and Geography Meet*. Columbus, OH: The Ohio State University Press.

Van Dooren, T. (2014) *Flight Ways: Life and Loss at the Edge of Extinction*. New York, NY: Columbia University Press.

Willis, A.-M. (2006). Ontological designing – Laying the ground. In: Willis, A.-M., ed. *Design Philosophy Papers, Collection Three*. Ravensbourne, Queensland: Team D/E/S Publications, pp. 80–98.

Websites

European Centre for the Experience Economy. http://www.experience-economy.com/

MA Narrative Environments. http://www.narrative-environments.com

1 Theory

This chapter introduces the tripartite network model developed to guide the design of narrative environments as a practice. The model, which interrelates three nodes, people, narrative and environment, was developed so that design practice can take into account the thinking about language, experience, the body, time and space that has occurred since the end of the nineteenth century. Developed in different disciplines, this research often took the form of dualistic oppositions: language and thought; experience and action; body and mind; and temporality and spatiality. The tripartite model seeks to overcome the limitations of such disciplinary and dualistic thinking. As it unfolds, the model enables designers to draw on research from other disciplines and thereby to enrich, both theoretically and practically, the design of narrative environments. In what follows, the emphasis falls on the environment node because the integration of spatial practices with theories of narrative and theories of subjectivity is the least well theorised, particularly the way in which narrative is embedded in space and place. The tripartite model posits that people cannot exist without place, nor can they exist without narrative and, consequently, they cannot exist without narrative in place.

One of the strands from which the model has emerged is thinking about spatial practices, which interweave material and social dynamics. As individuals and communities, we learn, live, struggle and reconcile our identities and differences through spatial practices. 'Spatial practice' is a term taken from the writings of Henri Lefebvre (1974) and Michel de Certeau (1984). Lefebvre argues that space is not simply a matter of physical dimensions and material structures, but, being purposefully constructed, spaces embody and enact ethical, political and cultural relations. Lefebvre developed a three-part dialectic of space which he describes as spatial practice, the representations of space and representational spaces, a "perceived-conceived-lived triad" (Lefebvre 1974: 40). He describes *representational spaces* as lived spaces that are comprehended through deciphering their symbolic language. For Lefebvre, representational spaces form systems of non-verbal symbols and signs which are more or less coherent. They are the architectural and spatial forms that people come to recognise as part of their everyday world and become part of their imagination. "Representational space is alive; it speaks" (Lefebvre 1974: 42). Spatial forms often vary according to geographic location and cultural norms, but the meaning and relevance of architectural and spatial elements are shared by residents, learned by tourists and typically circulated through the media. Representational spaces are "qualitative, fluid and dynamic" (Lefebvre 1974: 42). Lefebvre suggests that, by contrast, *representations of space* are the abstracted, encoded products that are used to manage space, that is, the maps, annotated ground plans and elevations that form rigorous systems of signs whether verbally or mathematically resolved. These diagrams are conceptions of space derived from technical and regulatory systems. They are produced and used by planners, engineers and architects. Lefebvre argues that these professions exercise enormous power and dominate the production of our everyday world.

Lefebvre describes *spatial practice* as the routines that people perform in their daily lives. Spatial practice establishes routes, networks and patterns of interaction that reproduce accepted codes of behaviour but which, because they are not wholly intellectually worked out or logically conceived, leave space for improvisation and innovation, potentially disrupting or subverting both representational spaces and representations of space. A simple example is finding a shortcut around a sign-posted official route. Michel de Certeau (1984) also discusses spatial practices in the context of everyday life. He says, "Every story is a travel story – a spatial practice" (Certeau 1984: 115), arguing that spatial practices can be used by ordinary people as a tactic to subvert institutional constraints. Spatial practices, as they are defined in the design of narrative environments, incorporate Lefebvre's three analytical categories and Certeau's contentions about their tactical and narrative status. As can be seen, spatial practices are not the sole domain of planners, architects and designers. Such professional activities intervene into an existing field of spatial practices. They are structured and produced, as described by Lefebvre, and enacted as analysed by Certeau.

Despite the work of Lefebvre, Certeau and others, space still often goes almost unnoticed because, as Georges Perec (1997) has highlighted, space is seen as banal, obvious, habitual and taken for granted as part of daily life. However, as other writers such as Gaston Bachelard (1994) have shown, desire, emotion and action are inextricably woven through space in the everyday. This brings to light one of the theoretical principles in the design of narrative environments: people cannot exist without place. Our imagination and our sense of self are, in part, formed through our spatial attachments. We express and perform our identities through the details and arrangement of our homes, through our negotiation of the spaces of the workplace, through the neighbourhoods we choose to live in and through a sense of belonging to a particular region or nation. We use space to establish status, power and social relations, in other words, our 'habitus', as French sociologist Pierre Bourdieu (1984) calls it. Habitus is an influential concept, with a strong spatial dimension (Fogle 2011). Bourdieu describes habitus as learned skills that enable us to function almost unconsciously in our familiar locale through customary behaviour. Bourdieu argues these skills are cultural and class-specific, and we may feel awkward and lost in different circumstances not knowing how to act or what different behaviours, objects and places mean. Bourdieu reinforces Lefebvre's and Certeau's understanding that space is not just a neutral given but, once established, material spatial forms and the way they are used act to perpetuate our conventions, divisions, fears, hopes, alliances and allegiances.

This postwar French debate opened up the discussion of space and place. Elizabeth Grosz (1995), for example, considers that it is important to distinguish space, which is mappable, explorable and therefore susceptible to becoming conceived space in Lefebvre's terms, from place, which implies occupation, dwelling and being lived in. She argues that the concept of space, rather than place, is privileged in Western thought. Furthermore, theorist J. E. Malpas (1999: 26) reflects that "space has been increasingly understood in the narrower terms that tie it to physical extension". He argues that this narrowing can be seen in the way that the concept of *kenon* or void has come to replace the Greek notions of *topos* (place) and *chora* (spatial interval) in the history of philosophy. This notion of void plays a significant role in the development of modern concepts of space because it implies the notion of the homogeneous domain of pure extension. Thus, Malpas (1999: 26) concludes,

> It is precisely this idea that lies at the heart of thinking about space in the work of Descartes and Newton. Thus, with Newton, we arrive at an understanding of space as a single, homogeneous and isotropic 'container' in which all things are located.

Once measured, space can be divided, amalgamated, bought and sold as a commodity in an economic system. Under these circumstances, land is valued as a functional asset, for example, for its proximity to a port or transport system, or valuable if it can be farmed or put to use for profit. This reduction of place to space as container permits particular places to be conceived as *terra nullius* (nobody's land) and legitimises acquisition of those territories as empty containers. The predominance of space as void permits a colonial perception of the world in which territories outside of Europe are void, because they do not contain European civilisation. As Grosz highlights, mapping is an essential tool in this objectification and commodification of space. Maps assume a particular orientation and hierarchy in the representation of space; for example, medieval European maps show Jerusalem as the centre of the world, while modern maps show Europe as the centre of the world. Mapping is a spatial practice that ensures the continued dominance of conceived space over other spatial practices which assert place as lived.

Often considered to be an unintended consequence, in fact, one of the major outcomes of the predominance of conceived space in spatial practices are 'non-places' (Augé 1995). Examples of these characterless, generalised spaces, as discussed by Augé, are airport lounges, bland shopping malls, large car parks and edges of motorways. They grow out of an era of mass production, mass transport and planning conventions that rely on conceived space. As a consequence, non-places have economic and functional value but lack social and cultural value.

Narrative environments bring these conflicts among different spatial practices to conscious attention in order to emphasise the importance of place as essential to human existence which is intrinsically tied to locality and spatiality (Malpas 1999: 10). The relationships among discourse, language, space, place and humans are fundamental to the key issues affecting societies across the world, from global environmental crises to social inequalities and political injustices. Space and place are fundamentally entangled with our values, desires and ethics, and it is hard to think of any issues that are not in some way played out through space and place.

In the design of narrative environments, both concepts of place and space are necessary. Place is not seen as a static, romantic, nostalgic or conservative affectation. Similarly to geographer Doreen Massey's (2005) conception of space, but rejecting her suspicion of the notion of place, place and space are understood to be in a constant state of change and therefore carry agency – the power to change that which exists within space or flows through place. Exploring space at a global and regional level, Massey reminds us that mountains and sea levels rise and fall over thousands of years while towns can grow or shrink more quickly, perhaps even over a generation. Designers of narrative environments are aware that urban public realm, for example, may change, over a matter of hours, from being a place to eat lunch to a place for a political protest or the stage for an art performance. Massey sees place as "a simultaneity of multiple trajectories" (2005: 61), as flows of people, money and power collide and adhere. She analyses space, place and power, unpicking the effects of spatial and economic divisions and resulting social inequalities. She sees space as not necessarily progressing inexorably towards modernity, reinforcing the apparent naturalness of nation states and regions, but open to other, as yet unknown, possibilities. This is important for the design of narrative environments which make interventions into these flows.

Given the potential for space and place to change, their powerful symbolic nature and their asset value, many different entities, from global industries to national governments, to local communities and each of us as individuals, may all desire to adapt our spatial environment in different ways. This sets off wave upon wave of complex cultural, political, social and design action as the interrelated forces struggle to shape space and place as they wish it to be. For example, a property developer employing conceived space as a spatial practice may view an empty lot in an inner city as a business opportunity to build high-rise flats, while a resident, understanding the lot as part of their lived space, might prefer it to become a community garden, a designated space to relax and socialise. Different communities may claim the same space, creating tensions, which, in extreme cases, may lead to armed conflict. One of the principles adopted by the design of narrative environments is that all spaces are contested in some way and the contestation is precisely what stimulates people to imagine the space in a different way – to negotiate and evolve the space. Contestation, which can be shaped into a dramatic conflict, is fruitful in terms of the narrative imagination. Narrative environments, in seeking to explore those dramatic conflicts, provide a challenge to prevailing functional and technocratic spatial orthodoxy, loosening space and using narrative as a route to creating new places.

As should now be clear, the spatial environment is not taken to be an inert backdrop. It acts upon us, through us and among us. Space and place not only embody our culture and traditions; they actively shape our bodies, feelings, aspirations and actions. Bruno Latour (2005) argues in actor network theory (ANT) that the material world and the world of concepts are inseparably intertwined and are always in a state of networked interaction through material semiosis. For the design of narrative environments, this notion of material semiotic network interaction is important for the conception of environment as an active process of environing (Parsons 2009).

> in earlier periods the advent of Reason was predicated on the non-local, nonsituated, nonmaterial utopia of mind and matter, it is now possible to dissipate those phantoms and observe them move inside specific spheres and networks.
>
> (Latour, 2009: 134)

Acknowledgement of the agency of the physical world of objects and spaces resonates deeply with spatial and product design practices, where it is held that materials, forms, light and spatial dimensions all play a part in shaping identity, atmosphere and action. Theorists such as Scott Lash and Antoine Picon (2009) concur with Latour describing architecture's ability to perform, enact and critique. Albena Yaneva (2016) argues that architecture is performative: it persuades, convinces, intimidates, enlightens, inspires and provokes action. While the design of narrative environments uses some architectural methods, it also applies methods from other design disciplines to shape the way space is enacted, dramatised and lived in order to encompass cultural, social and political factors as well as taking into account inhabitants' or visitors' agency. The collective entities, as agents, give rise to the distinctiveness of place, which is not just geographical or historical, but is carved from the struggle among the materials, weather, spatial affordances, people's use, action and interpretation. For ANT, the relations among people, places and things need to be repeatedly performed to sustain their existence, and for the design of narrative environments the network sustains meanings, as memory and history, constantly re-establishing, reiterating and adapting them over time.

In ANT, human and non-human agents are called actants. They all exist within, and perpetuate, the system through their actions in the network. This theory is a challenge to the idea that human will and intention are the sole forms of agency, arguing instead that non-human actants are active players in dynamic actor-networks or 'actant-rhizome ontologies' (Latour 1999: 19). Not unlike the tripartite model developed for the design of narrative environments, Latour (1993: 6) argues that "networks are simultaneously real, like nature, narrated, like discourse, and collective, like society".

In constituting a meaningful whole, the network is constituted as a 'world'. Jean-Luc Nancy (2007) distinguishes between 'world' as a disparate aggregation of all that exists and world as an interconnected meaningful whole. The further assumption is that any particular narrative environment, as a world, is part of a world of many worlds (de la Cadena and Blazer 2018). This characterisation draws upon another distinction that Jean-Luc Nancy deploys, that between globalisation and mondialisation. While globalisation formally links the world together as a single set or a category, mondialisation stands for incompleteness, becoming and openness, creating and maintaining the world as an interrelated, interdependent whole, conceivable in environmental, ecological, cyber-systemic or 'living' terms. It is the latter, mondialisation, which is relevant for the design of narrative environments. The networked character of narrative environments reveals how the dynamics of different scales, from the local to the global, play out in particular situations. Each element in a narrative environment can be seen as part of several networks. Objects in exhibitions, for example, are specifically used to bring other worlds to mind. They seek to change your perception of being in a present experiential moment to being part of a human history which may then open up to the diversity of distinct cultural geographies. This, in turn, may be understood as part of an imperial history, which opens up yet further to being part of an economic history. This then can bring you back recursively to a different perception of yourself and your ethical relation to those geohistories. The process of moving through the network of worlds enables people to reflect on and to change their habitual dispositions, actions or behaviours.

The design of narrative environments proposes that everyone experiences the conflict between their place-based subjective worlds and their complex relationships to the conceived spaces that make up globalisation. These conflicts are manifested through the lifeworld. The understanding of lifeworld here differs from that of Husserlian phenomenology which, in its initial formulations, centred on the transcendental ego and a consciousness which bracketed out the everyday. The focus in the design of narrative environments is on the many dimensions of experience to which networked, situated, everyday interaction gives rise.

Space Communicates

Another premise of the design of narrative environments is that space not only acts but also, being a material semiotic phenomenon, 'speaks'. Brian Lawson (2001: 5) argues in his book, *The Language of Space*, that "Space and architecture ... are a vital language central to human communication". Lawson sees buildings as social objects, describing how buildings, while having a technical function, can also appear secretive and forbidding, oppressive or moving, depending on your point of view. For example, the National Monument to Peace and Justice in Alabama, USA (Figure 1.1), by MASS design is, for

Figure 1.1 National Memorial for Peace and Justice, Alabama, USA, MASS Design Group 2018.

many, a humbling experience. It commemorates each of the black lives lost from lynching. Curator Teil Silverstein (2019) who visited the memorial said,

> The structural design is incredibly evocative, as these massive steel columns rise above your head when you descend into the Memorial. The hanging columns evoke the horrific act of lynching as well as the massive weight of this nation's history of slavery and racism, while the inscribed names of 4,000 plus victims make this history intimate and this site consecrated by remembrance.

As this example shows, we 'read' spatial, material and symbolic environments through our bodies. Phenomenologist Maurice Merleau-Ponty (2002) argues that, as moving, perceiving bodies, we are indivisible from the space around us. He maintains that our immediate environment is part of our body schema, which includes not only our physical body but also its relationship to the surrounding world. In other words, we carry with us a sense of depth, dimensionality, orientation, flow, movement, form, colour, tactility, texture and lustre, as perceptual-spatial qualities. Our body extends through our senses to include our immediate surroundings and we can feel violated or comforted by materials or actions that we perceive at some distance from our actual body. Embodied perception blurs the boundary between body, mind and things. Merleau-Ponty suggests we make meaning from our embodied perception of the immediate world around us prior to any overt conceptualisations. He suggests the body and the world intercommunicate:

"my existence as subjectivity is merely one with my existence as a body and with the existence of the world, and because the subject that I am, when taken concretely, is inseparable from this body and this world" (Merleau-Ponty 2002: 475). For the design of narrative environments, Merleau-Ponty's position is vital because he brings the body into the arena of communication, breaking down the dichotomy of inside and outside, integrating body, subject and space. In *The Poetics of Space*, Gaston Bachelard (1994) concurs with Merleau-Ponty's position. As summarised by Malpas (1999: 5),

> the life of the mind is given form in the places and spaces in which human beings dwell and those places themselves shape and influence human memories, feelings and thoughts.

Bachelard examines our subjective, psychological and emotional investment in the spatial universe of the home. He argues people need houses to dream and to imagine. Once again, space is shown to be key to human existence in line with the principles of the design of narrative environments.

Form, light, sound, space, smell and the activities of other people in the space all combine to create mood and atmosphere which can stimulate action, emotion and memory. In the last 20 years, the concept of atmosphere has become an important area of study in architecture, aesthetics and anthropology. A leading thinker in this turn is philosopher Gernot Böhme (2017), who describes atmospheres as intangible, tinctured interstices or in-between spaces, and we struggle to understand to whom or to what to attribute them. Environments resonate with us as a representation of social norms, hierarchies and values which brings insights from social science into the arena. Philosopher Peter Sloterdijk (2011) argues that sociability and atmosphere are intertwined and used as a way to connect and build bonds between those who live together. Sloterdijk conceives space as a series of spheres that we move among and within. The spheres immerse and insulate us from hostility and danger. Nevertheless, Sloterdijk contends, human beings oscillate between the desire to be insulated and the desire to break free, transgress, flow and mingle.

While spatial forms, rhythms and atmospheres implicitly communicate through various material semiotics and peripheral vision and sensing, explicit communication in space tends to be organised around linguistic and graphic semiotic forms. Environmental graphic design, in other words, signage, maps, packaging, leaflets and posters or projections, may use text, image, moving image and sound, or all of them together. Graphics in the environment help to create messages, communicate stories and contribute to the distinctive voice of a place. They vary in scale, from posters to the size of a building, as in the treatment for the Work in Progress pavilion, WIP Villette, in Paris by Intégral Ruedi Baur. In 2010, this former slaughterhouse was transformed into a cultural centre. Intégral Ruedi Baur added the red lines to symbolise wind and movement and to enhance the visibility of the building (Figure 1.2).

Ruedi Baur (2019) speaking of the relationship between architecture and graphics says, "for economic, functional or atmospheric reasons, graphics can take on a driving role … [however] I am more interested in a fair balance". The design of narrative environments sees graphic communication not as an imposition on space but as complementary to architecture and spatial design. Narrative environments often deploy a diverse range of semiotic means to communicate, from the implicit bodily address of spatial, atmospheric arrangements to the explicit address of graphics, moving image and sound. This extends the kind of semiotic analysis developed by Roland Barthes (1977) when he applies literary analytical techniques to aspects of everyday life in postwar France.

Figure 1.2 Signage for the WIP Villette, Paris, France, Intégral Ruedi Baur 2010.

A further dimension of explicit environmental communication is the ever-growing presence of digital media: text, sound, image, video and animation that we access in situ through our mobile phones. We expect to access digital maps, news sources, apps, blogs, games, commercial websites and social media anywhere, anytime. We rely on digital means to decide on choices for mobility, places to meet and things to do. The digital world has an enormous and growing impact on our spatial behaviour. The degree to which the internet, most often discussed as a virtual space, is integrated into situated spatial practice is often underestimated. Trip Advisor, for example, has changed our spatial routines. Whereas, formerly, we might have wandered around a neighbourhood to find interesting places to shop or eat and relied on serendipity to find them, now we check ahead and make decisions from a remote location. We pre-visit online which, Traxler (2011) argues, dilutes our sense of the here-and-now. Spatial wandering and exploration are diminished as wayfinding is delegated to locative media (Frith 2015). Nevertheless, digital communications can also overcome socio-spatial conventions that have previously restricted access to, and information about, places.

Finally, explicit communication in narrative environments relies on observing and interacting with other people as a means to gather information. We are ushered through airports, sporting events, theme parks, shops and museums by people performing their roles to greet, advise, surveille or reinforce the meaning of the place. This is an added layer of communication that is often carefully aligned to the architectural form, signage and atmosphere of place. For example, in the nineteenth century, German and French landscape designers, such as Peter Joseph Lenné, employed actors to have picnics in parks, such as Pfaueninsel Park near Berlin, to orient visitors' narrative imaginations and conceive of the park as a social space. In a similar spirit, luxury retail stores position smartly dressed security staff at their public entrances to signify that you are entering a domain of wealth and exclusivity. Rather than having active roles in apprehending shop lifters, their presence is intended to emphasise customers' high status. Human interactions and the spatial behaviour of others are enormously influential in the way narrative environments communicate.

Space Narrates

Space may communicate but how does spatial communication narrate? Indeed, why even consider narrative as a form that is appropriate for spatial communication? In answer to the first question, in trying to understand or create meaningful spatial experiences, we need to expand our attention beyond utilitarian concepts of functional structures that simply exist in static forms, such as ground plans and architectural models. We need to move away from a focus on designing objects, whether that be a frock, a kettle, a building or a public square. We need to consider how these are experienced by people and how those experiences can accumulate to create an experiential arc with transformative narrative qualities.

   In relation to human movement through space and place, bodily engagement with the immediate material environment is discussed by Christian Norberg-Schulz (1979) who envisions a three-part spatial scheme which combines sensations of proximity, continuity and change, leading to sense of place. Planner Gordon Cullen (1971) conceives serial vision and the sequential character of the built environment as central to the experience of townscape. He articulates a grammar of space suggesting we sense being outside, crossing thresholds and being inside spatial phenomena. We are suspended between here and there and we "journey through pressures and vacuums, a sequence of exposures and enclosures, of constraints and relief" (Cullen 1971: 10). The sequential quality of spatial experience has also been discussed by architects such as Le Corbusier (1995) in his notion of the architectural promenade (Samuel 2010) and Philip Johnson (1965) in his essay on the processional in architecture. Architect and theorist Christopher Alexander (2004) argues for the importance of the sensation of centrality: conceiving of the centre helps us understand where we are in relation to the patterns of the urban environment. Urban planner Kevin Lynch (1960) theorised that we develop mental models of the urban environment in making a case for the perception and legibility of cities based on five key elements: paths, edges, districts, nodes and landmarks. These elements help us to imagine the city, supporting orientation in the city and reinforcing its identity. Drawing on these sources, space and place can be conceived as a trajectory through multiple related spatial experiences. However, a narrative environment is more than just a spatial sequence; it is a triple, integrated unfolding of movement: through *space*, through *time* and through story *content*. Urban design scholar Mark Childs (2008: 185) embraces narrative directly when he argues that "storytelling is part of urban design ... stories of place can inform designers about the narrative fabric that is as much a critical part of the context of a site as the soil type". Childs maintains that stories and storytelling can support urban design in several ways: urban designers can curate the narrative landscape of a town so designers can more easily engage with place stories; urban planners can help connect stories of place, the built form and the resulting form of a settlement; and urban designers can create or dissolve master narratives to include multiple and diverse narratives.

   To return to the second question of why consider narrative for spatial communication, firstly, several theorists point to narrative as key to human thought processes. Frederic Jameson (1981), for example, argues narrative is the central function or instance of the human mind, claiming that it is a major part of the way we reason and believe. Paul Ricoeur (1979) is concerned with the relationship between time and narrative and suggests we do not only experience time as a linear succession of 'nows' but use narrative to create a coherent story of our lives and our history. In other words, we construct our identity using narrative. Jerome Bruner (2004) argues that stories are developed from the interplay of self, others and the world. According to Alistair Macintyre (2007: 216), "Man is in his actions and practice, as well as in his fictions, essentially a storytelling animal". Through narrative, we consciously incorporate and make sense of life experiences as they unfold. Narrative is constitutive of experience, memory and identity. At the cultural level, narrative also enables a discussion of temporality and history in three respects: the time of the story, the time of the telling and the experiential time of narrative environment as event. In narrative environments, the temporalities of both the story and the telling open up to the embodied spatio-temporality of events.

In understanding and designing narrative environments, theory and practice are complementary components. While drawing on narratology, it is one that is broadly conceived, such as that suggested by Roland Barthes (1977: 79) when he states that "Narrative is first and foremost a prodigious variety of genres, themselves distributed amongst different substances – as though any material were fit to receive man's stories". Stories and storytelling are not simply a matter of written or spoken language. Spatial narrative differs significantly from literary narrative, just as literary narrative differs from theatrical narrative, cinematic narrative, narrative in painting (Bal 2009: 166) or narrative in music (Ryan 2004). The design of narrative environments also builds on Marie Laure Ryan's argument that narrative is a medium-independent phenomenon. Ryan argues that no medium is better suited than language to make explicit the logical structure of narrative. However, it is possible to study narrative in its non-verbal manifestations without applying the communicative model of verbal narration. The design of narrative environments disputes this hierarchy, with the literary narrative at its apex, and the cultural processes whereby it is privileged, arguing that narrative is best understood as a necessary dimension of living. Narrative environments emerge from the interaction of the human subject, the environment and narrative discourse. Rather than producing total physical immersion in an unreflective reality, which discounts narrative, or being absorbed in reading a literary narrative, which discounts environment, the design of narrative environments aims for critical engagement with narratives as they are woven through lived environments.

While challenging the hierarchy of modes of narrative, the design of narrative environments accepts the value of different narrative modalities. A literary, theatrical or cinematic narrative is a highly crafted construction which communicates a story over time to a specific audience whereby, through dynamic alliances, actions and struggles, someone or something changes from one state to another. What is more, this transformation deliberately sets out to communicate a cultural message (Porter Abbott 2002). Interesting opportunities emerge in applying narrative as an organising principle to the analysis and design of places. First, the notion of dynamic struggle in traditional forms of narrative maps very well onto contested spaces with their multiple human and non-human actors. Second, a change of state in stories, whether that be emotional, intellectual or physical, or all three, maps very well not only onto the changes in the physical space as we walk through it but also onto the changes in the visitor's or inhabitant's experience as they move through the space. Third, the production of narrative, as an act of communication, subjectively positions an audience or reader. The goal of narrative environments is to create audience experiences, not just spaces. Narrative theory, it is argued, provides the design of narrative environments with methods to shift from making objects to composing and choreographing experience. Fourth, and very importantly, the constructed and purposeful character of narrative can, if applied to environment, prompt critical thinking. For example, it leads to questions such as: Who decided to make this space? Who decided to make it like this? For what reason? Where did they get their authority and authorisation? Applying critical questions about authorship and authority opens up the subject of power and of socio-political and environmental impacts. Thus, we move beyond technical, functional and aesthetic questions such as: What are the dimensions of this space or building? How was this built? What is its function? Is it formally beautiful? How much did it cost to build?, to such questions as, What values does it embody? How are they enacted, by who and for whose benefit? Narrative, therefore, is not simply a technical tool. It can be used to inform, to raise awareness, to reflect, to prove a point, to prompt empathy, to entertain, but also to assert power, to persuade and to lie. Use of narrative moves design from being solely a problem-solving service to an active engagement with the political, the moral and the ethical dimensions of specific societies.

Narrative environments are stories purposefully embedded *in* the environment that can be expressed *through* multiple explicit and implicit means. Examples of spatial narratives suggested by Ryan (2016) include a road name system, a landscape trail with signage or an exhibition. Narrative environments can be found in numerous other kinds of places as well, for example, in streets during religious festivals, in educational spaces, in public libraries, in care homes, in bars, restaurants, nightclubs, event spaces, brand spaces, work spaces, urban quarters. Narrative environments can be found almost anywhere, providing a story has been deliberately embedded to design the space with particular audiences in mind.

Because of the nature of space, visitors or inhabitants will tend to wander and construct their own narrative threads from the overall framing narrative. The visitors to, or inhabitants of narrative environments are not passive receivers but active participants moving, interpreting, speaking and producing their own experience in the space of their imaginations, physical space, social space and across the virtual spaces of digital media. Literary and film narratives have heroes, sometimes called protagonists, with whom we identify. In a conventional narrative, we empathise with the protagonist's struggle, pain and triumph. This positioning changes in a narrative environment. As we follow the spatial narrative, we not only empathise with a protagonist but we literally *become* a parallel embodied protagonist in our own story of discovery and identity building.

A Network Theory of Narrative Environments

As summarised in the Introduction, the design of narrative environments involves the articulation of three kinds of actants – people, narrative and environment – which form a network as an open, responsive, adaptive system. The design of narrative environments is enacted as each node calls upon, responds to and is interwoven with the other nodes. There is a two-way dynamic in each of the inter-nodal interactions, as each node acts upon the other two and simultaneously is acted upon. Hence, the network operates through processes of interaction among the subjective, the narrative and the placial, all of which are consequently distributed throughout the network. The intersubjective, for example, is mediated by story and place. Furthermore, depending on the character of the narrative environment, each of the three nodes at the top level can be further elaborated as a series of interrelated sub-networks to form an ever more complex system, with implications for the development of human, narrative and spatial communication (Figure 1.3).

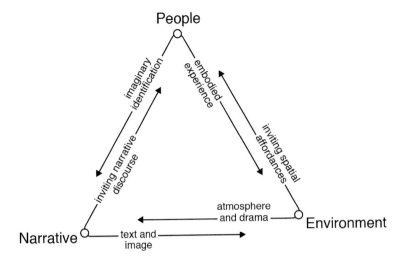

Figure 1.3 Interrelated actantial networks in the tripartite network model of narrative environments.

Taking the relationship between the people node and the narrative node first, the design of narrative environments is interested in exploiting the potential of the reciprocal ways in which the subjective networks of the people node are realised through the networks of narrative discourse and vice versa. In these sets of exchanges, dynamic networks of speech, writing, discourse as public expression of narrative are woven into the narrativisation of the internal expression of self, as a form of intersubjectivity. From the narrative side this relation operates as a mode of address inviting people into the world of its story and from the people side it is recognised as calling for a response, through the creation of the subject's own imaginary storyworld, as part of the subject's 'telos' or continual quest for narrative continuation of its purpose. People's response depends upon how semiotically literate they are, the extent and kind of their knowledge, what stories form the basis of their cultural understanding and so on, in other words, the relationship between the world of the story and their cultural repertoire. These techniques include their ability to understand literary, pictorial and graphic metaphors, to understand scientific and mathematical proofs, recognise literary, filmic and theatrical citations and an ability to follow and develop lines of reasoning and argumentation. Thus, the subjective grounds the narrative in desiring and imagining, while the narrative grounds the subjective in symbolic, rational order and narrative structure, drawn together by the environment from both directions into one place as a mediated, common lifeworld.

Second, moving to the relationship between the people and the environment nodes, the design of narrative environments is interested in exploiting the potential of the reciprocal ways in which the subjective networks of the people node are realised through the networks of the environment node, which include other people, and vice versa. In these sets of exchanges, dynamic networks of material semiotic systems, as common expression of environment, are woven into the body, as intersubjective environment. In other words, the subject is 'environmentalised', that is, woven into an environment, and therefore into an intercorporeal relation with other people in specific situations. From the environment side, this operates as a mode of address using the affordances of spatial arrangements to invite the subject as a body to participate in the situation. From the people side, it is a call to deploy culturally defined techniques of the body, as Marcel Mauss (1992) called them, to act in and upon the environment and with and upon other people. These techniques include aspects of the anatomical body, such as posture, proximity, gesture, touch and gaze, as well as voice as the materialisation of language expressed through intonation, volume, pitch and the vernacular aspects of language use. They also include the body as a vehicle for material cultural expression through clothing, jewellery, hair styling and body art. Such techniques further include ways in which the body is extended into, takes possession of and seeks to control the spatio-temporal environment through the choice of artefacts, technologies and inhabited spaces, marking out territories. The subjective grounds the environment in the body and sensory experience, while the environment grounds the subjective in phenomenal and situational order and material structure, drawn together by the narrative from both directions into one storyworld.

Third, moving to the relationship between the narrative node and the environment node, it is through event and situation that the environment node, as place, is connected to the narrative node, as story. In these sets of exchanges, dynamics of linguistic, graphic, pictorial and literary semiotics are woven into the material semiotics of space and place as processes of environing and intercorporeal interrelating. From the narrative side, the environment is named, categorised, referred to and inferred using signs as symbols to order space and create place by pointing, demarcating, inviting, prohibiting, promising, reasoning and so on. From the environment side, narrative is articulated through material semiotics. This includes form, colour, light, dimension, scale, and texture, generating atmospheres, visual drama, environmental affordances and events. Together, they configure pathways or construct barriers, thereby giving substance and material order to the symbolic processes of the narrative node. In this way, the narrative grounds the environment in symbolic, rational order and narrative structure, while the environment grounds the narrative in phenomenal and situational order and material structure, drawn together by the subject from both directions into one experiential lifeworld.

The integrity of the nodal network, therefore, is engendered by the way each node binds the other two into ecological relationships of interdependence. The relationship between the pairs of nodes is not just reciprocal but each node also acts to connect the other two. Since all three nodes act simultaneously, they create an ongoing flow and circulation from which the narrative environment emerges as material and experiential environment.

Taking a lead from ANT, and starting with a three-part network at the top level, the design of narrative environments develops a very specific understanding of the ways in which semiotic systems form and reform networks so that the whole network can be understood as a field of actanctiality. The design of narrative environments does not just rely on literary narratological semiotics but follows a designerly approach that conceives materiality, thought and action as thoroughly interconnected. In developing this semiotic system, the most adequate model is that of C. S. Peirce (1998). Peirce has a complex theory of semiotics but the important aspect, from the perspective of the design of narrative environments, is that he has a three-part scheme that allows the connection of sign and action, a position he defined as 'pragmaticism', a theory of practice. For example, his theory of the sign interrelates sign, object and interpretant. According to Peirce none of them exist until all of them exist. Using Peirce there is no necessary pre-existing relationship between story, as sign, and place, as object. They are brought into relationship by people, as interpretants. A humanistic interpretation of the narrative environment tripartite model would construe it as a tripartite relationship among 'I' at the people node, 'now' at the narrative node and 'here' at the environment node. This serves as the grounding of the narrative environment in symbolic abstraction and material attachment and provides the key to unlock orientation within and understanding of the narrative environment. 'Me', 'then', 'there' unfolds the past and future dimensions of subjectivity as it passes through the temporal dynamics of narrating alongside the situated spatial dynamics of placing. The tripartite network, seen from this perspective, is axiomatic for understanding starting position and for subjective orientation, spatial orientation, temporal orientation and their interrelationships (Figure 1.4).

To gain a more detailed understanding of the way each node binds and translates the other two, we look first in some detail at the 'people' node, initially employing the psychoanalytic theory of Jacques Lacan (1968; 1977). Lacan, interpreting Sigmund Freud, defines three interrelated dimensions of subjectivity: the imaginary, the symbolic and the real. In the adult person, these three orders co-exist, shaping and impacting each other. The imaginary is the reality that we consciously experience shaped around the image we have formed of ourselves. The symbolic is the social and cultural orders into which we are born, which the imaginary has to negotiate and navigate. The real is that to which we have no conscious access, in other words, the ways in which our desires are shaped through the interaction of the imaginary and the symbolic. According to Lacan, the imaginary is the image that the infant adopts to cohere its fragmented bodily experiences and form a self that over time becomes the centre of its future identifications and actions. The imaginary concerns pleasure, a domain in which fantasies, projections and identifications produce what we *take to be* reality. The symbolic is the societal order into which that self is inducted, once it assumes the form of an 'I' and adopts the conventions of linguistic and other bodily, social semiotics. The symbolic is a domain of control, where semiotic practices determine how you are perceived by others within specific interwoven cultural, economic and legal orders and, therefore, what roles you are permitted to take up. The Lacanian real, which is different from 'reality', is an unconscious, unknowable and indescribable realm. In Lacanian psychoanalytic theory, unconscious desire is sublimated or displaced, leading to the formation of a symptom, which is the observable side

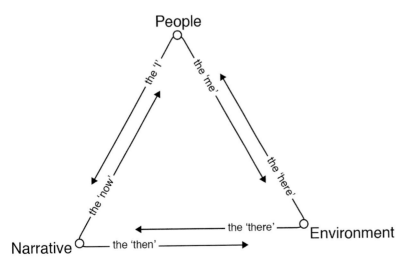

Figure 1.4 The play of conscious, spatial and temporal presence and absence in a narrative environment.

of the psychoanalytical object. The symptom, as the conscious object of an unknowable desire, can never be completely fulfilled. As the 'I' is not a self-contained identity (Lacan 1968; 1977) but a process of identification existing in a dynamic relation to its ever-changing environments, it is compelled to seek further imaginary identifications and, paradoxically, in endeavouring to remain the same, it finds itself involved in an itera-tive process of continual renewal. The imaginary 'I' seeks and follows a series of offers, invitations and promises and is thus developed and potentially transformed. Taking the Lacanian view of subjectivity, the design of narrative environments distinguishes between the conscious 'I', as articulated through linguistics and social semiotics, and the 'me', the imaginary process of bodily, objective self-identification. 'I' is self-consciousness and 'me' is the body, subject to the symbolic, societal order through its imaginary identifica-tions which shape its lifeworld. Together, 'I' and 'me' form an interwoven imaginary identity and a social self, the person as an actantial, networked being.

Following Lacan, we can link the unfolding of the 'I' to the narrative node through linguistic discourse and other semiotic media, as narrative discourse. In other words, one develops a sense of identity by constantly retelling the story of oneself to sustain a consistent self-identification (Bruner 2004). While one builds a unique identity, one does so by using the conventional resources of existing cultural narratives. One cre-ates a distinctive personal identity through one's individual articulation of conventional positions in language, semiosis and discourse. One chooses particular words in one's expressions, for example, slang words or regional words or a standard national lan-guage. Through these choices, one endeavours to position oneself through one's voice. This strategy may be accepted or not. If not accepted, one keeps negotiating, by altering one's expression and presentation, until one finds a position which is accepted. Vocal conventions intersect with conventions of the visual, the gestural and the sartorial, the way one uses one's body, the 'me', for example, proximity and touch and the way one projects onto and claims space, as the people node draws together the narrative node and the environment node. The example of the voice illustrates how difficult it is in practice to separate the conscious 'I' and the embodied 'me' but it is valuable to treat them separately for analytical purposes. Just as the 'I' is involved in processes of con-tinual self-renewal, the 'me', the embodied, socialised self opens up to the environment and gathers together an expanding set of spatial, temporal and material affiliations, allegiances and attachments, defining the space across which the 'me' is distributed. This would include, for example, clothing, material possessions, a sense of ownership of particular spaces and also more abstract senses of belonging such as to a neighbour-hood, a city or a country. One belongs not just to a specific locale; one is attached and shares allegiance to that culture, to that civilisation, to that history. The psychically invested lifeworld, through its embodiment sentiments, folds together the pragmatics of lived space and the more abstract semantics of material cultural history with its accom-panying politics of space.

The narrative node draws one in through identification with characters whose actions situate one in a particular place. For example, as a reader of *Ulysses* by James Joyce, one is initially drawn into the position of the character Stephen Dedalus, the artist hero seeking Christian transcendence, who appears to be on a journey from the suffering of this world to an eternal world of beauty, truth and freedom. After the initial scene setting, one stumbles across the figure of Leopold Bloom, an earthy and earthly charac-ter. Although Dedalus remains the narrative frame, one finds oneself following Leopold Bloom through the life of a Dubliner on a specific day, 16 June 1904. Far from a passage to the ethereal, one finds oneself caught in a mundane, corporeal journey. One switches from a passage towards the City of God to an entrapment within the city of Dublin. One follows Bloom encountering the people in his life as he walks through the streets of Dublin. Dublin, therefore, is characterised both as a field of social, personal and emotional relationships, an atmosphere, and as a geo-physical location. Together these form the world of the story. On the basis of the world of the story described by Joyce, one reconstructs 1904 as an imaginary storyworld. One imaginatively places oneself in the 'now' of 1904. As a reading subject, one is drawn into a position in a narrative in a particular place at a specific time: Bloom, Dublin, 1904. The narrative destination initially seems to be heavenly transcendence but becomes earthly entanglement. The narrative node identifies one as a 'he' in a 'now' in a 'here'. One does not go straight to Dublin but moves through an identification with 'he' as Dedalus and then to 'he' as Bloom who then transports one into the city. It is through narrative that the people node is translated to the environment node. The narrative node inscribes itself upon both the people node and upon the environment node, drawing them together in a particular imaginary and symbolic order through the telling of a tale.

In the present day, visitors to Dublin can follow Bloom's route as part of the Bloomsday festival. The city has taken Joyce's critical relationship to Dublin and turned it into a celebratory event. Initiated by a group of literary and cultural figures in 1954, the festival is now a major tourist event. People come to experience the 'then' and the 'there' as being intermingled with the 'now' and the 'here'. Thus, one characteristic of narrative environments is that visitors experientially oscillate to and fro between the 'now' and the 'then'; between the 'here' and the 'there'; and between who they are and who they imaginatively become. The story is evoked and made explicit through text, image, sound and performance in the physical environment. The importance of narrative as a way to bond people to place cannot be underestimated. It is an important theme in cultural geography, ranging from the discussion of foundational myths as a way to institute place to the use of storytelling in establishing urban identity (Tuan 1991), as well as in cultural anthropology (Fischer-Nebmaier 2015).

The environment node draws the people node onto the narrative node by translating subjective embodied experience into spatialised, materialised narrative. The elements of the environment node could be described as intercorporeal, interrelating bodies, both the living organic and the materially inorganic. The human body, understood through its subjective experiential dimension as 'me', takes part in enacting the intercorporeal through its attachments and allegiances to other people, physical objects and places. Other people's bodies are understood both as part of 'me', for example, as 'my friends', and as part of the objective environment, for example, as strangers. For example, in being a part of a demonstration, one feels an attachment to others in the crowd, they are like 'me', but you also see them as an undifferentiated mass, they are not 'me'. The intercorporeal includes relationships among people, who gather elements of the physical environment together to make a common world. An environment is not simply a set of materials or physical relationships but an active cultural form. The design of narrative environments shapes the intercorporeal into situations, events and places which inscribe cultural narratives. The environment node, understood as 'world', translates embodied experience of the 'me-here-now' into cultural narratives and histories of 'they-there-then' through enacting the material semiotics of place.

An example is the Brion Cemetery and Sanctuary, in San Vito D'Altivole, a small village not far from the Dolomite Mountains, Italy. It was designed from 1969 to 1977 by Italian modernist architect Carlo Scarpa. The tombs were commissioned by Onorina Tomasi, widow of industrialist Giuseppe Brion, the founder of the Brionvega company, for herself and her husband. There is no guide, no ticket, no signage to tell you where to go or what the space means. Scarpa said, "I have tried to put some poetic imagination into it, though not in order to create poetic architecture but to make a certain kind of architecture that could emanate a sense of formal poetry" (Kirk 2005: 204).

The visitor walks through the cemetery and enters the Brion Sanctuary through a towering two-storey concrete entrance facade and hallway. Three stairs and a double window formed by two large intersecting circles lead one into the space. It poses a question of whether the two circles represent a couple. You can then turn right or left down much narrower corridors with lower ceilings and hard surfaces which amplify the sound of your steps. The circles point towards symbolic narrative and the two directions posit a corporeal choice. If you turn right, a sense of claustrophobia grows and one has to push hard against a door at the end, which makes a loud grating sound. The bodily strength needed to push open the door as a resistant body generates an intercorporeal interaction which in turn opens up a sensory realm of sound. You emerge into a calm, quiet open space with a pond. You become more aware of the quietness and the stillness, in contrast to the noisy disturbance you have made in order to enter. You hear the sound of rhythmic dripping and the buzzing of flies over the smooth surface of the water. This is a place of contemplation.

If you had turned left down the other hallway, you would have emerged onto a lawn on the other side of the pond. You hear the sound of trickling as water flows through open concrete channels down to the two tombs on the far side of the garden. The motif of the pair is reiterated: two circles, two directions, two tombs. The tombs lean towards each other and are protected by a concrete bridge, with dappled light reflected on the underside. The concrete walls of the garden incline inwards, absorbing sound and forming a soundscape, a form of atmospherics. The pond and garden are meditative spaces punctuated only by the distant bells of the village church. The temporal punctuation of the bells' ringing highlights the endless 'now' of the sanctuary. You can see the village in the distance beyond the tombs giving rise to another pairing or duality: the village appears as a borrowed landscape, a 'there', reminding one of everyday life, yet setting one apart from that world in a bounded, protective 'here'. Beyond the tombs, up the hill, there is another building surrounded by water which you enter by walking across stepping stones. The door grates again upon opening. You find yourself in a simple space with concrete walls and a wood-panelled ceiling with an opening that lets in a shaft of light. Nowhere is this space explained as a chapel but you can sense its meaning from bodily being there. The unfolding narrative draws you into a story of what lives on after death but leaves you to resolve the paradox which the sanctuary poses between the eternal and the temporal.

In summary, the design of narrative environments proposes that the three-part network is axiomatic for the design process. The network incorporates the relationality and groundedness of Latourian and Peircian material semiotics. Insights are taken from Lacan's discussion of the psycho-dynamics of intersubjective and intercorporeal networks and knots and from Merleau-Ponty's demonstration that perception relies on the moving, sensing body. Lefebvre's thought is used to show how social practices are spatially and temporally produced. Barthes' and Ryan's arguments are heeded, that narrative is a medium-independent phenomenon and can be expressed through space and any material. Starting from three simple nodes, it can be seen from the above that the design of narrative environments gradually becomes more complex. The reason for developing the theoretical model is to provide a scaffolding for the progressive assembly of rich, evocative and engaging narrative environments.

References

Alexander, C. (2004) *The Nature of Order*. London: Taylor & Francis.

Augé, M. (1995) *Non-Places: Introduction to an Anthropology of Supermodernity*. London: Verso.

Bachelard, G. (1994) *The Poetics of Space*. Boston: Beacon Press.

Bal, M. (2009) *Narratology: Introduction to the Theory of Narrative*. Toronto; Buffalo; London: University of Toronto Press.

Barthes, R. (1977) 'Death of the Author' in *Image-Music-Text*. Glasgow: Fontana, pp. 142–148.

Baur, Ruedi (2019) interview with Tricia Austin October 31, 2019.

Bourdieu, P. (1984) *Distinction: A Social Critique of the Judgement of Taste*. London: Routledge.

Bruner, J. (2004) 'Life as Narrative' in *Social Research*, 71(33), pp. 691–710.

Böhme, G. (2017) *The Aesthetics of Atmospheres*. London, Routledge.

Certeau, M. (1984) *The Practice of Everyday Life*. Berkeley: University of California Press.

Childs, M. C. (2008) 'Storytelling and urban design'. *Journal of Urbanism*, 1(2), pp. 173–186.

Cullen, G. (1971) *The Concise Townscape*. Oxford, UK: The Architectural Press.

de la Cadena. M. and Blazer, M. (2018) *A World of Many Worlds*. Durham: Duke University Press.

Fischer-Nebmaier, W. (2015). Introduction: Space, narration, and the everyday. In: *Narrating the City: Histories, Space and the Everyday*. Fischer-Nebmaier, W., Berg, M. P., and Christou, A., eds. New York, NY: Berghahn Books, pp. 1–55.

Frith, J. (2015) *Smart Phones as Locative Media*. (Digital Media and Society Series). Cambridge, UK: Polity.

Fogle, N. (2011) *The Spatial Logic of Social Struggle: A Bourdieuian Topology*. Lanham: Lexington books.

Grosz, E. (1995) *Space Time and Perception*. New York: Routledge.

Jameson, F. (1981) *The Political Unconscious: Narrative as a Socially Symbolic Act*. Ithaca, NY: Cornell University Press.

Johnson, P. (1965) Whence & Whither: The processional element in architecture. *Perspecta*, 9(10), 167–178.

Kirk, T. (2005) *The Architecture of Modern Italy. Vol 2 Visions of Utopia, 1900-present*. New York, NY: Princeton Architectural Press.

Lacan, J. (1968) *The Language of the Self: The Function of Language in Psychoanalysis*. New York, NY: Dell Publishing.

Lacan, J. (1977) *Ecrits: As Selection*. London: Tavistock Publications.

Lash, S. and Picon, A. (2009) Agency and architecture: How to be critical? Scott Lash and Antoine Picon, in conversation with Kenny Cupers and Isabelle Doucet. Comments by Margaret Crawford. *Footprint Delft School of Design Journal*, Spring 2009, 7–20.

Latour, B. (1993) *We Have Never Been Modern*. Cambridge, MA: Harvard University Press.

Latour, B. (1999) On recalling ANT. *The Sociological Review*, 47 (S1), 15–25.

Latour, B. (2005) *Reassembling the Social: An Introduction to Actor-Network-Theory*. Oxford, UK: Oxford University Press.

Latour, B. (2009) Spheres and networks. *Harvard Design Magazine*, 30, 138–144.

Lawson, B. (2001) *Language of Space*. Burlington, MA: Elsevier.

Le Corbusier (1995) *Œuvre Complète = Complete Works*. Basel: Birkhauser.

Lefebvre, H. (1974) *The Construction of Space*. Oxford, UK: Blackwell.

Lynch, K. (1960) *The Image of the City*. Cambridge, MA: MIT Press.

Macintyre, A. (2007) *After Virtue: A Study in Moral Theory*, 3rd ed. Notre Dame, IN: University of Notre Dame Press.

Malpas, J. E. (1999) *Place and Experience: A Philosophical Topology*. Cambridge, UK: Cambridge University Press.

Massey, D. (2005) *For Space*. London: Sage.

Merleau-Ponty, M. (2002) *Phenomenology of Perception*. Trans. Colin Smith. London: Routledge.

Mauss, M. (1992) Techniques of the body. In: Crary, J. and Kwinter, S., eds. *Incorporations*. New York, NY: Zone.

Nancy, J.-L. (2007) *The Creation of the World, or, Globalization*. Albany, NY: State University of New York Press.

Norberg-Schulz, C. (1979) *Genius Loci: Towards a Phenomenology of Architecture*. New York: Rizzoli.

Parsons, A. (2009) Narrative environments: How do they matter? *Rhizomes*, 19. Online. Available HTTP: http://rhizomes.net/issue19/parsons/index.html. Accessed 27 October 2019.

Peirce, C. S. (1998) *Collected Papers of Charles Sanders Peirce. Volume 2: Elements of Logic*. Bristol: Thoemmes Press.

Perec, G. (1997) *Species of Space and Other Pieces*. London: Penguin.

Porter Abbott, H. (2002) *The Cambridge Introduction to Narrative*. Cambridge, UK: Cambridge University Press.

Ricoeur, P. (1979) The human experience of time and narrative. *Research in Phenomenology*, 9, 17–34.

Ryan, M. L., (2004) *Narrative across Media: The Languages of Storytelling* (Frontiers of Narrative). Lincoln: University of Nebraska Press.

Ryan, M. L., Foote, K. and Azaryahu, M. (2016) *Narrating Space/Spatializing Narrative: Where Narrative Theory and Geography Meet*. Columbus, OH: Ohio State University Press.

Samuel, F. (2010) *Le Corbusier and the Architectural Promenade*. Basel: Birkhäuser.

Sloterdijk, P. (2011) Architectures an art of immersion. *Interstices: Journal of Architecture and Related Art*, 12, 105–109.

Silverstein, Teil (2019) Interview with Tricia Austin October 5, 2019.

Traxler, J. (2011) The mobile and mobility: Information, organisations and systems. In: Pokorny, J. et al., eds. *Information Systems Development: Business Systemss and Services:Modeling and Development*. New York, NY: Springer. pp. 25–34.

Tuan, Y.-F. (1991) Language and the making of place: A narrative-descriptive approach. *Annals of the Association of American Geographers*, 81(4), 684–696.

Yaneva, A. (2016) *Mapping Controversies in Architecture*. London; New York: Routledge.

2 Precursors

In this chapter, the design of narrative environments is discussed as a transdisciplinary practice that draws together thinking and skills from many different sources. Its collaborative methods challenge deep-seated assumptions about hierarchies and boundaries in art and design. Art and design education have been shaped, in part, by the nineteenth-century *Beaux Arts* tradition in which fine art and architecture were granted the highest status. During the twentieth century, architecture consolidated its status by establishing its own institutions to safeguard and promote the profession. By contrast, design, even though it had been granted some legitimacy by the Arts and Crafts movement and the Bauhaus, was still confined in the mid-twentieth century to the status of commercial and applied art, and thus as secondary to fine art and architecture. However, more recently, design has shown that it is not just a technical practice driven by aesthetics and the market but rather is a principled practice that aims to shape a better world. The design of narrative environments espouses such broader socio-political and environmental goals and aims to consolidate and provide a coherent framework to address them. In seeking to flatten traditional hierarchies, the design of narrative environments embraces art and architecture but gives them the same status as other design disciplines, including communication design, scenography, product design and interaction design. It also adds to the mix by introducing writing, interpretation and curation. It combines aspects of different design disciplines which may in themselves be weighted more towards one of the nodes in the tripartite model. However, the design of narrative environments draws them into a vital and reciprocal network that supports critical and socially-engaged design. Although this may seem a new approach, the historical precursors of narrative environments are described below to show how script, space, objects, symbols and signs have been used to create sacred spaces, landscape narratives, amusement parks, world fairs, live action role playing, exhibition design, narrative architecture, retail and brand experiences, social innovation, critical and speculative design and design fiction. The range shows the versatility of the design of narrative environments as a newly established practice.

Design Practice Sources

As a multidisciplinary practice, the design of narrative environments draws skills and principles from several fields (Figure 2.1). From urban design and architecture, the design of narrative environments incorporates analytical skills and the ability to envisage forms and spaces that the human body can enter and pass through. Architectural scale can be used to express the divine, take steeples, domes and minarets, for example, or power and authority, as evident in the dimensions of government buildings, museums and law courts, which reach heights several times that of the human body. Expressive

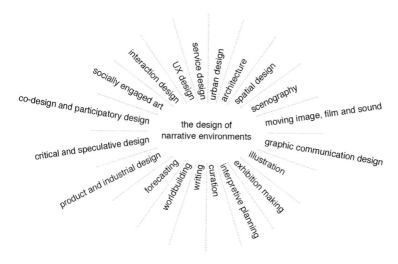

Figure 2.1 The network of disciplines that contribute to the design of narrative environments.

use of scale also requires an understanding of the relationship of the smaller parts to the whole, including zones, spaces, and their respective functions and details. Abstract organisational logic and sense of purpose are combined with physical structure and tectonics, building morphology, spatial dimensions, volumes and planes. Architecture involves an orchestration of adjacency, proximity and distance, levels, surfaces qualities and materiality. As spaces for people to visit and dwell, there are also concerns for air quality, temperature, sound, light conditions and atmosphere. These are all important to the design of narrative environments. Given human movement, machine movement, movement of sound, air and heat, there is a focus on thresholds, boundaries and means of orientation such as axes, landmarks and sightlines. Furthermore, architects take into account the relationship of buildings to their immediate environment plus their geographic and historical context. Urban design and architecture share a concern for flow, capacity and practical functionality as well for the social and economic impact of any changes to the built environment. Spatial or interior design is a closely related profession, traditionally concerned with the fit out and zoning of spaces once built, such as layout, materiality, lighting and atmosphere. More recently, however, it has taken a larger view, incorporating the design of physical aspects of external spaces, exhibition spaces and other public spaces.

While the design of narrative environments incorporates many of these approaches, it differs from urban design, architecture and spatial design for several reasons. Mainstream urban design, architecture and spatial design focus on functionality and production specification within specific legal, policy and commercial contexts. In terms of the tripartite network model, architecture, urban design and spatial design reside in the environmental node, defining it as an instrumental domain providing utility for the assumed inhabitant. However, these spatial disciplines do not explicitly engage with the social practices that they may reproduce or reinforce. Architecture, urban design and spatial design can create powerful visual impact, referencing past styles, but these are not typically regarded as communicating content or narrative, even while they may set up resonant metaphors. Urban design, architecture and spatial design usually anticipate content arising from human activity once the design is inhabited. In contrast, designers of narrative environments understand the spaces and structures to constitute particular behaviours that express key values shaping experience and playing a part in narratives. Urban design, architecture and spatial design are conventionally resolved as technical diagrams within specific traditions of architectural notation such as ground plans, elevations, axiomatic diagrams, cross sections, 3D renderings, fly-throughs or detailed illustrations or computer generated visualisations, physical or digital models of buildings or city quarters and sample materials boards. This range of outputs is, to an extent, prescribed by professional licensing bodies. The products of these disciplines typically represent structure and functionality but do not express time-based, content-driven, user experiences. These experiences are expressed in the design of narrative environments through storyboards developed from the perspective of the visitor or inhabitant. While elements of urban design, architecture and spatial design provide an important structural dimension of the design of narrative environments, other disciplines are also essential to incorporate visitor or inhabitant experience and narrative content.

From scenography, the design of narrative environments borrows an understanding of the unfolding of experience through clearly articulated zones of action and planned temporal sequences. This is the realm of ritual and techniques of performance that acknowledge other people's presence in a space as key to mood and action in any unfolding story. Scenography also brings a vast array of techniques in lighting, film projection and costume that immerse visitors in a fictional world. Scenography is concerned with transmitting meanings and narrative through relationships among acting, scripting and communication of symbolic meanings through the elements of the set. Both scenography and the design of narrative environments focus on how audiences become engaged, how that engagement is sustained over time and how audiences grasp and understand content. A scenographer typically produces scenic paintings and props as well as sound and light effects. The temporal nature of performance affects the choice of materials, using lightweight disposable supplies that are not necessarily handled by the audience. Scenography, like the design of narrative environments, appeals through sensory, intellectual and emotional means. However, it differs from the design of narrative environments in that it produces predominantly temporary performances, whereas narrative environments persist, in some cases for hundreds of years.

From graphic communication design, the design of narrative environments takes a concern for naming, informing, engaging, warning and persuading through static and animated text, illustration, moving image, film and sound. The visual logic of graphic design, based on information hierarchy and analogy, functions on a surface. Graphics occupies 'flatland', as information designer Edward Tuffte (1983) puts it. Nevertheless, in many ways, the principles of graphic language correspond to the principles of spatial language. Hierarchy is produced through scale and positioning. Headlines are bigger than, and set above, body text, just as front doors are larger than surrounding architectural features and are often elevated with steps leading up to them. Books, posters and websites are arranged on underlying grids to give coherent visual sequences, using rhythms and repetition, just as, for example, built cloisters or arcades do. Graphics also uses juxtaposition, contrast, gaps, clustering and framing to emphasise, align, surprise and sometimes unsettle viewers, while relating the parts to the whole, just as spatial designers and scenographers do. Graphic designers, illustrators, film makers and sound designers also work especially with connotation. In other words, they use the evocative qualities of colour, light, form, sound and recognisable objects and places to evoke supplementary meanings. Particularly clever and resonant combinations are described sometimes as wit or poetic expression, while associative metaphor or deliberate symbolic disruption of norms is core to graphics. Graphic designers recognise a typeface, for example, not only for its formal qualities but also for its associations that enrich and embody messages, just as specific choices of materials in architecture communicate through sensory means and association. A key difference between architecture and graphics is that graphics is about explicit communication and legibility, while architectural communication is often much more implicit. In terms of the tripartite narrative environments network, graphics emphasises the people and narrative discourse relationship. The important difference between communication design and the design of narrative environments is that the graphics in narrative environments are interwoven with the spatial context to articulate the experiential flow of content through space over time, drawing the environmental and the narrative nodes together.

The design of narrative environments also integrates skills from the world of museology, because one manifestation of the design of narrative environments is exhibition-making. Museologists are those who are concerned with any aspect of museums and other informal learning-based organisations such as zoos, parks, heritage sites and science centres. Curation, writing, interpretive planning and management are vital to exhibition making. The curator cares for the collection, is a subject expert and often proposes the exhibition topic and key messages. Interpretive planners and interpretation managers help to create a story as a vehicle to communicate topic and key messages to the target audience. They produce a written narrative, an interpretive plan which acts as the organising principle and guide sometimes for architecture, often for exhibition development, marketing and management of audiences. This means interpretive planners and managers need to understand the goals and mission of their client and their client's business model. Interpretive planners and managers are required to analyse diverse kinds of content. They need to understand what audiences already know and what audiences want to know, in order to synthesise the different dimensions and create a relevant storyline. A full narrative environment requires input from curators, designers and specialist suppliers in considering the best ways to communicate and engage audiences by, for example, using objects, images, maps, text and signage, film, sound, interactives and immersive digital media. The interpretation needs to include a sense of who is speaking and hence the tone of voice of the exhibition or environment. Interpretive planners and managers also suggest how museums, parks or neighbourhoods might measure the success of the design through, for example, footfall, dwell time, press coverage, knowledge gained by visitors or new perceptions of the organisation or area.

From product and industrial design, the design of narrative environments incorporates the knowledge of materials, production techniques, bodily and emotional interaction with objects and their symbolic values. Product designers have focused on user experience since the development of human-centred design in the 1980s, an approach in which design decisions are driven by an empathy with the people for whom you are designing. Product designers are also interested in narrative. Researcher Silvia Grimaldi (2015) explores domestic objects' ability to tell stories, in other words, their potential to elicit narrative responses from users, and how the narrativity of film discourse can be integrated into products. Grimaldi argues that objects can be designed to provoke personal narratives and that doing so adds to their technical, functional or aesthetic value. Her work belongs to the critical and speculative approaches (Malpass 2017) that have been developed in product and interaction design in the last 20 years. Critical design is generally that which goes beyond market-driven problem-solving and provokes critical reflection on the socio-political context of design. Speculative approaches

(Dunne and Raby 2014) are future-focused explorations of how forecasting research may play out in the everyday. In the UK, Tony Dunne (1999) pioneered critical practice and speculative design practice. His work raises issues of environmental sustainability, privacy and identity, using satire and recontextualisation to disrupt normative readings and prompt critical thinking in audiences. Although it shares an interest in critical approaches to design, the design of narrative environments differs from product design in that it focuses on the relationships of objects to space and to human interaction, demonstrating a greater emphasis on the environmental node in the three-part network.

Speculative designers Eva Knutz, Thomas Markussen and Poul Rind Christensen (2014) deploy design fiction (Bleeker 2009; DiSalvo 2012; Grand and Weidmer 2010) as a research method to develop new products. Design fiction envisages speculative and provocative 'what if' futures populated by fictional personas. The resulting scenarios give rise to radical new products and services. For example, the Kolding team set a student brief in 2013 starting from Kaspar Nielson's novel *Civil War in Denmark*, which itself is set in the future. They asked students to immerse themselves in that fictional world in order to envisage objects and interactions appropriate to that world. In this case, the students produced a proposition, 'Recycling Humans', that challenges current moral and ethical norms by envisaging ways of recycling dead human bodies, victims of war, to make garments and artefacts in an era of scarcity. These fictions were materialised through products. Had they been spatially materialised, they would become narrative environments.

In Los Angeles, designer and professor Alex McDowell produces future world narratives. McDowell established the World Building Media Lab (WbML) (2012–2018) which allows scientists, storytellers, artists, programmers and conceptual thinkers to create future scenarios on urgent issues, such as rapid urbanisation, environmental sustainability and the worldwide refugee crisis. The WbML describes its method as developing a world from which threads of narrative logic emerge. The WbML produces immersive physical environments, film and virtual realities, while contributing to the development of new business models, policies and patentable technologies. This practice aligns closely with the design of narrative environments which also produces 'what if' future scenarios and objects, such as the scenarios created by MA Narrative Environments students in collaboration with Arup Foresight and Innovation.

The narrative environments programme shares some features with service design, which emerged in the 1990s as an 'interdisciplinary, collaborative and holistic field of design' (Prendiville 2016). Service design was, in some ways, a response to the burgeoning service economy but it was also an opportunity to shift systems of production and consumption towards environmental and social sustainability. Service design deliberately steers the focus of design from being about the development of material artefacts to the design of interactions between service providers and consumers (Service Design Network 2017). It looks for inventiveness and creativity among 'ordinary people' to solve daily life problems related to such themes as housing, food, ageing, transport and work, and develops collaborative services and business models helping to shape new forms of community and new ideas of locality. It is concerned with improving the quality and delivery of services, such as transportation, banking and health services, that weave socio-technical structures and power relations into everyday life. Services are understood as a time-based physical and emotional interaction with objects, places and information (Sangiorgi 2009). Service designers map stakeholder and customer journey maps, fictional personas and storyboards showing touch points, that is, where and when the user comes into contact with or is reminded of the service or brand. Service designers use collaborative workshops with users and stakeholders as a way to democratise information-gathering and decision-making. They also prototype and test services using an iterative design process. There has been widespread adoption of service design among both commercial and public sector organisations. Many design techniques used in service design are also used in the design of narrative environments. The main difference is that service design propositions tend to resolve as diagrams of systems and products, whereas narrative environments resolve as narrative spatial experiences, emphasising both the narrative and the environmental nodes in the tripartite network.

From interaction design, the narrative environments incorporate a concern for seeing the world through the eyes of the user and inviting dialogue and participation. Interaction design developed in 1990s, emerging from the sphere of computing. As a result, interaction design is often considered a screen-based practice that enables human interaction with machines to be more user-friendly, intuitive and pleasurable. The internet of things, however, has opened the door to interacting verbally with smart objects, such as Amazon's Alexa. The design of narrative environments acknowledges that the physical environment can be seen as an interface, and includes the making of computer-enabled environments. User experience design (UX) has evolved from interaction design. It is particularly relevant to the design of narrative environments because UX designers use scenarios and storyboards to envision experience, opening productive questions concerning the relationship between digital 'materiality' and other kinds of material environments. They focus on people as their primary frame of reference and explore how to achieve high levels of engagement and satisfaction from a product service or space. Like the design of narrative environments, UX designers may collaborate with non-designers, such as sociologists, psychologists and data analysts, iteratively testing their ideas on their anticipated users. The designers of narrative environments differ from UX designers in their specific focus on the potential for the combination of narrative discourse and embodied perception in a physical environment.

The design of narrative environments also practises co-design or participatory design, where designers develop propositions in partnership with the people for whom they are designing. The word co-design first appears in the UK (Sanders and Stappers 2008) in 1971 but the practice gathered pace around the millennium and is being widely adopted and developed by many design disciplines. Co-design implies sharing authority in decision-making. The user assumes the role of expert in their area of experience and designers work within a plural context negotiating with others' positions. In architecture, peer-to-peer urbanism or participatory urban activism developed in Scandinavia, the USA and Europe (Krivý and Kaminer 2013) to overcome traditional architectural consultation processes, perceived as top-down tokenism. Co-design or participatory design techniques are frequently used when working on complex social innovation projects where citizen expertise is vital to developing propositions and where co-ownership with inhabitants is key to maintaining new systems that aim to sustain communities or overcome social divides in harsh conditions. Such designers not only need strong research skills, lateral and creative thinking but also strategic planning and mediation skills. Some art practices also apply participatory practice, particularly in issue-based, socially engaged projects. The critical and inventive approach of fine art overlaps with the design of narrative environments. However, socially-engaged art is not necessarily narrative. In fact, artists often raise questions rather than tell stories. Socially engaged art research does not systematically integrate skills and processes from architecture, performance, graphics, product design and interaction design. Art tends to be rooted in the individual artist's preoccupations.

In summary, twentieth-century design disciplines differentiated themselves on the basis of discourses and practices involving specific materials, media and technical processes related to particular industries. So, for example, architecture pursued design for construction using drawing, working with wood, stone, glass, metal and cement and exploring tectonics, the art of framing construction; while graphic design emerged as the articulation of word and image on printed matter and produced design for the publishing and advertising industries, amongst others. By contrast, more recent holistic approaches, such as service design and the design of narrative environments, add temporal, spatial, user-centred and action-based dimensions, while relying on multidisciplinary practice to open to the outside world beyond professional conventions. As such, the design of narrative environments does not have a defined subject matter but can apply its processes to the subject at hand through the tripartite network, situating the design in terms of narrative discourse, demographics and place. It becomes relevant to a much broader range of industries and cultural, commercial and social enterprises. That is not to say that the traditional design skills are outmoded. Multidisciplinary teams require specific expertise in a wide range of material skills and knowledge to create effective propositions. However, in the design of narrative environments technical skills are reframed, treated less hierarchically and in a less predetermined order.

Narrative Environments *Avant La Lettre*

Historical precursors of narrative environments are numerous. Although not conceived as narrative environments, they demonstrate the integral interweaving of story, space and people. They can be understood as spaces that fulfil a range of purposes from the expression of the sacred; of political power; of conventional values; of commercial, educational and social practices; and of critical commentary and protest. Figure 2.2 shows a genealogy with examples named or discussed in the book.

Sacred places are environments that combine script, sound, image, light, music and architecture. From the towers of Angkor Wat in Cambodia to the cathedrals of Western Europe, they are some of the most historic precursors of narrative environments. St John's Cathedral in Valetta, Malta, for example, is one of the world's most significant Baroque churches. St John's Cathedral is an architectural metaphor for the Order of the Knights of St John, who built it between 1573 and 1578. The plain post-siege facade suggests the knights' military pragmatism, while inside the lavish gilded vaults, polychrome marble floors and fresco ceilings evoke the power and wealth of the Order. Stories of the Bible and the Saints are communicated through huge paintings, alongside inlaid floor mosaic showing angels and skeletons. The Cathedral works on at least three levels. Firstly, it expresses the Christian story. This story also spills out onto the streets of Valetta in a more populist form, as parades, fiestas and processions with effigies. At a second level, the Cathedral provides a strand in the history and identity of Malta. At a third level, the Cathedral contributes to an international history of art, because the oratory houses several paintings by the renowned sixteenth-century painter Caravaggio. Further levels could be added concerning the preconditions for the emergence of capitalism and the modern world. The connections and layers of all these stories are most strongly defined by the narrative node, the biblical narratives that position the human subjects and develop spatial languages that encode theological and emerging power relations.

On the other side of the world, in Hong Kong, the Chi Lin nunnery and park in Diamond Hills, Kowloon, immerses you in a different tradition, Buddhism. Nevertheless,

	6c.BC–5c.	6c.–14c.	15c.–19c.	20c.	21c.
The sacred *places of wonder that tell sacred stories*		Angkor Wat, Cambodia	St John's Cathedral, Valletta, Malta The festival of Ganesh Chaturthi, Pune, India	Chi Lin Nunnery and park, Kowloon, HK Villa Savoye, Poissy, France	
The political *places designed to impress and tell stories of power*	The Ishtar Gate, Babylon	The Arch of Titus, Rome, Italy	Temple of Ancient Virtue, The Elysian Fields, Stowe, UK		Skopje city centre, North Macedonia
The conventional *places that express or enable people to enact deeply held value systems using narrative*			Bournville Village, UK	Cazenovia, New York, USA Kentlands, Maryland, USA	ReGen village, Netherlands
The commercial *commercial places that use narrative to provide an escape to fictional worlds*			Steeplechase Park, Coney Island, USA	Luxor, Las Vegas, USA Huis Ten Bosch, Nagasaki, Japan	Sky City, Hangzhou, China Helmut Lang Hollywood store, LA, USA
The educational *places that primarily tell stories to educate*			The Great Exhibition, London, UK Futurama exhibit, New York World's Fair, USA	US Holocaust Memorial Museum, Washington, USA Play Zone, Millennium Dome, London, UK	The Blur Building, Swiss EXPO, Switzerland The Seed Cathedral, Shanghai EXPO, China
The social *places that primarily tell stories to increase sociability*			Pfaueninsel Park, Berlin, Germany		Granary Square, London, UK Musical Shadows, Mesa, USA
The critical *places that primarily tell stories to critique normative values and market driven value systems*				Stalker/ Osservatorio Nomade collective walking, Italy	Giants: Border Mexico, Tecate, Mexico–USA Extinction Rebellion, multiple sites worldwide

Figure 2.2 Genealogies of narrative environments.

the three-node network can still be seen to be at play as Buddhist narratives run through the temple design. The temple was renovated in the 1990s in the style of the Tang Dynasty. There are 16 halls in total inside the temple, and it is approached through a traditional Chinese garden. The entry and passage into the Buddhist temples is a sequence of gateways and courtyards that pace the experience as they lead you to the centre as a sanctuary. Each courtyard houses sculptures, for example, the Sakyamuni Buddha, the goddess of mercy, Guanyin and the Bodisattvas, which are made of gold, clay and wood. Each space is a scenographic tableaux of symbolic narratives communicated through path surfaces, vistas, carvings, sculptures and rituals (Barrie 2010).

Moving to India, the festival of Ganesh Chaturthi, which originated in Pune, demonstrates how whole cities can be temporarily but utterly transformed into narrative environments. The festival lasts 10 days. On the first day, families bring home the idol of Lord Ganesha. There are parties and, over the following days, rituals are carried out in his name. On the last day, crowds fill the streets and block all other movement as the idol is paraded in public. Loud music, dancing and coloured smoke marks the approaching culmination of the festival, when the effigy is tipped into the river Ganges. The immersion is called 'Ganesh Visarjan', and it is believed the Ganges carries Lord Ganesha back home to his parents Lord Shiva and Goddess Parvati who live in the Himalayas. Hinduism is rich with festivals that enact the stories of the religion. Each festival has particular rituals, traditions, songs, foods and clothes. There are also gender-specific ceremonies. All of these communicate complex interconnected layers of narrative. Space and time come together in unique ways in a purposefully constructed narrative environment. The Russian literary theorist Mikhail Bakhtin coined the term 'chronotope', a combination of *chronos* meaning time and *topos* meaning space, to express this merging of time, space and event: "space becomes charged and responsive to the movement of time, plot and history" (Bakhtin 1981: 84). This underpins the time-space experiences of such events as rituals, festivals, processions and journeys, confirming the three-node network. It informs our perception of landscapes, cityscapes and buildings that become temporal-spatial and narrative events for believers.

Narrative religious and political rituals weave together the architectural form, the moving body and the unfolding stories into a cohesive narrative environment, for example, the Ishtar Gate which was the eighth gate to the inner city of Babylon. It was built circa 575 BCE by order of King Nebuchadnezzar II. The design of the gates is layered so that the opening gradually reduces in size, visually drawing you in and attracting you into the space. The brick walls are covered in a blue glaze representing lapis lazuli, a deep-blue semi-precious stone that was highly prized in antiquity. The Processional Way, which was lined with walls showing lions, bulls, dragons and flowers, symbolised the Goddess Ishtar. The gate itself depicts the gods and goddesses Ishtar, Adad and Marduk. Such processional urban design persists to the present day. Large broad roads are designed as festival routes and military parades. Take the Mall in Washington, Pall Mall in London or Red Square in Moscow. These forms can spring to life as narrative environments when they are animated by people with a common purpose. Their narrative can also be transformed if they become places of protest or riot (Kaika and Karaliotis 2014).

Political narratives can be embedded in the city and the landscape. Adam Scott, co-founder of FreeState, a London-based design company that specialises in narrative experience master planning, cites Stowe Gardens in Buckinghamshire, England, as an inspirational example. In the eighteenth century, the influential Lord Cobham commissioned the gardens which were designed by landscape architect William Kent as a spatial narrative. Stowe Gardens articulate an argument for a new political order based on classical ideals of freedom. Kent added hills, valleys, lakes, temples, ruins, monuments and statues that formed trails depicting, for example, stories of vice, virtue, love, lust and sea-faring. In one section, the Elysian Fields, a Temple of Ancient Virtue looks across to a Temple of British Worthies built in the newly fashionable Palladian style, equating famous English figures with classical poets and scholars. Cobham also employed a hermit as a performer to complete the narrative. Kent commissioned a special book for Stowe Gardens, possibly the first ever guide book, which featured two characters, one a pragmatist and the other a poet. This book was given to Cobham's guests, the richest and most influential men in England, if not the world, at that time. As visitors strolled through the gardens, landscape, sculptures and architecture, the book evoked the political struggles of the eighteenth century to prompt debate.

A rich history of parks and landscapes designed as spatial narratives can be delineated. American academics Matthew Potteiger and Jamie Purington discuss these phenomena in some detail in their book *Landscape Narratives* (1998). Potteiger and Purington fold together literary theory, cultural geography and visual art to create a framework for understanding the design of landscape narratives. They critique new regionalism and neo-traditionalism in the USA such as can be found in Cazenovia, New York. Cazenovia constructs its narrative of resistance to the homogenising effects of mass production, controlled by long-distance capital, but it does so through nostalgia. Bournville in the UK, designed in the nineteenth century to look like a medieval village as a reaction to industrialisation, might also be critiqued as nostalgic. Potteiger and Purington go on to discuss Kentlands, Maryland, which was planned and built in the latter half of the twentieth century to look like a traditional rural American town. Kentlands was modelled on towns such as Cazenovia. The developers wrote a town charter, established a town newspaper and town parade to assert its fictional history. They even created brochures that featured an old estate and pictured children in period dress. Potteiger and Purington argue that the design professionals and corporate developers built Kentlands as a replica that plays on sentimentality and, as such, is a closed narrative. Potteiger and Purington, in analysing open and closed narratives, suggest that open narratives are indeterminate, public, participatory, layered with multiple temporalities and interpreted somewhat differently by different users. Closed narratives, alternatively, are determined, private, commodified, use selected time frames and are controlled by authors. Current initiatives of civic environments such as ReGen Villages in the Netherlands have strong narratives. The first high-tech eco village "will collect and store its own water and energy, grow its own food, and process much of its own waste. Also: no cars" (Peters 2018). Although focused, this narrative is not closed; it is open to the ongoing economic, ecological and social context.

In a more explicitly commercial context, moving away from civic environments, Norman Klein (2004) introduces the notion of scripted spaces. Klein traces a history of lavish spectacle, optical illusion, cinematic effects and the engineering of the real using shocks, surprises, fakery, applying narrative collage to the service of powerful entities which seduce us with appealing myths. By analysing the Luxor in Las Vegas, Brian Lonsway (2009) discusses the spatial articulation and materialisation of fictionalised history, mixed with the functions of a resort hotel. He explores how this requires collaboration among developers, architects, film makers and ride designers. Lonsway also discusses Huis Ten Bosch, a public park in Kyushu, Japan, modelled on Dutch architecture and social practices, suggesting that it is a type of theme park that builds on the tradition of tourist villages to represent otherness or foreignness. He locates it "somewhere

between the western models of world fairs, living history museums and theme parks"
(Lonsway 2009: 88). In terms of the visitor experience, these environments are more
temporary than the civic; the duration relates to the financial contract made between the
visitor and the park operator.

The last 10 years have seen an acceleration in whole-town themed environments.
Take for example, Sky City, a replica of Paris on the outskirts of Hangzhou, China,
with an Eiffel Tower, Champs-Élysées and Haussmann-style apartments, or Liaoning's
Holland Village, also in China, which installed windmills and canals to replicate The
Hague. This is happening all over the world. For example, in the pedestrian resort village
of Mont Tremblant in Canada, developed by Intrawest, the architecture is reminiscent of
old Quebec while also evoking traditional German and Swiss styles. Like Disney, Mont
Tremblant village is expertly staged and managed. Care is taken that you always feel safe
and it is a very successful enterprise. Within the range of narrative environments, these
resorts cite previous styles and eras but not with any critical intention.

The interlinking of narrative and space in the Disney phenomenon has been discussed
by others at length (Vanderbilt 1999). The layout, with a central motif or 'honey pot',
attracts people to the centre and avenues reaching outwards prevent visitors from feeling lost. Events are timed approximately every half hour to attract and distract people.
Staff are always moving towards visitors to offer a helping hand. The slightly smaller-
than-life-size scale of the buildings intimates that people have entered a fictionalised,
out-of-the-ordinary world. It is comfortable, safe and entertaining. While the experience
is clearly packaged, nevertheless, its popularity indicates that it is engaging, despite the
expense and the long queues which introduce a certain frustration and exhaustion. From
the point of view of the design of narrative environments, the questions that arise concern what sustains Disney's continuing success: Is it, for example, that Disney's stories,
being rooted in children's literature, are moral tales in which evil is always defeated and
good always triumphs, asserting moral certainty in an uncertain world?

Disney exploits, while sanitising, the Bakhtinian notion of the carnivalesque. Mikhail
Bakhtin (1968) discusses the medieval European tradition of the carnivalesque, suggesting it was a ritual spectacle where common people could experience a world which
opposed official truths upheld by the church and the feudal lords. Hierarchies, norms
and prohibitions were suspended through satire and parody. Kings became fools. You
could laugh at authorities and ritually subvert everyday norms. Bakhtin argued the car-
nival offered renewal and revival. Something of the same spirit persists in early amusement parks such as Luna Park, Dreamland and Steeplechase Park on Coney Island, New
York. Coney Island projected a world of exotic otherness, freeing people to behave in
non-conventional ways. In its heyday, in the late nineteenth and early twentieth century,
Coney Island offered thrilling rollercoaster rides and exotic and voyeuristic freak shows.
In 1885, James Lafferty built the 'Elephant Hotel', a 122-foot-tall animal with tin skin
and glass eyes that straddled the beach like a Colossus of Brooklyn. The hind legs hid the
staircase to the torso's 31 rooms and ocean views. It was known for its hedonism. Coney
Island was a place where people could transgress conventional mores. While being a kind
of narrative environment, Coney Island's relationship to the everyday was more one of
escapism rather than of reflection.

After the Second World War, competition from other leisure experiences reduced
the appeal of Coney Island. The last section to close was Steeplechase Park in 1964. It
was the end of an era for Coney Island but narrative-led leisure experiences are still in
demand. For example, Secret Cinema offers spatialised cinematic experiences, combining film screenings with interactive performances in found settings that evoke the film

that provides the theme. Screenings are set up almost like a game with strict rules of play. Ticket holders must keep the destination secret; they are not told the name of the film they will eventually see; they must dress up in a code prescribed by Secret Cinema. On arrival, the audience explore the site, read the multiple strands of narrative through the architecture, objects, images and performances which reflect modes of film construction (Atkinson and Kennedy 2016). Finally, they are ushered into a space to watch the film.

In recent years, several ludic narratives have been spatialised, such as, notoriously, Pokemon Go. Live action role playing (LARP) has also emerged, where people don costumes and physically perform characters' actions in narrative games that can last for several days. This is an interesting extension of digital game playing and improvisational theatre. In this kind of narrative environment, the screen and the script dominate the visitor experience.

At the same time that Coney Island was emerging, spatial narrative was also developing through world fairs. The first was the Great Exhibition in London in 1851, which brought trade and industry to the masses in a celebration of 100 years of the industrial revolution. It was advertised as an opportunity to see the world for a shilling. It was hugely successful and since then numerous world fairs and expos have set out to celebrate the achievements of nations. World fairs have provided opportunity to experiment with the design of novel buildings and provide extraordinary new spectacles. The Eiffel Tower was part of the 1889 World's Fair. The Futurama exhibit at the 1939 New York World's Fair is one of the most renowned examples. It was designed by the industrial designer and theatre set designer Norman Bel Geddes. Visitors were moved in their rows of seats over a huge diorama of a fictional section of the USA. Arthur Herman (2012: 58) explains that the exhibit

> was designed with a stunning array of miniature highways, towns, 500,000 individually designed homes, 50,000 miniature vehicles, waterways, and a million miniature trees of diverse species. These elements of the diorama gradually become larger as the visitors, seated in chairs overhead, moved through the exhibit, until the cars and other elements of the exhibit became life-size.

Other remarkable and innovative narrative structures built for expos include Diller and Scofidio's Blur building at the Swiss Expo in 2002 and the Seed Cathedral by Thomas Heatherwick at the Shanghai Expo in 2010. The Blur building was an open pipe structure that sat in Lake Neuchâtel. Pumps circulated lake water through the pipes. Sprays on the pipes released mist. It looked like a cloud sitting on the lake. It was a most evocative structure. Visitors could walk to it across a bridge and venture inside, dressed in plastic raincoats, to find a water bar. The Seed Cathedral, 20 metres high, was made from 60,000 transparent fibre optic rods, each containing one or more seeds at its tip. It was a poetic expression of Kew Royal Botanic Gardens' Millennium Seed Bank Project and evoked the main theme of the expo: nature and the city. This kind of narrative environment aims to inform but also promote specific nations. They have a social, political and economic purpose.

Public museums also emerged in the eighteenth and nineteenth centuries. Their original mission was to educate and civilise the public. Tony Bennett (1995) discusses how museums were seen, in the nineteenth century, as having a transformational educational role, albeit from a paternalistic, monocultural perspective. They communicated a singular view of what was thought to be universal and timeless truth through the systematic display of objects. Imposing museum architecture was designed and built to symbolise material certainty and authority. Mark O'Neill (2008) argues that historical research into the development of museums reveals a long-standing conflict between museums as instruments of social reform and museums as defenders of traditional values and hierarchies. He writes that, in the late nineteenth century, museums became detached from their foundations as instruments of social change and entered a long period when they catered only for an educated few. Large museums housed collections in dark, imposing Victorian buildings, such as the Victoria and Albert Museum in London, often with taxonomic displays arranged in vitrines in somewhat gloomy halls dimly lit by glass skylights. For much of the twentieth century, many museums focused on the conservation and display of what were considered by expert curators to be important objects. It was not until the mid-twentieth century that museums started to change, instead focusing more on their visitors' needs and what this meant for the design of the space.

The forerunners of this change include the Bauhaus, where the white cube minimalist feel in exhibitions was developed in the 1920s. Famously adopted by Alfred Barr, Director of the Museum of Modern Art in New York, the white walls and geometric spaces eradicate site-specific references and the curator and artist step in to hang the art with generous space between each exhibit and carefully considered sight lines. However, the aesthetic quality of such spaces quickly became associated with good taste and was appropriated by up-market stores, who often display goods as art objects. Elitism was sustained, indeed expanded, in retail environments. These narrative environments illustrate how forms devised for one purpose are borrowed and applied in other contexts for quite different purposes.

In the late 1990s, story-driven exhibition-making in museums became firmly established. At this time, there was a growing concern among museologists that museums should do more to communicate to wider audiences and be much more inclusive (Sandell 1998). Exhibition design, formerly undertaken by in-house teams, was becoming more often outsourced (Gurian 2014). As a result, exhibition design companies began to spring up in Europe and America. American designer Ralph Appelbaum critiqued what he described as the old-style display of objects ranged along the perimeter of a great hall. He argued that the objects needed to be linked together and framed as a serial experience so that visitors could relate objects to each other and learn about their context through the display of contextualising material, such as image or film. Appelbaum argued furthermore that narrative experiences would engage visitors on an emotional level and appeal to wider audiences. His company went on to design the exhibition of the world-renowned Holocaust Museum in Washington.

Storytelling became increasingly important in exhibition design in the UK and the USA in the 1990s, when the role of interpretation manager emerged alongside the closely related practice of interpretive design. The term interpretive design superseded exhibition design for some years because exhibition design was considered too narrow a term, as it suggested simply specifying the dimensions and production processes for plinths, lighting and functional spatial layout. Interpretive design, by contrast, included the practice of researching and developing an overall story-led design concept which then requires additional materials, such as film, graphics and interactives, to contextualise the objects on display and engage a broad range of audiences through storytelling rather than simply display of collections. Interpretive design is a conceptual, user-centred, creative practice. Thus, design claimed storytelling as a new territory, which moved it beyond being a purely technical practice.

The 1990s also saw the emergence of new digital technologies that expanded the palette of exhibition design so that sound, image, film and internet connectivity could be used together to enhance the sensory dimensions of exhibitions. In the UK, Land Design Studio led the way in applying digital media in exhibitions. Co-founder and Co-director of Land Design Studio, Peter Higgins, cites the Festival of Britain, 1951, as a key moment in the development of narrative space because it established a method which brought together script writers to work with a designer, James Gardner, and an architect, Sir Hugh Casson. Another inspirational precedent that Higgins identifies is the Fun Palace designed by the influential architect Cedric Price and the renowned theatre director Joan Littlewood. Price (quoted in Matthews 2007: 73) noted that,

> Its form and structure, resembling a large shipyard in which enclosures such as theatres, cinemas, restaurants, workshops, rally areas, can be assembled, moved, rearranged and scrapped continuously.

The Fun Palace was seminal in its combination of media and flexible architecture. In the mid-1990s, Higgins visited Ars Electronica in Austria and ZKM Center for Art and Media in Germany, both centres of digital innovation, and the result was Land Design Studio's groundbreaking visitor experience, the Play Zone, in the Millennium Dome. The story-based interactives brought artists and designers from all over the world and set the bar for the content-driven interactive exhibitions that followed. Among the leading exemplars is Atelier Brückner, a distinguished exhibition design company set up in the 1990s in Germany, who specialise in immersive, scenographic experiences. Studio Azzurro in Italy has also developed a strongly poetic application of digital media in exhibition design. Kossmanndejong in the Netherlands is greatly admired both for its design and its publications, for example, *Narrative Space: On the art of Exhibiting* (Kossmann, Mulder and Oudsten 2012). Other notable exhibition design companies in the Netherlands are Tellart, Opera and Tinker IT. Duncan McCauley in Germany is another pioneering exhibition design company that specialises in synthesising film and architecture. Casson Mann, Metaphor, MET and Event Communications are all eminent exhibition design companies in the UK with remarkable track records for using multi-modal forms to unfold stories in space.

Marie Laure Ryan (2016) examines exhibitions as spatial narratives, but also text, inscriptions and historical markers and trails in the environment. She extends her study of spatialised narrative to include place names and road signs, creating useful categories and classifications. Guided walks are another popular form of spatial narrative, not unlike oral histories, in that they depend on the guide to be an expert performer, an environmental interlocutor. Precedents for walking as poetic spatial narrative include Aboriginal Australians who, Bruce Chatwin (1987) explains, sing chants as they move through the landscape. The song lines establish location, each landmark being assigned a particular chant, so, through performance, Aboriginal Australians continuously enact a relationship with the surrounding environment. The chants are passed down through the generations.

Architects have also explored narrative. Although narrative in architecture has a long history, going back, for example, to '*architecture parlante*', speaking architecture, in fifteenth-century Europe, with Francesco Colonna's *Hypnerotomachia Poliphili* (Leon Van Schaik, 1985), a novel in which the main characters are buildings, it was largely marginalised in the twentieth century. However, there are some exceptions. For example, Aldo Rossi, drawing an analogy between urban design and theatre, was interested in how memory is embedded in built forms (Livesey 1994: 115–121). John Hejduk described how characters become buildings in the architectural process

(Vilder 1994: 209). Jonathan Hale (2017) describes some buildings as actively telling their own story of construction and history, for example, the way steps on stairways are worn away by use over the years. Jennifer Bloomer (1993), who is interested in the relationship between architecture and text, argues that architecture can tell a story. German architect Bernhard Franken conceives of the narrative and communicational powers of architecture (Morgan 2008). Architects interested in narrative often look to the work of American architect Bernhard Tschumi (1995), who produced influential reflections on sequential, experiential space in *Manhattan Transcripts* in which he challenges convention by arguing that action and event should be considered as part of architectural discourse. He translates devices such as plotting, foreshadowing and fading into architectural form.

Tschumi taught at the Architectural Association in London in the 1970s, and his ideas were developed by his students. They formed a movement called Narrative Architecture Today (NATO). As documented by Claire Jamieson (2017), the work was a celebration of the abject, an aesthetic of entropy and a do-it-yourself provisionality. One of the NATO members, Carlos Villanueva Brandt, traces a trajectory from Situationism to NATO, explaining how he and fellow architect, Mark Prizeman, worked in the 1970s with the grittiness of the streets, found their way into abandoned warehouses, made films and objects mixing low culture and high culture in the spirit of punk. They rejected the intellectual world of architectural discourse in favour of the implicit narratives in the city that they remixed as acts of '*détournement*', turning ordinary things that had an allusive story into provocative objects, films, paintings and manifestos. In the Gamma City exhibition in London in 1984, the group showed objects that had animal qualities, for example, a mosquito chair, dog towers and wolf housing, where people lived like wolves. They maintained their narratives were open ended; people could interpret as they wish. They saw their work as an architectural equivalent to the novel *Ulysses* by James Joyce. It was Nigel Coates (2012) who coined the name NATO. Coates was interested in narrative as myth and used classical references to make overt metaphors working within architecture and fashion. He conceived the city not as layers of planning, but layers of narrative, and maintained that architecture cannot help but express the cultural eco-systems that make cities. Coates argues that architectural design evokes personal experience and collective political and social values. Sophia Psarra (2009), architect and academic, examines spatial experience and meaning, arguing that "architecture carries meaning through the arrangement of spaces, social purposes and cultural meanings with which it is invested" (2009: 1).

Narrative architecture and urban planning have also been addressed by other architects and theorists. Sociologist Richard Sennett (1990), for example, makes an argument for a concept of narrative space. Sennett explains he is seeking a humane urban design and he refers to Bakhtin's chronotope, the inseparability of time and space, stating that the urban environment needs to be designed to allow for events to begin and unfold. In his vivid description of Manhattan, he asks how planners can make room for the narrative qualities of ambiguity and surprise. He advocates the design of weak borders rather than strong walls, so that spaces can be appropriated and used by different groups at different times. He critiques functional disaggregation which, he suggests, originates in the garden city movement. However, rather than creating peaceful pleasant spaces, Sennett argues, the movement created sealed communities where people are diminished in their development. In his view, planners should lift fixed zoning regulations, allowing activities and encounters in spaces which "are simple enough to permit constant alteration" (1990: 191–196). He describes these as displacements and argues, by analogy from fiction, that a narrative of place emerges as these displacements are advanced, resisted and negotiated. Urban theorists such as Mark C. Childs (2008), Leone Sandercock (2011) and Matthew Carmona (2015) have reiterated that stories and storytelling can inform and condition the design of places in multiple ways. The relationships articulated by the three-node narrative environment network model, with different configurations and different emphases, can be seen in all of these architectural and urban design examples above.

Several design-led architectural practices use forms of narrative in their work, for example, Sarah Featherstone of the London-based practice, Featherstone Young. At the start of the design process, Featherstone draws inspiration from small-scale spatial clues that connect to the past and to the use and feel of the space. This might be washing hanging on the line at street level, showing how a public space, which is assumed to be unsafe, turns out to be an extension of the home. Featherstone explains that clues accumulate and reveal the events and stories of people's lives. Responding as an architect to these clues, even in small ways, can completely transform a space. For example, in Wrexham, Wales, where she was commissioned to design a new art gallery in a former car park, she noticed that the building could function as a shortcut between the centre of the town and the shopping centres on the outskirts of the town. She framed the entrances on each side and placed the gallery on the path of the shortcut. She also designed what she calls 'baggy space' (Featherstone and Marsh 2018), in other words, space for people to do what they want, such as meet, hold workshops or have birthday parties. She is designing non-controlled environments where individuals' stories can be played out, much as Sennett called for.

By contrast, control is highly valued in brand and retail environments. Customer journeys are envisaged and planned as engaging sequential experiences. Christian Mikunda (2004) suggests marketers have created a third space, in addition to home and work, where every habit relates to sales and consumption, whether that be consuming landmark architecture or encouraging strolling to discover merchandise and services. Mikunda talks about designers creating concept lines with 'brain scripts', which play on people's media literacy or the stories they already know. These are used to draw people onto routes with clear axes, hubs, mnemonic points and districts that, while establishing a cognitive map, also arouse people's curiosity and desire. Recent large-scale experiential design for retail includes Madrid Xanadu, designed by Kiku Obata & Company, which contains Europe's largest indoor snow sports facility, or the Fashion Catwalk in The Dubai Mall which consists of five, 7-metre diameter rings, each 0.5 metres high. The rings hold full-colour video LEDs and move up and down and can be choreographed with live video feeds and music.

This sector produces immersive narrative brand experiences for multinationals, such as Ford, Volkswagen, Samsung and Guinness, but also reaches into other spaces, such as hospitals. For example, in 2016, at the Juliana Children's Hospital in The Hague, Tinker Imagineers was contracted to add an experiential layer to the existing clinical design. The company created an 'adventure journey' with an overall narrative for the patients. Games, play sets, interactives, drawings and puppets were installed to surprise, distract or relax the children. Other examples of thematic experiential architecture include the Hyundai Card Music Library + Understage experience in Seoul, South Korea, designed in 2016 by Gensler and an immersive environment for the Wushang Zhongyan Mall International Cinema in Wuhan, China, designed in 2015 by One Plus Partnership. Visualising scenes from movies like *Independence Day* and *The Day After Tomorrow*, One Plus Partnership created scenes that could easily convince theatre-goers they had walked into a real film setting. In Kyoto in 2015, Glamorous Co. Ltd. developed a forest of lanterns concept for Randen Arashiyama Station. In 2015, Heine Jones created a family of interpretive sculptures for the multicultural city of Dandenong, Australia, to celebrate the city's common language, English.

This brings us back to placemaking and place branding. It is worth revisiting as it is such a contentious area. On the one hand, placemaking is embraced by property developers as a profit-making venture, modernising and beautifying districts and attracting new, wealthy residents in line with what they describe as a narrative of place. The critique of this commercially driven gentrification is that financial profit is privileged over the well-being of existing citizens and often results in many local residents becoming marginalised and forced to move on. Commercially-driven placemaking can rob local residents of their social networks and situated ways of life, simultaneously effacing their histories. By contrast, 'placemaking', as understood by socially-engaged designers, is driven by joint efforts among all stakeholders or actors in an environment, including its citizens, artists, businesses, visitors and local government, to produce convivial places to live which support multiple narratives, an example being Participatory City in London's East End. Socially-engaged placemakers argue that they increase social cohesion, cultural, educational and economic opportunities; foster well-being and active civic engagement; and make the location unique and desirable to visit as well as environmentally sustainable. These kinds of narrative environments are powerful sites for discursive practice and social innovation, addressing all three nodes of the narrative environment network model.

The examples above show how spatial narrative, like other narratives, can be used as a route to spirituality, a commercial tool, a critical device and/or a means to create socially inclusive, creative environments. They show that the role of the designer can be that of guardian of traditional values, critical agent provocateur, entrepreneur and/ or researcher, but also co-creator, as a story listener and a story teller (Austin 2016). Designers of narrative environments take part in the creation and re-creation of place. There are many different kinds of narrative environment but the programme at Central Saint Martins takes a critical and relational perspective, addressing matters of concern to support politically aware and socially motivated creators of stories, social interactions and human experience.

The emergence and legitimacy of a new practice needs to be seen in the context of existing practices and assumptions. It may seem that, by using the word narrative, the design of narrative environments seeks to place itself in the tradition of literary narrative and belles-lettres, and to take up a position in the cultural high ground. Equally, in drawing on literary studies, which borrows its legitimacy from the practice of literature, the design of narrative environments may seem to be situating itself as an academic discipline in the humanities. Further, in drawing on film studies, itself borrowing its legitimacy from the study of literature, the design of narrative environments may seem to be positioning itself in the academic realm of media studies. Rather, the design of narrative environments starts from the position that people are constantly engaged in interpreting their world and narrative plays a crucial role in this process of generating interpretations, understandings and knowledge as the basis for situated interaction. The design of narrative environments seeks to restore the recognition that narrative and environment are inseparable; and inseparable from the constitution of human subjectivity as an environmental phenomenon that narrativises itself. In as far as the study of literature, film, architecture and other design practices can contribute to understanding how narrative, environment and subjectivity interrelate in practice, they contribute to the design of narrative environments. However, the legitimacy of the design of narrative environments does not lie in borrowing their academic authority, but in providing practical insights into how we do, and how we might live together, and how we might understand the processes of environing and narrating upon which we depend.

References

Atkinson, S. and Kennedy, H. (2016) From conflict to revolution: The secret aesthetic, narrative spatialisation and audience experience in immersive cinema design, *Participations*, 13 (1), 252–279.

Austin P. (2016) Narrative environments and social innovation. In: Bertolotti,E., Daam, H., Piredda, F. and Tassinari, V. eds. *The Pearl Diver*. DESIS Network, . Dipartimento di Design, Politecnico di Milano. Milan. pp. 155–164.

Bakhtin, M. (1981) *The Dialogic Imagination: Four Essays*. Austin, TX: University of Texas Press.

Bakhtin, M. (1968) *Rabelais and His World*. Bloomington, IN: Indiana University Press.

Barrie, T. (2010) *The Sacred In-Between: The Mediating Roles of Architecture*. New York, NY: Routledge.

Bennett, T. (1995) *The Birth of the Museum*. London: Routledge.

Bleeker, J. (2009) Design fiction: A short essay on design fact and fiction. *Near Future Laboratory*. Online. Available HTTP: http://blog.nearfuturelaboratory.com/2009/03/17/design-fiction-a-short-essay-on-design-science-fact-and-fiction/. Accessed 14 April 2018.

Bloomer, J. (1993) *Architecture and the Text: The (S)crypts of Joyce and Piranesi*. London: Yale University Press.

Carmona, M. (2015) Re-theorising contemporary public space: a new narrative and a new normative, *Journal of Urbanism: International Research on Placemaking and Urban Sustainability*, 8(4), 373–405.

Chatwin, B. (1987) *The Songlines*. London: Vintage.

Childs, M. C. (2008) Storytelling and urban design. *Journal of Urbanism: International Research on Placemaking and Urban Sustainability*, 1(2), 173–186.

Coates, N. (2012) *Narrative Architecture*. Chichester: John Wiley and Sons.

DiSalvo, C. (2012) Spectacles and tropes: Speculative design and contemporary food cultures. *Fibreculture Journal*, 20. Online. Available HTTP: http://twenty.fibreculturejournal.org/20 12/06/19/fcj-142-spectacles-and-tropes-speculative-design-and-contemporary-food-cultures/. Accessed 14 April 2018.

Dunne, A. (1999) *Herzian Tales: Electronic Products, Aesthetic Experience and Critical Design*. Cambridge, MA: MIT Press.

Dunne, A. and Raby, F. (2014) *Speculative Everything: Design, Fiction, and Social Dreaming*. Cambridge, MA: MIT Press.

Featherstone, S. and Marsh, J. (2018) Designing and Programming in 'Baggy' Space: A case study of the Oriel Wrecsam People's Market project In: MacLeod, S., Austin, T., Hale, J. and Ho, O, eds. *The Future of Museum and Gallery Design*. London: Routledge.

Grand, S. and Weidmer, M. (2010) Design fiction: A method toolbox for design research in a complex world. In: *Design and Complexity: Conference Proceedings*. Online. Available HTTP: http://www.drs2010.umontreal.ca/data/PDF/047.pdf. Accessed 19 November 2019.

Grimaldi, S. (2015) Narrativity of object interaction experiences: A framework for designing products as narrative experiences. In: *Experience Design: Concepts and Case Studies*. London: Bloomsbury Academic, pp. 57–68.

Gurian, E. H. (2014) Skimming along: A reflection on fourty-five [sic] years of exhibition issues. *reXD*. Online. Available HTTP: http://choasforum.weebly. com/uploads/2/4/5/3/24530080/e hgurianapril2014.pdf. Accessed 14 April 2018.

Hale, J. (2017) *Merleau-Ponty for Architects*. London; New York, NY: Routledge.

Herman, A. (2012) *Freedom's Forge: How American Business Produced Victory in World War II*. New York, NY: Random House.

Jamieson, C. and Poyner, R. (2017) *NATO: Narrative Architecture in Postmodern London*. London: Routledge.

Kaika, M. and Karaliotis, L. (2014) The spatialization of democratic politics: Insights from Indignant Squares. *European Urban and Regional Studies*. Online. Available HTTP: http://jour nals.sagepub.com/doi/abs/10.1177/0969776414528928. Accessed date 14 April 2018.

Klein, N. (2004) *The Vatican to Vegas the History of Special Effects*. London: New Press.

Knutz, E., Markussen, T. and Christensen, P. (2014) The role of fiction in experiments within design, art & architecture – Towards a new typology of design fiction. *Artifact*, 3(2), 8.1–8.13.

Kossmann, H., Mulder, S. and Oudsten, F. (2012) *Narrative Space: On the art of Exhibiting*. Rotterdam: 010 Publishers.

Krivý, M. and Kaminer, T. (2013) The participatory turn in urbanism. *Footprint*, 13, 1–6. Online. Available HTTP: http://footprint.tudelft.nl/index.php/footprint/article/view/766. Accessed 10 May 2017.

Livesey, G. (1994) Fictional Cities. In: Pérez-Gómez, A. and Parcell, S., eds. *Chora 1: Intervals in the Philosophy of Architecture*. Montréal: McGill-Queen's University Press, pp. 109–122.

Lonsway, B. (2009) *Making Leisure Work: Architecture and the Experience Economy*. London: Routledge.

Malpass, M. (2017) *Critical Design in Context: History, Theory, and Practices*. London: Bloomsbury Academic.

Matthews, S. (2007) *From Agit-Prop to Free Space. The Architecture of Cedric Price*. Berlin: Blackdog Press.

Mikunda, C. (2004) *Brand Lands, Hotspots and Cool Places*. London: Kogan Page.

Morgan, C. L. (2008) *Franken Architekten: Spatial Narrative*. Av edition.

O'Neill, M. (2008) Museums, professionalism and democracy. *Cultural Trends*, 17(4), 289–307.

Peters, A. (2018) The world's first "High-Tech Eco Village" will reinvent suburbs. *Fast Company*. Online. Available HTTP: https://www.fastcompany.com/90207375/the-worlds-first-high-t ech-eco-village-will-reinvent-suburbs. Accessed 9 August 2018.

Potteiger, M. and Purington, J. (1998) *Landscape Narratives: Design Practices for Telling Stories*. New York, NY: Wiley.

Prendiville, A. (2016) Connectivity through service design. In: Sparke, P. and Fisher, F. eds. *The Routledge Companion to Design Studies*. Abingdon: Routledge, pp. 40–53.

Ryan, M. L., Foote, K. and Azaryahu, M. (2016) *Narrating Space/Spatializing Narrative: Where Narrative Theory and Geography Meet*. Columbus, OH: Ohio State University Press.

Psarra, S. (2009) *Architecture and Narrative: The Formation of Space and Cultural Meaning*. London: Routledge.

Sandell, R. (1998) Museums as agents of social inclusion. *Museum Management and Curatorship*, 17(4), 401–18.

Sanders, E. and Stappers, P. (2008) Co-creation and the new landscapes of design. *Codesign*, 4(1), 5–18.

Sangiorgi, D. (2009). Building up a framework for service design research. *8th European Academy of Design Conference Proceedings*, 1–3 April, pp. 415–418.

Sandercock, L. (2011) Out of the closet: The importance of stories and storytelling in planning practice. *Planning Theory & Practice*, 4(1), 11–28.

Sennett, R. (1990) *The Conscience of the Eye: Design and the Social Life of Cities*. New York, NY: Norton.

Tschumi, B. (1995) *Manhattan Transcripts*. London: Academy Editions.

Tuffte (1983) *The Visual Display of Quantitative Information*. Cheshire, CT: Graphics Press.

Vanderbilt, T. (1999) It's a mall world after all: Disney, design, and the American dream. *Harvard Design Review*, Fall 1999. Online. Available HTTP: https://web.archive.org/web/2008101 0203142/, http://www.gsd.harvard.edu/research/publications/hdm/back/9onplace_vanderbi lt.pdf. Accessed 20 October 2019.

Vilder, A. (1994) *The Architectural Uncanny: Essays in the Modern Unhomel*. Cambridge, MA: MIT Press.

Websites

Arup Foresight. https://www.arup.com/expertise/services/advisory-services/strategy-and-insights/foresight

Atelier Brückner. http://www.atelier-brueckner.com/en

Casson Mann. https://cassonmann.com

Duncan McCauley. http://www.duncanmccauley.com/en/

Event Communications. https://www.eventcomm.com

Featherstone Young. http://featherstoneyoung.com

Land Design Studio. http://www.landdesignstudio.co.uk

Participatory City. http://www.participatorycity.org

MA Narrative Environments. http://www.narrative-environments.com

Metaphor. https://www.metaphor-design.co.uk/

Ralph Appelbaum Associates. http://www.raany.com

Secret Cinema. https://www.secretcinema.org/

Service Design Network. https://www.service-design-network.org

Studio Azzurro. http://www.studioazzurro.com

World Building Lab. http://5dinstitute.org/people/alex-mcdowell

3   Dramatic Conflict

Stories are very particular forms. Although they contain descriptions of everyday life they are purposefully constructed by writers or playwrights and, in the case of narrative environments, by multidisciplinary teams of designers in collaboration with scriptwriters, interpretive planners and sometimes end users or inhabitants. Taking the three-node network explained in Chapter 1, it could be argued that all spaces tell a story; for example, the seashore tells a story of erosion, a busy high street tells a story of consumerism or a village fete tells the story of a rural community. If so, all environments would be narrative environments. However, this definition would be too broad to be useful in developing the practice and theory of the design of narrative environments (Austin 2012). Narrative environments would be the same as the everyday or the lifeworld. In contrast, narrative environments are taken to be places which have been *deliberately* designed to tell a story. As such they correspond to literary stories which are purposely crafted to convey a message (Aristotle 1996; Bal 1992; Chatman 1978; Porter Abbott 2002; Propp 1958). So, just as stories are not daily life, neither are narrative environments, although you might come across them in your daily life. Narrative environments are intentionally structured, content-rich spaces or situations that communicate particular stories to specific audiences and that seek to induce an emotional impact, particular behaviour, social or commercial exchange, an inquiring or critical frame of mind in the visitor or inhabitant, or a combination of some or all of these. Narrative environments are envisaged, debated, designed and funded by individuals or communities, companies and governments. They are produced by an alignment of multiple stakeholders in a complex set of steps that are negotiated in order to transform an environment, tell a story but also to produce socio-economic and cultural change.

This leads to the question, how do narrative environments arise? While individuals generate literary stories and plays, narrative environments are developed by creative teams usually in response to a client brief. However, in instigating the proposition for a narrative environment, creative teams, like literary authors, observe and reflect on frictions in the world at large. Frictions or tensions excite the imagination, so that we produce stories or dramas about the origin of the friction or what may happen as a result of the friction. Writers may respond to inner tensions, interpersonal tensions, societal or political tensions, and designers of narrative environments do much the same, although they are particularly rooted in tensions that exist in specific physical locations and will include physical and material stresses as well as social and political dynamics. Screenwriters call these frictions *dramatic conflicts*, tensions that cause people to act or something to happen. Some screenwriters suggest all storytelling is based on conflict: "Without conflict there's no drama. Drama is conflict" (Flattam 2013). Writers craft their narratives around a driving conflict and envisage their hero or protagonist progressing through a series of conflicts, in a struggle for resolution. Indeed, creative writing instructor Robert McKee talks about 'the Law of Conflict'. McKee says, "nothing moves forward in a story except through conflict" (1999: 210–13). Literary theorist David Herman (2004: 83) also suggests conflict is constitutive of narrative, although its source, manifestations and relative pervasiveness will vary from story to story. Empathy with characters and their struggle to resolve conflicts is one reason audiences sustain emotional engagement in stories (Zillmann 1991).

The concept of dramatic conflict can be traced back to theories of agon in classical Greece where the word *agon* meant a purposeful gathering. However, its meaning evolved over time in a number of ways. For example, Aristotle (1996) writes about agonistic nature of Aeschylus' play the *Oresteia*, where the characters are engaged in struggles over justice and power, while in another of his plays, *The Eumenides*, agon is clearly related to athletic contest and legal proceedings. Debra Hawhee (2002: 186) writes that agon or struggle is central to the act of learning and self-development in ancient Greece. As such, struggle is evidence of virtue, skill and courage. It was considered insufficient just to be virtuous. Virtue had to be demonstrated or performed in public. Some years later historian Thucydides (Marincola 2007) describes agon as extreme anxiety and the notion of conflicting emotions producing agonising states of mind still persists. In the English language the word 'agonist' has, since the seventeenth century, been taken to mean someone involved in struggle and has given rise to the words protagonist and its opposite, antagonist, as core roles in narrative.

Twentieth-century philosopher Hannah Arendt (1958: 199–207) takes inspiration from ancient Greek politics and theatre in formulating her concept of action. As well as paying attention to narrative, she develops the notion of a 'space of appearance', which occurs whenever people gather together and through their speech and interaction reveal their political character. Arendt's understanding of agonism is important to the design of narrative environments because she suggests political agonism is not confined to parliaments or official buildings. It can arise in any public space. For Arendt, human plurality is the basic condition for action and speech. In distinguishing herself from Arendt, political theorist Chantal Mouffe (2013) argues that Arendt's concept of agonism, although based on human plurality, is without antagonism. Mouffe explores antagonism, agonism and hegemony. Hegemony is a process whereby those disadvantaged by hierarchical power relations nevertheless agree to live by such social orders, making a pact that is against their interests. In *Hegemony and Socialist Strategy* (2014), Ernesto Laclau and Chantal Mouffe argue that political struggle is pervasive and ever present. Thus, antagonism can erupt at any time. Social and political order is not fixed but temporary, precarious and constantly subject to challenge. This approach resonates with Doreen Massey's description of space as being in a constant state of change, constituted by the interaction of multiple agents, each one moving along their own trajectory. Massey and Mouffe both envisage a pluralistic world, critiquing liberalism's and neoliberalism's assumption of the free individual. Instead, they see society and space as the outcome of practices, struggles and decisions made by multiple actors, a world that encourages some flows but constrains or obscures others. This pluralist, dynamic view can also be made to resonate with some of the insights from Actor Network Theory (ANT). Although initially seemingly apolitical, ANT is pluralistic. It envisages multiple situated actors engaged in constant negotiation and the constant formation and reformation of alliances. Drawing on these sources, the three-node narrative environments network understands agency, power and responsibility as distributed across people, narrative and space.

These ideas are important to design, particularly in its critical mode, because design is no longer, if it ever was, just a technical process. Design is increasingly being deployed in important strategic social and political processes. This may not be evident at first glance because there is a dominant view of design as the market-driven presentation of goods, services and experiences. Since its emergence in the industrial revolution, design has evolved in different directions. One direction, to produce the face and form of products, has become closely associated with market economies. In this model, designers develop products and services to sustain or expand mass production and consumption, for example, through eye-catching packaging, seductive advertising, spectacular lighting, fun interactive screens and awe-inspiring architecture. These designs help to attract an increased number of customers or, in the case of commercial narrative environments, an increased number of visitors to shops, restaurants, leisure attractions, museums, events and regenerated urban quarters. The designer in this realm is envisaged as a problem solver, at the service of the client, working on new products, services and experiences that address the client's needs. In the design of narrative environments, examples of this are commercial, experiential and place branding, where a strategic narrative is often circulated as a promotional video to appeal to customers, and events are curated to draw people to spaces that shape and enhance their emotional attachment to the location.

Market-driven problem-solving is the dominant view of design across the creative industries. The issue is that it positions the designer as a technical expert, albeit creative, but does not allow for the designer to express any political, environmental or social position. Nor does it necessarily question in much depth the suitability or benefits of the design solutions to the visitors or inhabitants (Peart 2017). It limits design, which has the capacity to deal with many more dimensions of human life than marketing. Dunne and Raby (2013) also point out that problems are conceived of within specific systems and working within the same system inadvertently reinforces those systems and therefore could be argued to perpetuate the problem in a different form.

In his book *Dark Matters & Trojan Horses: A Strategic Design Vocabulary*, designer and urbanist Dan Hill (2012) outlines some practical strategies that designers can use to work beyond the problem-solving paradigm. Dark matter is a phrase borrowed from physics to describe the vast majority of matter in the universe which is undetected. However, it is only when this dark matter is brought into the frame that systems can be more fully understood. Hill's analogy makes the case for the consideration of a wider context in the design process so that, as well as market forces, other factors, or actants as they would be called in the design of narrative environments, are taken into account. These include organisational culture, policy environments and governance structures, which are often overlooked in the development of artefacts and services. Hill advocates a more comprehensive and strategic design process. This matters as much in commercial design as in social or critical design.

Market-driven design obscures the important tradition that emerged from the Arts and Crafts movement in the nineteenth century, and whose legacy can be traced through the twentieth century, which advocates social and political reform and envisioned the designer contributing to a more egalitarian world. Social purpose, in an industrialised context, was a guiding principle at the Bauhaus in the 1920s and the 1930s. It was rearticulated in a different form in the 1970s by Victor Papanek (1971). Papanek connected product design, architecture and anthropology, arguing that design should meet people's needs within the finite physical resources available in the world. Recent developments in critical design and participatory design continue to position the designer as an active advocate in the democratic process.

Problems do exist but so do opportunities. By simply focusing on problems designers may overlook potential ways to innovate. However, the design of narrative environments argues that the point is to investigate what gives rise to those problems and opportunities, to look at the underlying tensions or dramatic conflicts. This leads to a wide variety of propositions in addition to those addressed to problem-solving. The kind of dramatic conflicts identified will depend on the perspective taken. For example, the current health crisis triggered by obesity could be viewed as a tension between the priorities of urban planning, based on the car, and the need for bodily exercise. If destinations are spread far apart, we drive and therefore exercise less, creating obesogenic environments. This conflict takes a spatial form, highlighting a conflict between urban design for cars and urban design for human bodies. Alternatively, obesity could be seen as an effect of poverty. People on low incomes tend to buy cheap, processed foods, high in sugar, salt and fat content. In this case, the conflict arises from the economic divide between rich and poor and the ways it is embodied in the food production, distribution and marketing systems. Part of this underpinning dramatic conflict is the recognition that it is a deliberate ploy on behalf of food producers to add sugar, salt and fat to many foods, exploiting our predilection for these ingredients despite their adverse effects on health. The conflict here is between corporate goals to achieve profit and customers' opportunity to buy healthy foodstuffs. These three different perspectives on obesity prompt three different visions of how practices might be changed in order to combat obesity. In the design of narrative environments, the decision to focus on any one of these dramatic conflicts would drive the form and content of the design. As these examples show, design teams need to develop a sophisticated perspective that incorporates political, technological, organisational, social and environmental dimensions of the world at large so that they are designing in an informed way.

Researching Dramatic Conflicts for the Design of Narrative Environments

In order to understand the multiple qualities and meanings of spaces and places, initial research into the dramatic conflicts they embody is essential for the design of narrative environments. A critical perspective can be developed by implementing what Michel Foucault (1972) called discourse analysis, a term he used to describe the way groups of statements structure, regulate and perpetuate institutions and their power, and produce objects, places and practices in those institutions. For example, the discourses of law give order to legal regulations, the legal profession, and courts and prisons as places of legal enactment. The discourse of medicine articulates relationships among doctors, patients, bodies, hospitals, treatments and medical research. The discourse of art practice interrelates art galleries, museums, artists, audiences, collectors, curators and reviewers. Sociologist Gillian Rose (2011), in advocating discourse analysis as a visual research methodology, describes two main approaches. The first is to look for the kinds of assumptions, values and knowledge expressed in and through paintings or visual objects. She gives the example of Lynda Nead's (1988) research on the depiction of prostitutes in European nineteenth-century engravings and paintings showing how prostitutes contravened contemporary bourgeois notions of femininity. Nead argues that prostitutes were portrayed as evil or as victims of an evil society. Engravings show prostitutes paying the price for their so-called deviance by gradually losing their looks, their glamorous clothes and frequently choosing suicide by drowning. While the images stem from prevailing views, their production and circulation serves to institutionalise and validate this view as truth.

Applying this kind of discourse analysis to site research means looking for repeating patterns visible *in* the environment that normalise a particular value system. An example might be noticing the city skyline is peppered with high-rise buildings and assuming that means the city is an active participant in the global economy and a vibrant place to live. On closer examination, however, many high-rise flats may belong to foreign investors who have no intention of living there. Consequently, sites of major urban development can be virtually uninhabited and can carve a void in the social and physical fabric of the city.

The second approach Rose takes is to look at the way paintings are produced, owned and exchanged to reveal the institutional apparatuses and powers at play. So, for example, she examines how museums legitimise the collection of certain objects and not others. The question of the power and purpose of museums has been explored in some depth in recent years. Elaine Heumann Gurian (2006) and Suzanne MacLeod (2017) discuss museum architectures as powerful tangible frames that inflect or directly influence the institutions they house and the way they are understood. The architecture of museums embodies assumptions that influence the collections, the interpretation strategies, the attitudes of staff and visitors and the museum's civic role. For example, the scale and solemnity of nineteenth-century European and American museum architecture asserts the role of Western museums as state-sponsored guardians of a singular 'civilisation'. Tony Bennett (1995) criticises such museums for speaking from a position of unquestioned authority.

Theorists in the twentieth century such as Mieke Bal (1992) and Eileen Hooper Greenhill (1992 and 1999) have disputed the single voice and the assumed neutrality of museums. Bal compared the Metropolitan Museum of Art (the Met) on the Upper East Side in New York, which it says on its website houses "a treasury of rare and beautiful objects" and the American Museum of Natural History, on the Upper West Side, which houses Asian, African, Oceanic and Native American art. Bal makes the point that an object in the Met is revered while a similar object in the American Museum of Natural History is perceived as "an instrumental cognitive tool, anonymous, necessary, natural" (Bal 1992: 559) and therefore of lower cultural value. Bal's analysis shows how the anthropological frame is intricately shaped by colonialist values. Although in one sense, the Met and the Natural History Museum frame their collections differently and seem to present contrasting views, in another sense, they can be seen to materialise a single overall, hierarchical, conceptual frame in which the former is taken to be the domain of humanity and high culture while the latter is assigned to the realm of the lesser human, the non-human and 'primitive' culture. To put it in its simplest terms, one key dispute around museums concerns whether in practice they reproduce cultural elites or whether, in challenging this elitism, they are working as agents of change to establish a more democratic society. The application of this approach in the research of public spaces means asking questions about what constitutes the contextual frame and how it is maintained, probing the management and governance of space. Debates such as these highlight the importance of the framing context for meaning production. In the space, what objects, lights, street furniture have been installed to sustain the meaning? This process also brings to the fore the positioning of the researcher in relation to these questions.

Apart from discourse analysis, dramatic conflicts of place can also be uncovered through information-gathering using visual research methods, such as observation, sketching, photography and video documentation. Visual research can be synthesised through map making, which re-presents all manners of characteristics for reflection. Maps may include the quantitative analysis of dimensions and materials at a particular location but this is just a baseline for a more comprehensive analysis. Sensory mapping is another technique where special attention is paid to the moving body and its responses to the surrounding materiality, sound, scale, light and so on. This is a very demanding exercise because you are observing two experiential dimensions at once: sensing the physical world, and also your own bodily and emotional responses to that sensing. This kind of mapping, in producing multilayered diagrams of zones and transition spaces, can capture a sense of the atmosphere of a place. Behavioural mapping is another kind of mapping. It records the use of space by specific groups in particular places at particular times. In memory mapping, another valuable technique, members of the public are asked to draw a map of their journey to and through a location from memory. This reveals just how much people omit from maps. Whole buildings and roads disappear and only salient paths and landmarks are noted. Memory maps give form to cognitive models of space, as Kevin Lynch (1960) discusses.

The design of narrative environments, in being concerned with the movement of bodies through space, also adopts walking as a critical research method for exploring the urban environment. Variants of this method can found in the practices of the nineteenth-century flaneur, the Dadaist event, the déambulations of the Surrealists, the urban explorations of Walter Benjamin, the dérives of the Lettrists and Situationists, the wanderings of the land artists in the 1960s, experimental practices such as the Italian Stalkers in the 1990s right up to contemporary psychogeographical expeditions (Bassett 2004). This tradition emphasises following a route which is not predetermined, often through city streets, leaving yourself open to the guidance of the environment. It is the drift of the ambulating body through space in ways that break routine, overcome boundaries and provoke new situations. Author and philosopher Sadie Plant (1992: 95) writes, "to dérive was to notice the way in which certain areas, streets, or buildings resonate with states of mind, inclinations, and desires". Using this process to subvert the dominant orientations in the space enables researchers to discover places they otherwise might not have found. This exploratory, open-ended, playful approach to space is related to certain kinds of spatial narrative research where the researcher goes with an open mind and through immersing themselves in a place allows stories to develop in their imagination. These are action-based research methods that invite happenstance and interaction. They can be extended and amplified into temporary physical interventions that bring to awareness the 'dark matter', noted by Hill (2012), that regulates space.

Seeking to understand the dramatic conflicts of spaces and places also requires an understanding of the people who live in, work in or use that environment. Narrative environment researchers may install unexpected objects to gauge people's reactions. Minor disruptions to the everyday can reveal assumptions about the use and purpose of particular places. They may set up installations that help to engage passers-by in conversation or make temporary interactive games to attract their audiences. Slightly disruptive performance is another creative option that can reveal the conventions in a space. Other productive social research methods for engaging with everyday spatial practices include taking part in online chat rooms and blogs. Cultural probes, as developed in visual sociology, can be used, such as when researchers give people disposable cameras and ask them to photograph things they like or dislike at regular intervals during their day. More ethnographic-style inquiry may lead design researchers to seek to empathise with inhabitants by following local customs. This might involve role play which is useful to shift the researcher's mindset from detached observation to active engagement. Deeper immersion in the social dimensions of the environment might involve researchers living among the people they are researching, but this can work well only if the researchers establish the trust of the community they are studying. Much time is required for meeting and talking to communities and explaining the intentions of the research. Participatory designers usually gain access to local groups through community leaders. They work strategically to avoid any sense of intrusion. In some areas, communities may suffer from consultation fatigue and feel disappointed if their expectations are raised but not met. Well managed, socially engaged research for the design of narrative environments has the potential to bring about long-term change but it needs time and careful planning to undertake research that is thorough and productive.

Narrative environment researchers will also use desk research to gather relevant case studies, histories and socio-political context to feed into an exploration of the dramatic conflicts of place. The analysis of data collected will call into account the world view of the design team and this requires self-reflection and agreement among the team. The practical process of identifying dramatic conflicts of place involves literally laying out the data collected and moving elements such as photographs, testimony and maps to identify frictions, gaps and clusters. The skill here is pattern recognition. It is a rational process but it relies on relational thinking across the three nodes of the tripartite network.

Dramatic Conflict as the Basis of Narrative Placemaking

Once dramatic conflicts have been identified they can then be employed at a number of scales to develop narrative environments. In recent years, there has been a surge in city regeneration placemaking activities across the world. Some of these are superficial and lack authenticity, partly because they lack an understanding of the drama of place. Numerous examples of flawed schemes, which seek to impose a positive marketing message on a space without engaging with its specific characteristics or frictions, can be found. Genuine city narratives stem from the dramatic conflicts of specific locations. You cannot impose any brand on a place indiscriminately. Brand identity grows from a place and the unique characteristics and dramas of that place. As urban strategist Thomas Sevcik says,

> Cities are not T-shirts or cars onto which you can simply paste a logo. Cities are living things, with their own particular dynamics and dramas.
>
> (Sevcik 2018)

Residents, whether temporary or permanent, are part of this dynamic and are key to any city's evolving identity. So, while marketing departments may issue polished images, residents will say whatever they want about their city and so will tourists. This communication process has never been so pervasive as it is at present, facilitated by social media. Although it is in the interest of policy makers, government communications departments and businesses to characterise cities in glowing terms, official media are now often ignored or suspected of producing fake news. Local communities, individuals and tourists have turned to more granular sources of information in search of authenticity or depth of information. The power of top-down communications is diminishing and peer-to-peer communications are on the rise.

So how can local governments elevate their cities in the eyes of the world? Many governments commission 'starchitecture', for example, gigantic museums in a 'culture-led' strategy for city regeneration that does not engage with tensions within the city. They focus on attracting the attention of global tourists, often overlooking the needs and desires of their own populations. As Graeme Evans (2003) writes, the success of Bilbao, for example, was infinitely more complex and layered than the building of the

Guggenheim Art Museum. Nevertheless, it has become a point of pride and indeed competition among cities across the world to have enormous, spectacular new art galleries and museums which serve as walk-in city logos and events in a city narrative. The dramatic conflicts at play are rooted in global city competition for status and its accompanying economic rewards. This is perversely at odds with the democratic mission of museums to nourish the creative lives of citizens (MacLeod 2017). These museums are the display themselves. They are often unfit for internal display with curved or sloping walls, for example, where exhibits cannot be hung. These structures have more to do with city governments competing with each other for status and media attention than nurturing and growing their own cultural producers.

Local government has to be clever to shine on the world stage for any length of time. Economically, cities are in competition, and do need to be distinctive, especially from neighbouring competitors. It is not enough for them to rely on starchitecture or architectural heritage, which are fast becoming stage sets for selfies. City governments need active local artists and designers, engaged with personal and place-based dramatic conflicts, at the heart of their initiatives. Antagonisms around, for example, immigration, housing, the interpretation of history and the numerous other concerns that preoccupy us should be seen as useful because they can prompt new thinking and act as narrative drivers that unfold into new strategies and designs that have significant potential to enrich cultural production and enhance everyone's lives. However, the managers of such places need to be wary of them becoming commercial spectacles, which hollows out their meaning. An example of how this can happen is the gallery district 798 Art Zone, or Dashanzi Art District, a complex of 50-year-old decommissioned military factory buildings, located in the Dashanzi, Chaoyang District of Beijing. It houses numerous galleries and artist studios. It was established in 1995, instigated by Beijing's Central Academy of Fine Arts who were responding to a growing number of artists exploring what modern Chinese art might look like, while reflecting and commenting on Chinese culture. The 798 Art Zone was also a response to an international demand for Chinese art and for some years it was an important driver in the Chinese art market for experimental art. It elevated the reputation of Beijing as a creative centre. However, 798 Art Zone has, in recent years, become quite gentrified with numerous restaurants and tourist visitors. Rents have risen. It has become a place of consumption rather than a place of production that responds to the dramatic conflicts of China's rapid development.

Dramatic Conflicts and Story Dynamics in Exhibition Making

We now turn from placemaking to look more closely at dramatic conflicts in spatial narratives in museum exhibitions. The notion of dramatic conflict as manifested in stories leads us to A. J. Greimas' (1983) studies of the dynamics of story and an exploration of how dynamic story tensions translate into spatial experience. In his narrative model, Greimas conceived of three pairs of contraries: sender vs. receiver; subject vs. object; and helper vs. opponent. He argued that these contraries generate three types of relations: knowledge, constituted by communication between sender and receiver; desire, which is experienced by the subject for the object; and power, exercised in the subject's agonistic struggle, eased by the helper and aggravated by the opponent, to acquire or achieve the object of desire.

A literary example is the medieval Arthurian legend *The Search for the Holy Grail*. The Grail itself was thought to be the cup from the Last Supper and Christ's blood was supposed to have run into it at the Crucifixion. It was deemed to have magical powers that would bring happiness and eternal youth. Legend had it that the Holy Grail was hidden in a far-off castle somewhere in England. In the story, the sender is a mysterious force that creates an apparition which appears in front of King Arthur and his knights, the receivers. The apparition opens up the axis of knowledge by telling the knights about the existence of the Holy Grail. The knights then become the active subjects, setting out to find the Holy Grail. The axis of desire is activated. Galahad, one of the knights had a further vision that it was God's will that they should take the Grail to the Holy City of Sarras in the Middle East. The axis of power is populated by those helping the knights find their way to Sarras and opponents who obstruct the knights' pursuit of the object of desire. The opponents may be, for example, a mountain range, a desert or the Saracens. Neither helpers nor opponents are necessarily human characters.

Greimas' scheme is appealing as it captures the interweaving of significant dynamics of knowledge, desire and power at play in narrative and we can use these story dynamics to make more engaging narrative environments. This three-pair dynamic can also be used to analyse media narratives and narrative environments, as in the case studies below. It is not claimed that all stories can be reduced to these three axes. Nevertheless, this scheme enables us to consider story dynamics that capture emotion and the imaginative aspects of narratives. It complements structuralist approaches to narratology whose 'story grammar' focuses on story components such as the naming of roles (functions) and analysis of sequence and order (Genette 1980).

Louis Hébert (2011) discusses the work of Greimas on linguistics and semantics, particularly Greimas' development of an abstract diagram of meaning production called the semiotic square. Starting from the semiotic square, Allan Parsons (2017) suggests that Greimas' theory can be used to examine the spatial dynamics of different 'worlds'. Similarly to Philip E. Wegner (2010), Parsons has interpreted the semiotic square, in alliance with Jacques Lacan's theory of the human subject as divided, to develop a tool for analysis of the three-node model, people, narrative and environment. Parsons envisages 'the world' as constituted by active relations among four kinds of worlds: 'My world', 'Your world' 'Our world', and 'Their world'. 'My world' is both imaginary and symbolic, the way I imagine myself and the way that that imaginary identity is distributed spatially and symbolically, through my identifications with, and attachments to particular languages, specific material objects and particular locations. 'Your world' arises from the mutual perceptual divisions among the 'My worlds', brought into relationship through shared languages, objects and locations, recognising mutual claims on those material media of communication. Such material media are either held in common, as the ground of community in 'Our world', or in public, as the ground of society, in which 'Our world' related to but distinguished from 'Their world'. The emerging intersubjective and intercorporeal network is a continual negotiation of these boundaries which in narrative environments are rendered explicit so there can be a conscious renegotiation of conflicts and alliances. The second important aspect of this theorisation is the potential dominance, through hegemonic incorporation or otherwise, of one world, for example, 'Their world', over another, for example, 'My world', which the design of narrative environments also brings to the surface by showing how particular languages, objects and locations articulate potentially hierarchical relations among the different worlds.

This theory allows us to conceive, through negotiation and dramatic conflict, the spatialisation and materiality of thresholds and territories, constituted through identification with, or alienation from narrative content and material place. Parsons argues that 'the world' is neither undifferentiated nor singular. We sense when we are leaving the comfort of our own world venturing into a wider world, whether that be a shared world, with its sense of belonging, where one can be 'self-possessed', or an alien world, with its discomfort, uneasiness and sense of dispossession. We need to feel safe, in 'Our world', but we also desire new knowledge and power, from 'Their world'. For exhibition design, the implication is that the exhibition will belong to 'my', 'your', 'our' or 'their' world depending on who the visitor is, but it is never a neutral representation of 'the world' or 'the history of the world'. The analysis of different psychodynamically experienced and materially realised worlds applied to literary stories, spatial narratives and lifeworlds can reveal the possible gaps and connections among individuals, groups, organisations and institutions.

To exemplify the use of this approach, the following section examines two case studies. The first is an exhibition, *Their Mortal Remains*, that took place in 2017 at the Victoria and Albert Museum (V&A), London. It was one in a series of hugely successful blockbusters that included exhibitions on Alexander McQueen in 2015 and David Bowie in 2016. The V&A was established as a Museum of Manufacturers in 1852. Its mission is to be recognised as the world's leading museum of art, design and performance and deepen the relevance of its collections to the UK creative and knowledge economies. It is an immensely influential and well-regarded institution, housed within an imposing Victorian building. It focuses on design and its application in the world at large, and, as such, exhibitions of popular culture are fitting, although since its founding the V&A has become a symbol of high culture, despite its initial aims to celebrate design as part of the emerging industrial society.

Their Mortal Remains, which showed the career development of the musicians Pink Floyd, from the 1960s until the year of the exhibition, 2017, was staged in the V&A's temporary exhibition space. The exhibition was conceived and designed by Stufish Entertainment Architects, founded by the late Mark Fisher. The studio is renowned for combining architecture, theatre and live music events. It designed every Rolling Stones show since 1989 and every U2 concert since 1992 and the opening and closing ceremonies at the Beijing Olympics in 2008. Stufish worked with Pink Floyd over many years. They designed the Wall Tour in 1980 and the Division Bell Tour in 1994. *Their Mortal Remains* was designed as a touring exhibition to be produced in other capital cities across the world.

The temporary exhibition space at the V&A is linear and therefore lends itself to chronological accounts. The space is U-shaped, so visitors encounter a distinctive half-way mark as they step through a lobby and turn almost 360 degrees into the second half of the space. This spatial shift needs to be incorporated into the storyline. In *Their Mortal Remains*, the first half of the exhibition was divided into several distinct spaces. At the threshold, the audience entered the exhibition through a psychedelic bus, evoking youth travel in the 1960s (Figure 3.1).

This was followed by several smallish spaces: the immersive psychedelia of the UFO nightclub; the Sid Barrett story; the move to more instrumental music; the release and impact of *Dark Side of the Moon*; the technology the band used to experiment with sound; and the graphics and stage sets the band developed. The second half of the exhibition was highly theatrical. A huge space housed 5-metre high simulations of Battersea Power Station with enormous replicas of floating inflatables, referencing one of their album covers. This was followed by scenographic settings of walls with missing brickwork evoking the Wall stage show. The exhibition culminated in a large immersive media wrap-around room where visitors could sit, surrounded by projections and music. Throughout the exhibition there were video projections, video screens with talking heads, objects and music graphics, photographs and graphic information panels and

Figure 3.1 Entrance to the exhibition *Their Mortal Remains*, the Victoria and Albert Museum, London, 2017.

labels. Each visitor was given headphones which played Pink Floyd music. The music faded into the sound of talking when visitors approached the screens. Overall, the exhibition moved from the intimacy of the UFO club to the wide-open space of a stadium, increasing in scale as visitors moved through the space, mirroring the scale of the band's performances and fame (Figure 3.2).

The dramatic conflict of the story was Pink Floyd's struggle with the music industry to become famous, not for mainstream pop but rather for being independent and continuously innovative musicians. However, the key flaw in the exhibition is that it did not show or evoke the machinations of the music industry or the context of popular culture against which the band positioned themselves. Equally, the major rifts among the band members over the years and the reasons for them were minimised. The dramatic conflicts in the story barely surface. Instead, visitors encounter a series of successes, reinforcing an already circulating mass media and public relations story of Pink Floyd as superstars. As a consequence, for example, young musicians would be unable to learn a great deal from the exhibition about how the music industry works or how they could position themselves.

If we take Greimas' narrative model to examine the axes of knowledge, desire and power, we see the knowledge axis manifested through the band's increasing technical accomplishment in sound, light effects and graphics. The band triumph through their determination and skill, reaffirming the overarching brand narrative. The desire axis manifests as a drive to be renowned for their musicianship and creativity, and not simply for wealth or celebrity. Some photographs and text in the exhibition show Pink Floyd

Figure 3.2 Inside the exhibition *Their Mortal Remains*, the Victoria and Albert Museum, London, 2017.

filming a performance at Pompeii to an audience of none, in the process locating themselves firmly in Western high culture, in contrast to their musical peers who were at the time performing at Woodstock to a mass audience. The aspirations of Pink Floyd to create high culture and not produce mass culture were not discussed explicitly enough in the exhibition, which reduced any critical engagement with the story. The power axis in Greimas' model is manifested in the relationship between the music corporations and music bands, the outcomes of which determined their career paths, and in the struggles among band members over creative direction. Neither was discussed in any detail. The net result was a flattening of the story.

The exhibition itself, being at the V&A, a centre for high culture, confirmed that Pink Floyd had reached their goal of being considered artists, while simultaneously demonstrating the standing of the V&A as a frame that validates aspirants' cultural credentials. So, ironically, although the V&A appears to be bringing popular culture into a place associated with high culture, thereby making it more democratic as a museum in creating a more inclusive 'Our world', the power of the V&A's reputation is so great that instead it actually shifts Pink Floyd into the realm of high culture. Famous national museums, unless they somehow deconstruct themselves, cannot help but produce and sustain the framing spatial narrative of high culture which is bestowed by the government and embodied in the grand and imposing architecture and operational practices of those museums. The environment here speaks loudly and with propriety.

Moving from an analysis of the content of the exhibition to an analysis of the spatial aspects of the narrative environment from the visitor's perspective, we can apply Greimas' pairs of contraries: the subject and object, the sender and receiver, the helper and opponent. From a content perspective, the band members were couched as subjects whose acts and works visitors followed through their hand-written letters, video interviews, music, films and pictures of performances but from a visitor perspective, the visitor is the subject seeking the object. A crucial point is reinforced here. In narrative environments, there is a shift in the role of the visitors. You, *the visitor*, are not only the recipient of the messages you also become the subject seeking the object. In this case, you literally set out on a path to find out what 'Pink Floyd' means.

The headphones were helpers providing music to immerse visitors in narrative space but also to punctuate the visitor's journey by broadcasting the spoken words from film and video as they walked close to the screens. The physical divisions of the space acted as physical opponents pacing the journey, preventing visitors from seeing the next section, acting as concealing, revealing and spatial modulation devices.

From the perspective of Parsons' analysis of relationships among worlds, the audience stayed in their own world partly because they were insulated by their headphones, except perhaps at the end, when visitors sat together on the floor in the wrap-around media room where some people may have felt a sense of 'us' literally as an audience. In the hermetically sealed world, the sound, images and staging took people on a nostalgic journey drawing up associated emotions from their memories. From the perspective of embodied experience the rhythm and flow of the space was articulated through the gradual increase in scale, corresponding to the success of the band but also offering more and more physical drama for visitors to discover as they progressed through the show.

The collection of historical objects, letters, posters, photographs, albums, CDs, items of clothing, musical instruments and so on did not build a wider network of relations to invite you to participate in the world of Pink Floyd. This was perhaps because they were displayed behind glass which minimised their physicality and as a consequence they lacked presence.

They were also arranged in rows with labels using conventional museum display techniques which jarred with the sound, light projections and scenography which were immersive and experiential.

Overall, *Their Mortal Remains* relied on sensory stimulation to engage visitors and drive them through the space. The experience was largely market-driven nostalgia and consequently rather questionable in terms of the museum's mission to educate and inform its visitors. The exhibition demonstrates how dramatic conflicts underlie the transformational capacity of both the story and the spatial narrative and that minimising struggle in the story weakens the narrative, reducing it to a slick brand narrative. In this case, the irony is that the band wish to be known for their musicianship and innovation but the polished brand narrative reduces them to a commodity.

Dramatic Conflicts and Story Dynamics in Critical Narrative Environments

By contrast, the narrative environment, *Citizenshop – Buy Your Way into the Country*, created in 2016 by designer Nele Vos, is a critical commentary on immigration and nationality which she installed in a small empty shop that sometimes functions as a gallery on the busy Bethnal Green Road, London. Vos, who was a student of MA Narrative Environments at the time, was exploring themes of national identity, international mobility and their relation to the refugee crisis in Europe caused by conflicts in Syria, Afghanistan and African countries such as Somalia. Vos devised a two-part story contrasting the privilege afforded to those wealthy enough to purchase nationality with those who have become stateless. Her research revealed that different countries sell their nationality for different prices. At the time, an Argentinian passport cost $26,000, an Australian passport cost $3,557,000 and an American passport cost $500,000. The opportunity for those who can choose whichever tax and financial regimes best suit their circumstances stands in stark contrast to the plight of refugees who, through no choice of their own, belong to no state. Vos's project is a critique of the inequities of a neoliberal, international economy, the capture of the nation state by private interests and the technocratic protocols that sustain the system. The project exposes double standards between the post-Second World War human rights-based regime and the international economy organised around nation states-based rights regimes. The project questions what having 'rights' means.

Applying Greimas's model, the sender of the message, that you can change your nationality, is financial rationality, channelled through official governmental communications, financial media publications or personal financial advisors. The receiver is anyone who has the capacity to act on that information and advice. The message transforms them into a rational economic subject seeking to move to a location where their financial interests are seemingly better served. Rational subjects seeking optimal conditions are assisted by legal and financial systems which act as helpers by defining and defending their property rights. Opponents are two-fold. Firstly, they are countries who are seeking to defend themselves against international flows of capital, and, secondly, those seeking to uphold the global human rights regime and, in consequence, to undo the identification of human rights with financial rights, a process that is coordinated by and across nation states.

According to the human rights narrative, all subjects have rights. The sender is the UN convention of human rights; the receivers should be everyone. However, if the subjects are displaced people, who therefore become stateless, the universal story is rendered impotent as the displaced discover that, without wealth or state, they have no rights and effectively disappear. They seek therefore to become citizens of another state. Helpers might be humanitarian organisations who assist them in gaining refugee status, on-line campaign websites and family who provide money for travel. They then become visible as claimants. Opponents might be human traffickers, legal systems, anti-immigrant governments, the sheer distance needed to travel to reach safety and the dangerous nature of the terrain.

There are two levels of dramatic conflict: the political-economic conflict between neoliberalism and other forms of organising society; and the conflict between the universal idea of each human being as endowed with rights and the actuality of rights being attached to states. The two conflicts are tied together by the capture of the state by financial capital.

Vos brings these two conflicts to the surface by designing a two-part spatial narrative which is informative, critical and humorous. She describes the work as an interactive travelling installation. The first iteration took place in Bethnal Green Road at the heart of a bustling multicultural area in London's East End. She installed a freestanding sign on the pavement outside the shop offering passports for sale. The showcase window of the *Citizenshop* was also designed to attract pedestrians. It displayed what appeared to be passports. On closer inspection, passers-by would notice the crest on the cover of the passport had been exchanged for an ISBN code and that images inside the passport illustrated the dramatic benefits of having a passport. Here were the clues that this was a critical commentary rather than a shop. Signage in the window which said CITIZENSHOP and 'WHAT DOES CITIZENSHIP MEAN TO YOU?' also indicated this was not a typical shop. Nevertheless, the typography looked commercial, so the graphic design acted as satire, simultaneously sending two different messages. It was anticipated that people would suspect the shop to be a performance or installation of some kind, that this might pique their interest and encourage them to enter but also mentally prepare them for an unusual experience. Passers-by could look in and see there were computers, colourful signage and other people browsing the installation. A friendly sales person appeared at the door to invite visitors in. In Greimas' model, the sender was the freestanding street sign and the window display and the receivers were the passers-by, who become subject to the desire to know what 'Citizenshop' means (Figure 3.3).

Working with the principle of a two-part story, Vos divided the internal space into two, the front and back of the shop. When you ventured into the front of the shop, the sales people welcomed you into the international zone of the Republic of Nowhere. You were given a passport which served as a physical token to engage you and commit to staying in the premises by playing a role. The passport functioned as an invitation to start the journey. On the passport for the Republic of Nowhere, visitors found an individual username and password so they could go over to the computers and sign into the online portal of the *Citizenshop*.

The shop was designed like a smart travel agency to give the impression that commercial transactions would occur. The decor functioned as a narrative schema, preparing visitors for the familiar unfolding of a purchasing experience. In Greimas's model, the visitors become the subject, seeking a passport at a fictional level but also seeking the meaning of the installation. The sales people were helpers and the obstacles were

Figure 3.3 Citizenshop installation, London, Nele Vos, 2016.

the tasks visitors had to perform to progress through the space and the physical division of the space. The role play was engaging and people stayed to find out what the point of the shop was. In their role as customers, visitors were shown how to browse through the on-line international collection of investment programs in the *Citizenshop* catalogue. There was a provocative question on the wall behind the computers saying 'What can you afford to buy in Citizenshop?' On the website, visitors were confronted with current citizenship by investment programmes, which they could not afford, and alerted them to the way citizenship has become a commodity which opens up a different world only available to the wealthy. The costs, duties and bonuses governments apply to their offers were revealed and the variations among countries were also surprising to many (Figure 3.4).

Visitors were then ushered into the back of the shop past a large graphic banner that divided the space and concealed the parallel world. Visitors now entered the second part of the two-part story structure. They saw a series of demonstration boards holding individual opinions about the meaning of citizenship. As opposed to a commercial sales pitch, they started to encounter individual stories. The tone of voice changed from one of marketing to one of personal testimony. The light changed from warm to cold and the colour scheme was reduced to greyscales. Banners were hung on the wall with data on migration, displaced persons and statelessness. The banners also showed research from sociologists and policy makers discussing how the world might move beyond the neoliberal organisation of nation states. At this point, visitors were left to digest the information. Here the obstacle became the struggle to understand the multiple ethical, financial and human dimensions of the situation and relate these back to their own experience. Having read the banners, visitors noticed an invitation to contribute to the data

Figure 3.4 Citizenshop – a visitor is confronted with citizenship investment programs, London, Nele Vos, 2016.

Figure 3.5 Citizenshop – a visitor is exploring the meanings of citizenship, London, Nele Vos, 2016.

collection around citizenship by writing a note in response to the question: What does citizenship mean to you? (Figure 3.5).

In Parsons' scheme, the passers-by move by invitation from the 'My world' of Bethnal Green High Street into the 'Their world' of the *Citizenshop*, becoming a visitor. Entering and being given a passport for the Republic of Nowhere is, on the one hand, a displacement to the Nowhere world. On the other hand, the personalised passport prompts a reflection between being in 'My world' and being 'Nowhere'. While, on the computer, the world of neoliberal transactions is laid bare as another 'Their world'. As the world of those who can afford to buy citizenship becomes apparent, visitors realise their assumptions about citizenship being a right are being challenged by the information about citizenship being a commodity. Moving on to the second section of the installation, the facts and commentaries bring the visitors to a realisation that this is a shared issue. They are invited to consider the possible constitution of 'Our world'. Writing their personal response prompts them to reflect on the relationships among 'My world', 'Our world' and 'Their world'. The several shifts across different thresholds from 'My world' to 'Their world' to 'Our world' are an important aspect of the spatialised engagement. The sequencing of the movement through different worlds is transformative and provocative. This example highlights the importance for the design of narrative environments of the ongoing tensions between the nation state as a concrete territorial entity and globalisation as an abstract, universalising space.

While the V&A exhibition offered an immersive sensory experience that apparently gripped visitors through physical delight, triggering memories and heightening emotions, in the end it was a brand story that avoided confronting dramatic conflicts and, ironically, in itself lacked the innovation that the band claim for themselves. It was an extraordinary technical and aesthetic production and a secure business opportunity for the museum but it did not provoke or inform or indeed encourage people to share ideas or reflect on the world of Pink Floyd in relation to their own worlds. By contrast, *Citizenshop* highlighted an important issue and used an artful combination of playfulness and confrontation to reveal vital issues and prompt people to discuss them further, and possibly even act on them.

Irrespective of whether a narrative environment is commercial, cultural, social or critical, it needs a dramatic conflict to establish its relevance, authenticity and power. Through the dramatic conflict, people are engaged in thinking about how worlds are sustained or rendered invisible and how worlds include or exclude. Narrative environments prompt people to consider in which world or worlds they stand and how they are acting in relation to the way those worlds are produced and sustained. The design of narrative environments heightens people's awareness of their situatedness and how their actions are capable of changing that situation. They gain a greater awareness of the dramatic conflicts that structure their worlds and their lives. In this way, the design of narrative environments can provide insights into the situated, grounded and contested character of lifeworlds. It is not enough simply to present a set of related artefacts in chronological order or thematic clusters, or related architectural or urban design schemes, and imagine they will have significant impact. The three-node network model, aligned with the Greimasian model of narrative dynamics and the Parsonian model of the constitution of interrelated but differentiated worlds, provides a way of discovering and articulating dramatic conflict, such that inhabitant, visitor or participant engagement is enhanced through the design of narrative environments.

References

Arendt, H. (1958) *The Human Condition*. Chicago, IL: University of Chicago Press.

Aristotle (1996) *Poetics*. London: Penguin.

Austin, P. (2012) Scales of narrativity. In: MacLeod, S., Hanks, L. and Hale, J., eds. *Museum Making, Narratives, Architecture and Exhibitions*. London: Routledge, pp. 107–118.

Bal, M. (1992) Telling, showing, showing off. *Critical Inquiry*, 18(3), 596–594. University of Chicago.

Bassett, K. (2004) Walking as an aesthetic practice and a critical tool: Some psychogeographic experiments. *Journal of Geography in Higher Education*, 28(3), 397–410.

Bennett, T. (1995) *The Birth of the Museum*. London: Routledge.

Chatman, S. (1978) *Story and Discourse: Narrative Structure in Fiction and Film*. Ithaca, NY: Cornell University Press.

Dunne, T. and Raby, F. (2013) *Speculative Everything*. Cambridge: MIT Press.

Evans, G. (2003) Hard-branding the cultural city: From Prado to Prada. *International Journal of Urban and Regional Research*, 27(2), 417–440.

Flattam, J. (2013) What is a story? Conflict – The foundation of storytelling. *Script*. Online. Available HTTP: www.scriptmag.com/features/conflict-the-foundation-of-storytelling. Accessed 14 April 2018.

Foucault, M. (1972) *The Archaeology of Knowledge and the Discourse on Language*. London: Tavistock Publications.

Genette, G. (1980) *Narrative Discourse: An Essay in Method*. Ithaca, NY: Cornell University Press.

Greimas, A. J. (1983) *Structural Semantics: An Attempt at a Method*. Lincoln, NE: University of Nebraska Press.

Gurian, E. H. (2006) *Civilizing the Museum: The Collected Writings of Elaine Heumann Gurian*. London; New York: Cledge.

Hawhee, D. (2002) Agonism and arete. *Philosophy and Rhetoric*, 35(3), 185–207.

Hébert, L. (2011) *The Semiotic Square*. Signo: Theoretical Semiotics on the Web. Online. Available HTTP: http://www.signosemio.com/greimas/semiotic-square.asp. Accessed 14 January 2018.

Herman, D. (2004) *Story Logic*. Lincoln, NE: University of Nebraska Press.

Hill, D. (2012) *Dark Matters & Trojan Horses: A Strategic Design Vocabulary*. Mosco: Strelka Press.

Hooper-Greenhill, E. (1992) *Museums and the Shaping of Knowledge*. London: Routledge.

Hooper-Greenhill, E. (1999) *Museum, Media, Message*. London: Routledge.

Laclau, E. and Mouffe, C. (2014) *Hegemony and Socialist Strategy: Towards a Radical Democratic Politics*. London; New York: Verso.

Lynch, K. (1960) *The Image of the City*. Cambridge, MA: MIT Press.

MacLeod, S. (2017) Image and life: Museum architecture, social sustainability and design for creative lives. In: Greub, S., ed. *New Museums: Intentions, Expectations, Challenges* Munich: Hirmer Verlag, pp. 175–183.

Marincola, J. (ed.) (2007) *A Companion to Greek and Roman Historiography*. Oxford, UK: Wiley-Blackwell.

McKee, R. (1999) *Story: Substance, Structure, Style and the Principles of Screenwriting*. London: Methuen.

Mouffe, C. (2013) *Agonistics: Thinking the World Politically*. London: Verso.

Nead, L. (1988) *Myths of Sexuality: Representations of Women in Victorian Britain*. Oxford, UK: Basil Blackwell.

Papanek, V. (1971) *Design for the Real World*. London: Granada.

Parsons, A. (2017) *Actant and Actantiality* [Unpublished lecture at Central Saint Martins, UAL. October 2017].

Plant, S. (1992) *The Most Radical Gesture: The Situationist International in a Postmodern Age*. London; New York: Routledge.

Peart, R. (2017) Why design is not problem solving + design thinking isn't always the answer. *AGA Eye on Design*. Online. Available HTTP: https://eyeondesign.aiga.org/why-design-is-not-problem-solving-design-thinking-isnt-always-the-answer/. Accessed 17 November 2019.

Porter Abbott, H. (2002) *The Cambridge Introduction to Narrative*. Cambridge, UK: Cambridge University Press.

Propp, V. (1958) *Morphology of the Folktale*. Bloomington, IN: Indiana University Press.

Rose, G. (2011) *Visual Methodologies: An Introduction to the Interpretation of Visual Materials: An Introduction to the Interpretation of Visual Methods*. London: Sage Publications Ltd.

Sevcik, T. (2018) *City Positioning* [Unpublished lecture at Central Saint Martins, UAL. November 2018].

Wegner, P. (2010) Greimas Avec Lacan; or, from the symbolic to the real in dialectical criticism. *Criticism*, 51(2), 211–245.

Zillmann, D. (1991) Empathy: Affect from bearing witness to the emotions of others. In: Bryant, J. and Zillmann, D., eds. *Communication: Responding to the Screen: Reception and Reaction Processes*. Hillsdale, NJ: Lawrence Erlbaum Associates, Inc., pp. 135–167.

Websites

Citizenshop. http://www.citizenshop.org

Stufish Entertainment Architects. http://www.stufish.com

4   Story Content

This chapter explores some of the ways narrative content is understood from a theoretical perspective and how it is sourced and shaped in practice in the design of narrative environments. It examines how story content is defined in narratology as event, character and setting and explores how these three core story elements play out in narrative environments. Events can be represented literally in image, text or video or embodied in, and enacted through, the physical environment. Characters may be human, but they may also be non-human actants, for example, in stories about the technological, the historical or the political. What is more, spatial environments can also become characters themselves, for example, the landscape, fauna and flora on nature trails. Settings are also crucial to framing the narrative by providing context and modulating the pace and structure of the unfolding drama. The case studies below show some of the roles, processes and techniques used in the commercial and cultural industries to develop narrative environments, and, despite having very different goals, they both emphasise the importance of adopting a strategic approach and employing expert facilitation to enable multiple stakeholders to find consensus in the content development process.

The Elements of Story

Narratologists argue that the word 'narrative' is used to refer to both story (histoire) and telling (narrative discourse). The relationship between the story and its expression has exercised many theorists and produced other terminology such as 'fabula', to mean the story, and 'sjuzet', to mean the way events are woven together (Propp 1968; Shklovsky 1917). MA Narrative Environments has adopted the terms 'story content' and 'story telling'. The relationship between story content and story telling can be exemplified through the various tellings of Shakespeare's *Romeo and Juliet*. Originally a play, it was also the basis for Prokofiev's ballet in 1935 as well as over 24 operas, numerous films, a real-time series of tweets in 2010 by the Royal Shakespeare Company and the Mudlark Production Company, and, in 2018, as a walk-in immersive experience staged by Secret Cinema. Each time, the content of *Romeo and Juliet* took a different form, but nevertheless it remained recognisable as the same story. This demonstrates the versatility of story content. Story content and story telling cannot exist without each other: a story does not exist until it is told, and telling cannot take place without the story content. Even so, it is useful to look at them separately in order to uncover some of the ways narrative environments are generated and structured in principle and in practice.

From a theoretical perspective, structuralist and narratologist Seymour Chatman (1978) asserts that the key elements of story content are event, character and setting. There will be constituent events that move the story forwards and supplementary events

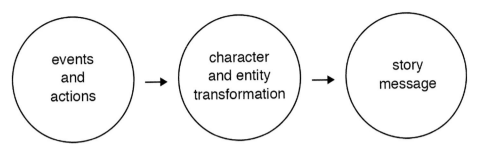

Figure 4.1 The dependency among events, character transformations and overall story message.

(Barthes 1977: 79–124; Chatman 1978: 53–6) that act more as context. Settings also provide context but can sometimes act as characters. There may be multiple characters who sometimes change roles. As characters experience events, they are transformed. The accumulated character transformations infer particular messages, morals or arguments. In narrative environments, there is always a consideration of the overall message, moral or otherwise, and meanings may have psychological, social, ethical or political dimensions (Figure 4.1).

Taking events first, the representation of events, or changes of state, is crucial to narrative environments. Story events are depicted in narrative environments by the use of timelines, text, pictograms, illustrations or photographs; as objects acting as evidence of events; as video showing the events; as scenographic staging of atmospheres to convey events through holograms, AR or VR, architectural and material interventions, or the addition of sounds and smells; or interactives, live performances and the behaviour of other visitors. All or any combination of these representations of events can move the story forward, but those which are spatial, material and sensorial signify the agency of the setting. The visitor or inhabitant experience is formed as a series embodied events, as people move through the narrative environment, experiencing changes in their surroundings as they proceed, sensing and reading the cues and consequently interpreting the story being told. This bodily movement and engagement does not happen in text-based, television, theatre or film narratives, where the audiences stay still.

In most narrative environments, physical changes to the space, a change in lighting, sound, temperature, dimension, materiality, for example, are designed to correspond to the events in the story and create a parallel set of physical events experienced, in the present, through the sensing body of the visitor. An example is the increasing scale in the Pink Floyd exhibition, which re-marks the increasing fame of the band, as discussed in Chapter 3. From a theoretical perspective, there is a question posed by geographer Doreen Massey (2004) about whether space itself should be considered as event. Massey critiques the popular assumption that space is static, a backdrop for chronological happenings. She sees space as dynamic, constituted by the overlapping trajectories and flows of people, politics and money. Taking Massey's perspective, thresholds, zones and edges all constitute events, since these are where moving humans encounter changes in spatial phenomena and atmospheres.

Massey's perspective provides grounds for arguing that narrative environments extend the double temporal order or the chronologic of narrative, as Chatman (1978) calls it, by which he means the disjunction between the time taken to absorb the narrative and the time represented in the narrative. Reading a book or watching a film may be a matter of minutes or hours, but the time the narrative represents could be years or decades or, alternatively, just a few seconds. In narrative environments, the moving visitor also experiences designed, embodied spatial events. The physical environment and moving body in narrative environments add an additional layer to the reading or interpretation of the narrative. The physical experiences are of a different order from the intellectual reading of the story and they take a different amount of time to absorb and accumulate. Thus, the physical nature of narrative environments gives rise to an additional spatio-temporal dimension of narrative experience. Creating an engaging spatio-temporal rhythm, therefore, is an important skill in the design of narrative environments.

H. Porter Abbott (2002) says that, in written or verbal stories, settings are not always necessary. It follows that setting would take the third place in the hierarchy of events, characters and settings. However, the word 'setting' needs further interrogation in the design of narrative environments, where environment plays an active part in the story, as an actant. This is evident in the example of the Gobbins walking trail in Northern Ireland, which is discussed in Chapter 6 and shown in Plate 6. The intrepid visitor walks along bridges suspended high above the sea, along paths hugging the cliffs or tunnelled through the rock. The geology *is* the story and the landscape *is* the entity that has undergone and is still undergoing transformation, grasped through bodily experience as the walk progresses.

Moving on to the role of characters in narrative environments, as in literature, theatre, film and television, human characters play an important role in the content of stories. According to scholar Marie Laure Ryan (2004), who compares literature to other narrative forms, literature allows the inner thoughts and feelings of human characters to be communicated and therefore is very well suited to stories based on psychological development. The reader identifies and empathises with the character, following the character's emotional journey. While in theatre, film and television, audiences also identify with characters, they do so in a more visual and visceral way. Usually, in theatre, film and television, characters act out their feelings through gesture or facial expression or discuss them explicitly in dialogue. There are exceptions where the audience has access, through breaking the fourth wall, to the characters' inner thoughts or to the contextual framing that cannot otherwise be said or acted.

Some narrative environments are also human character-focused, such as the homes of famous figures. At the Freud Museum, London, for example, the visitor can enter Sigmund Freud's consultation room, see the famous couch and imagine themselves being treated by Freud or perhaps even being Freud. Freud and his family are evoked through the authentic interior fit-out of the house, itself a re-creation of Freud's Vienna home, deploying the furniture that they used, objects they collected, photographs, text panels and written labels which describe the objects. Tours, events, videos and lectures are used to tell stories verbally but the physical objects make visitors feel close to the character and this enables them to transport themselves back in time in their imaginations (Beneker 1958, Bedford 2004). The act of imagining yourself in the past, prompted by the environment and the historical objects, creates a sense of being in another world which, in turn, creates a sense of narrative temporality. Visitors may well know aspects of the character's story which they may replay in their heads but, in many ways, the character in this kind of narrative environment is more like a setting in which visitors immerse themselves. Examples of such spaces exist all over the world, such as, to name a few, the Frida Kahlo Museum, Coyoachan, Mexico; Leo Tolstoy House Museum, Moscow; the Jackie Chan Museum, Shanghai; and Graceland, Elvis Presley's home, Memphis, Tennessee.

Another example of using character in an inventive way is the character in residence programme for Rainham Hall, an eighteenth-century merchant's house in Havering, London, owned by the National Trust. From 2013 to 2016, Creative Director Sam Willis led the development of Rainham Hall. Based on initial social and site research and concepts developed by MA Narrative Environments students, Willis commissioned architectural practice Studio Weave to work with her. The team immersed themselves in the local environment, developing participatory approaches to content development involving the local residents and creating a community of interest that would live on after the project. Rainham Hall presented a dilemma. It had no collection of objects. This was unusual for the National Trust, a charity first and foremost concerned with the conservation of its buildings and their objects. However, the lack of a collection allowed Willis and Studio Weave to move away from conservation as their key driver. They looked into the lives of the people who had lived at Rainham Hall rather than looking at the collections they had left behind them. Willis (2018) explained she and the team devised the overall strategy 'Who's living at Rainham Hall?' that worked particularly well because of the large number of different people, over 50 in total, who had lived in the house. Normally, at historic houses, multiple and changing occupancy would be viewed negatively because a large number of inhabitants suggests that the sites will have been bastardised, lost their authenticity and clear lineage. A rolling programme was devised whereby different inhabitants would be in residence for two years, consequently updating the display regularly, thereby attracting repeat visits. The strategy also allowed the National Trust to bring in other collections, for example, in the first two years, they brought in loans from the National Maritime Museum. In addition, the strategy allows the freedom and flexibility to change and respond to different audiences and current issues.

French artist JR uses characters as well. He is renowned for pasting giant black and white photographic portraits of ordinary people at an architectural scale in the urban environment. The monumental images often occupy the same space as the very people he is depicting. He pastes on walls, rooftops, the side of trains and container ships. His work sets out to address urgent social, political and environmental issues. He has worked all over the world. One of his early works, 'Women Are Heroes', took place in cities in Africa, Brazil, India and Cambodia. Huge images of women's eyes stare out across the city in a dramatic and thought-provoking way. JR says the goal of the project was to "highlight the dignity of women who occupy crucial roles in societies, and find themselves victims of wartime, street crime, sexual assault, and religious and political extremism" (JR 2008). Although 'Women Are Heroes' is very dramatic and resonant, a more fully narrative intervention was 'A Child Caught Between the US-Mexico Border', which took place in October 2017. JR installed a 70-foot image of a one-year-old Mexican boy peering over the border fence. Hundreds of people came to see it from both sides of the border and exchanged cameras through the fence to take pictures for each other. JR then instigated a cross-border picnic with a table extending on both sides. During this performative narrative environment people from each side of the border sat together, shared the same food and the same water in a gesture that symbolically dissolved the wall.

Returning to narrative theory, an enormous amount of thought and discussion has gone into the thinking about characters and their roles in stories. In the seminal book *The Morphology of the Folk Tale,* folklorist Vladimir Propp (1968) analysed 100 Russian folk tales. He concluded that all the characters could be categorised into seven broad character functions: the villain, the dispatcher, the helper, the princess or prize, the donor, the hero and the false hero. His structuralist approach to narrative was very influential in subsequent narratological research, such as that of A. J. Greimas and Gerard Genette, both of whose theories are used in the design of narrative environments. Propp's character functions have also been very influential in media education and the film industry.

American scholar of mythology and comparative religion, Joseph Campbell (1949) believed all mythic narratives were variations of a single story or monomyth. In his book *The Hero with a Thousand Faces,* he maps the movement of the hero in 17 stages and 3 acts. In the first act, the hero moves from the ordinary world into the special world or unknown world of adventure. In the second act, the hero, battling against enemies and adversity, wins a decisive victory. He then crosses back, in the third act, into the ordinary world with heightened knowledge, awareness and freedom to live. In the 1970s, Hollywood script analyst Christopher Vogler (1998) synthesised Propp's analysis and Campbell's model of 'The Hero's Journey' to create a practical guide for scriptwriters, *The Writer's Journey: Mythic Structure for Writers.* Numerous related tutorials have since proliferated on the internet. 'The Hero's Journey' has become part of the infrastructure of film making, with standard screenwriting software using 'The Hero's Journey' as a template. This has led critics to argue that Vogler and story consultant and author Robert McKee (1997) are simplistic and formulaic (Yorke 2013) (Figure 4.2).

McKee's criticises 'The Hero's Journey' for being, in essence, a spiritual quest. He argues, instead, that a story is a problem-solving process involving numerous characters. Maureen Murdock (1990) has also highlighted that the Hero's Journey presupposes a male protagonist acting in a stereotypically masculine manner, devoid of ethnographic context. In response, she developed a 10-stage Heroine's Journey where the Heroine battles prejudice against women. For the design of narrative environments, the Hero's and Heroine's journey can help to question and develop a story structure. However,

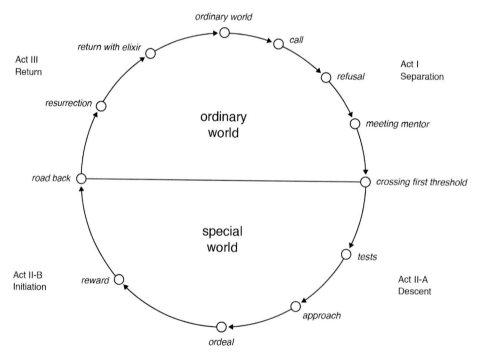

Figure 4.2 The Hero's Journey.

a slavish adherence to the formula will only produce predictable results. Furthermore, the formulaic structure of the Hero's Journey lacks the capacity to respond to the spatial and material qualities of narrative environments. Finally, the Hero's Journey needs to be treated with some caution so that it does not become a tick-box exercise that perpetuates certain societal biases and clichés.

Another reason the Hero's Journey does not provide a universal model for the design of narrative environments is that, in narrative environments, characters can often take the form of more abstract phenomena such as locations, regions or whole countries. The notion of hero is too anthropomorphic to deal with this understanding of character. One example is the enormous scenographic exhibition about India at Mumbai Airport (Shah 2014). Objects, architectural fragments and images tell stories of Indian culture in a highly textured and elaborate display and visitors are engaged in a complex, multi-level history on a sensory level. Similarly, visitor centres, science centres, art installations and brand experiences tend to focus on entities rather than human characters. Such narrative environments may focus on non-human actants in stories as aspects of topical issues. To capture the human and the non-human manifestations of characters and entities, the design of narrative environments uses the notion of actant, borrowing it from the work of Greimas (1987) and Latour (2005).

The two detailed examples below show how story content plays out in the practice of the design of narrative environments. Looking at the practice raises additional questions: How is content sourced and analysed, and how is it shaped in the design of narrative environments? Who is responsible for the narrative in narrative environments? How does the practice vary across different sectors and institutions? The first example is from the commercial sector and the second from the cultural sector. These spheres of practice differ in their priorities and purposes. Commercial narrative environments, such as brand and hospitality experiences, need to produce an explicit business benefit to the companies or investors involved; cultural narrative environments, such as exhibitions and cultural events, set out to fulfil their mission to educate and inform. It is interesting to note, however, that their respective challenges, methods and goals overlap. They foreground narrative but show how the other two nodes in the tripartite network, environment and people, are implicated through the narrative. There is a common concern for engaging audiences by communicating content through embedding stories into spaces and often creating spaces which prompt further storytelling. All the case studies incorporate story as a key driver in contrast to style-led, technology-led, finance-led design or purely functional design.

Cisco House, London Olympics 2012, and Casa Cisco, Rio Olympics 2016

The client in the first case study is the global technology giant Cisco, which develops, manufactures and sells internet infrastructure, communications hardware, high-tech products and services. Cisco designed and installed the network connectivity for both the London Olympics and the Rio Olympics and, as sponsors, sought to create at each Games, exceptional VIP hospitality experiences to influence their stakeholders. Cisco holds annual, place-based 'Cisco Live' events hosting tens of thousands of their employees, suppliers, partners and clients. These events offer hundreds of simultaneous activities, such as talks, courses, student programmes, workshops and networking sessions. However, for the Olympics Games, Cisco envisaged a different model, a hospitality hub targeted at C-level executives, that is Chief Executive Officers (CEOs), Chief Financial Officers (CFOs) and Chief Technology Officers (CTOs), for example. In the past, hospitality tents staged by some companies would put a drink and a sandwich in people's hands and then take them to the Games. For the 2012 'Cisco House' at the London Olympics, Cisco wanted an inspirational showcase and a marketing opportunity. Cisco called in their long-term partners, the global experience marketing agency George P. Johnson (GPJ), to lead on the concept development, design and installation of the bespoke experiences. The questions were: What content would help create an enthralling experience and how would that relate to the location of the hospitality hub?

Andy Bass, Creative Director on both the London and Rio hospitality hubs, explained the development and delivery process. The foundational principle was to create a 'Strategic Experience Development Map'. This is a tool invented by David Rich from GPJ, who was at that time the Olympic global account management lead on GPJ's relationship with Cisco and later led the Casa Cisco project in Brazil. The Strategic Experience Development Map crystallises the client's picture of success in terms of a business outcome. In a nutshell, it describes what the visitors need to feel, think, know and do before, during and after the event to be moved to the desired perceptions and actions. In this case, Cisco sought outcomes such as enhanced brand affiliation, new brand ambassadors, renewed commitment to the brand from employees and increased purchases from customers.

Ideally, the Strategic Experience Development Map lays the ground for the content development and physical design, which are therefore rooted in a strong understanding of both the client's objectives and the human dimension of the project, the visitors' needs and desires. Rich developed this tool in the mid-1990s after he had noticed that, all too often, companies were leaping to design decisions, for example, deciding on a thematic focus or production elements, based on personal preferences. They would come to a decision before identifying what would be most effective for the attendees and discussing, developing and agreeing the key strategic, experiential and business goals. With no clear and agreed rationale some clients would, shortly before the critical moment of delivery, request changes that did not align. Last-minute erratic changes, Rich explains, overload the development team, causing undue stress that puts quality execution in danger; create contradictory, confusing, or ineffective messaging; and produce additional costs and potential overruns. When combined, these factors generate considerable business risk. He points out, "The commercial world is unforgiving. In projects like these, millions of dollars of investment are at stake and livelihoods are on the line" (Rich 2018). Rich realised that a Strategic Experience Development Map with staged sign-off was needed to reduce risk and ensure greater success. The process would involve the whole team including the client using "strategy as a tool of governance" (Rich 2018).

Bass (2019) and Rich (2018) explain that successful marketers always look first at audience needs in relation to business objectives and brand. Audience research is vital to achieve their business objectives. The experience marketing team also have to bring new concepts to the table, otherwise people will tend to refer back to previous or well-known examples of experiences. Rich explains that very skilled facilitators are needed to enable senior business people, leading experts in their own field, to embrace perspectives they had not expected and to suspend their personal preferences. Rich's team run iterative charrettes with up to 30 people at a time from all over the world, meeting to clarify objectives for each audience segment, analyse audience status and needs, brainstorm ideas and then meeting again to filter and focus on specific ideas. The London Olympics hub, Cisco House, was a two-year project and the Rio Olympics hub, Casa Cisco, was a three-year project. During these periods of time there were several changes in the client team, so being able present the Strategic Experience Development Map was essential to create continuity.

Nevertheless, in Cisco House London the key variables, site and budget, were unknown at conception, and content was continuously juggled for 18 months, during which time Bass produced numerous experience concepts and visuals to keep people's imaginations engaged and the project on schedule. Bass explains that the site was important as its affordances and location would shape the content to some extent. Bass's team visited a great number of potential sites around London looking for one that provided a logical link to both Cisco and the Olympics and eventually settled on the Westfield Shopping Centre, next to the Olympic Park. Cisco installed a new two-floor, 20,000-square foot, semi-permanent pavilion. The Cisco House balcony gave visitors a panoramic view of the Olympic Park, a dramatic moment for the visitor experience. The construction was a technical challenge but, with a team of up to 60 people working on it every day, the building was completed in 70 days. A Cisco high-speed, state of the art network was installed to support digital interactives, live streaming video, early forms of augmented reality, a 3D 'Tube Train' experience, an 'Innovation Tunnel' and a 360° 'Future Theatre' with a wrap-around screen.

As soon as the venue was decided, content had to be developed as a parallel process to determine the visitor experience. Although the client knew they wanted a VIP hub which functioned as a showcase, they needed facilitation from GPJ to focus on what content would be included and how it would unfold through the building. There were many ideas from a huge range of experts in Cisco but an organising principle was needed. Bass pointed out that the audience would ostensibly be visiting the Olympics. This was a day out for them; they would want fun, and many would be dressed in shorts and t-shirts, often accompanied by their spouse. They would want to soak up the euphoric atmosphere of the Games and often that was just as important, if not more important, than seeing a particular sporting event. In this context, Bass argued that visitors would not be seeking technical demos but an exciting experience. He therefore proposed that inspiring case studies should serve as the heroes of the story. Screens and interactives showing the impact of Cisco technology also aligned to the central concept that the GPJ team identified as core to Cisco's message, "it's not what we make, but what we make possible". The view from the balcony and the visit to the Games themselves served as a live expression of the impact of Cisco's capabilities.

Bass recognised that visitors would be coming from all over the world and would possibly be unaware of how the Cisco House location fitted into the overall context of London and the Games. He conceived a threshold orientation experience where guests walked across a large floor graphic showing the river Thames, their hotel, the Games and the Cisco offices. The graphic was accompanied by augmented reality views of London that aimed to orient and connect visitors to the network of sites shown on the floor. All experience elements were hosted, with host scripts as conversation starters. This set the tone for the whole experience to be a series of social interactions. Hosts were positioned in all the zones.

After the threshold experience, visitors went up to the first floor of the pavilion. Two extra steps were designed so that people entering could see over others' heads to the balcony. On the balcony, the view was augmented by live camera views of the Olympic Park and overlays which guests could touch to bring up information about the Games in that location. Guests could then work their way down ramps to the bar, lounge and balcony, looking at the displays and talking to the hosts and each other as they descended (Figure 4.3).

Figure 4.3 Cisco House at the London Olympics, 2012.

At the end of the ramp, visitors were allocated to a group and given time to do a tour, the immersive media element of the experience. Bass adopted the London Tube as a metaphor for the core Business Transformation Experience, making a parallel between one of London's iconic features and Cisco as the architect of a transformative digital network. A 3D film took visitors on a journey viewing a number of projects where Cisco had supported business transformation before they were pulsed through an Innovation Tunnel taking them on a trip to the future, showing a timeline of Cisco's development. This brought them into the 360° Future Theatre which displayed information about the coming digital revolution and the effects of big data, AI and 3D printing, which were all cutting-edge ideas at the time.

The tour, which was the peak of the experience, was quite quick and when it was complete guests were free to go into the Olympic Park or back upstairs to the balcony and lounge. In summary, the experience interlinked four zones with an overall theme of the transformational power of networks, while delivering subsections about London, the infrastructure of the Olympics as well as the live video of the Games, case studies of the way Cisco had impacted the world, the company's history and a vision of the future. In parallel, visitors were able to grow their business networks: 13,000 invitation-only, executive guests visited Cisco House while it was open over a period of five months. It was an award-winning project that led to Casa Cisco at the Rio Olympics.

Bass and Rich started developing Casa Cisco in Rio in January 2014 with much the same objectives as London: to foster brand loyalty, build relationships and stimulate new business. The geographic context was very different. There was no central Olympic space because the Games were dispersed across four different locations in the city. Cisco also knew that, although it had been operating in the country for two decades, as an American company it needed to stress the point that it was committed to and understood the Brazilian market. Consequently, the team looked for an iconic Rio location that would become a fifth location for VIP Cisco stakeholders. They found a military officers' club on the beach at the foot of Sugarloaf Mountain with a remarkable view of the bay. It was safe and not far from downtown and Copacabana beach. They negotiated with the colonels who managed the property on behalf of the government to gut it and fully refurbish it, making several additions over the two years leading up to the Games so that, as a legacy, they would leave an exceptional facility after the Olympics. One point of difference between the approach to London and this design was the blending of Cisco corporate design cues with authentic Rio visual culture. These cues identified Cisco as the host while reflecting the company's integration into the local culture and community. This entailed blending the corporate colour palette, Brazilian design forms and materials to make a custom-commissioned 80-metre mural that reflected the style of Brazilian street art, while depicting story elements of the Games. This created a thread of continuity in the tone of voice for the whole experience and proved so effective that the mural artwork served as the basis for the marketing collateral that supported the experience. Aside from this Rio look and feel, the GPJ/Cisco team followed many of the same principles as Cisco House in London. They provided first-class internet connection, security, a bar, a new gallery space, three new lifts for disabled access and a new balcony. However, they also disguised older parts of the structure and created new zones through the staging provided by the snaking 80-metre-long mural that created a thread of continuity for the whole experience. The space was hosted throughout in the same spirit (Figure 4.4).

The mural related to the cultural context. Casa Cisco needed to be designed to reflect the way business is done in Brazil, it needed to have local relevance and authenticity, but still communicate global messages. There would be a local audience, an international visitor segment, academics, press attendees and trade attendees, and the hub experience needed to resonate with all of them. Bass describes imagining Cisco as a Brazilian company, and therefore what their headquarters would look like. The elements were designed with the Brazilian context in mind. For example, the Boteca bar and its furnishings and service was designed after typical bars in Brazil where business conversations take place accompanied by plentiful food and drink. Bass also commissioned a local graffiti artist, 'Ficore', to design and paint the mural. In order to bridge cultures, Bass commissioned the artist to paint using the Cisco colour palette and crisp geometric forms so that the mural had the life and rhythm of Rio but also communicated a cool, crisp, corporate feel. The other strong Brazilian influence was Anderson Felício, the local designer Bass commissioned to bring an authentic flavour to the make-over of the venue. As it turned out, Anderson Felício also became a lynch pin for the production, overcoming language barriers and helping to source local suppliers.

GPJ developed and agreed to the Strategic Experience Development Map through an iterative development process early on in the project. Having identified a location early in the

Figure 4.4 Casa Cisco at the Rio Olympics, 2016.

whole process, Bass says the project was easier than Cisco House. The team knew that over the two years, things would change, and they decided to create Casa Cisco as a blank canvas with a beautiful location, knowing the content would be developed over time. Six months before the Games, they eventually ran with Cisco's new brand advertising message 'There Has Never Been a Better Time', which provided a strong creative direction for the content.

Casa Cisco was finally resolved into six chapters. First, a reception space communicated a warm welcome to come in and have some refreshments. Second, the Boteca bar had videos about Cisco and live coverage of the Games, while the street art wall continued along one side. Third, a Transformation Bar area featured interactives and immersive video that told the story of Cisco's digital transformation of Rio's Porto Maravilha area. Visitors came to a short flight of stairs which were modelled on the iconic Selarón steps in Rio. This was a popular photo opportunity. Fourth, upstairs, the global advertising campaign was brought to life through videos showing visitors the beneficial impact people like themselves were making around the world. In the penultimate zone, there were video kiosks and connections to live events at the Games with inset information about the Cisco technology used to create the connectivity and data flows tracking social media usage, indicating peak moments of mass excitement. There was an account of the real-time systems Cisco had developed for the Games set in this room which also had a graphic timeline on the wall showing the 22 years Cisco had operated in Brazil. This graphic flowed into a huge floor plan of Rio showing the locations of different projects. Finally, visitors moved to the balcony for refreshments and photos against the backdrop of the sea view.

Every care was taken to encourage visitors to chat and a great deal of thought was given to the positioning of the Cisco hosts. After the balcony, visitors could visit the Games or stay and make further use of the Boteca. The Boteca had a small stage which made the space very suitable for presentations over the course of the Games. At times, it was used for presentations by Olympic athletes who shared with Cisco's guests what it was like to compete in the most high-profile sports competition in the world, while at other times it was used by Cisco executives to welcome their guests with special presentations. The narrative environment was so successful in achieving its design goals of balancing a corporate and local feel, and creating a business setting with local hospitality features that prominent organisations, such as the Brazil Foundation, sought it out as the site for its annual, celebrity-laden celebration. The once run-down building is now a favourite place for community events and a favourite venue for wedding ceremonies and celebrations. In addition to achieving its business objectives, the programme garnered six premiere marketing awards, evidencing the value of taking the strategic approach.

Experience design of VIP hospitality hubs is a niche market but the award-winning Cisco House and Casa Cisco are clear examples for all sectors about the importance of a strategic framework in structuring such complex projects and developing relevant content. The case studies show just how important it is to align content with audience needs and desires, the physical space and a consideration of the timing and interaction. The examples highlight the need to negotiate and agree the overall narrative messaging at all levels with all stakeholders. A high-level organising principle and powerful metaphor is then needed to create narrative unity among the story sections unfolding in multiple zones. At this point, specific content can be sourced or developed. In as far as Rich's Strategic Experience Development Map gathers together narrative, visitor experience and a concern for venue and location in order to achieve business goals, it clearly bears a close relationship to the narrative environments tripartite model, indicating that the model can be used as a 'wireframe' from which a strategic plan can be developed.

The Tower of London

The client in the second case study is Historic Royal Palaces (HRP), the self-funding charity which looks after six iconic royal palaces: Tower of London; Hampton Court Palace; Kensington Palace; Kew Palace; Banqueting House, Whitehall; and Hillsborough Castle in Northern Ireland. Historic Royal Palaces host over four million visitors per year. Their mission is to invite the public into extraordinary palace settings in order to explore how the monarchy has shaped British society. Historic Royal Palaces is a leader in experimental, innovative interpretation, creative programming and content creation. They are interested in broadening their reach, impact and relevance. An example of their innovation is the famous artistic commission 'Blood Swept Lands and Seas of Red', the Poppies project, which took place in 2014, at the Tower of London. A sea of 888,246 ceramic poppies, commemorating all of the British soldiers who died in the First World War, encircled the Tower. The installation was described as "the most popular art installation as well as arguably the most effective expression of commemoration in British history" (Heathcote 2014). Historic Royal Palaces aims to pursue a culture of change and development so that in all areas and at all levels they have a mindset receptive to innovation.

The example below describes the development of a unifying, content-driven framework for revising the visitor experience at the Tower of London. The development of the framework took place from May 2015 to April 2016. The final Tower Core Story was launched in April 2017 and is now the Interpretation and Design plan that informs future projects at the Tower. Since then, Historic Royal Palaces has developed Core Stories for Hampton Court Palace and Kensington Palace and work is currently underway on the Banqueting House, Whitehall. Polly Richards was the Interpretation Manager who led the process at the Tower of London. Richards explains that, in the museum world, the curator has responsibility for the collection of objects and sometimes a building or group of buildings. Curators are seen as the experts or keepers of the knowledge while the interpretation managers make that knowledge accessible to the public. They tease out the nub of the story, matching the curator's vision with what might interest the visitors, bearing in mind initial briefings and discussions about who the visitors are. The key messaging is then tested with target audiences and the feedback is integrated into the scheme of content, as it is worked and reworked, so that the curator's goals and audience's needs are gradually brought into alignment. Richards (2018) says, "I want visitors to feel the passion that the curators have for their subjects". She believes successful museums provoke conversation among visitor groups and that museums should be places of inspiration.

Richards explains how this process worked at the Tower of London. The Tower has a 1000-year history and is known all over the world. However, audience research undertaken at the time revealed that visitors did not know very much about the Tower before they visited except that it is historic, that the Crown Jewels are housed there, that it was a prison and that executions and murders took place there. Audience research also showed visitors were not connecting these facts. Another problem was that, due to the long and varied history of the Tower, visitors were faced on arrival with a substantial volume of material and a complex set of buildings with numerous choices about which way to go. Visitor evaluations revealed excitement levels fell off after half an hour because visitors became confused by too much information that did not allow them to construct a coherent story for themselves.

In order to make the Tower more comprehensible to its audiences, Polly Richards knew she had to find a clear key message under which all other information could be clustered. She also knew visitors to historical sites, such as this, need to access and digest content at speed because an average visit is no longer than two hours. The key message had to summarise the whole and serve as a reference point from which all aspects of the displays, event programming, internal and external communications could flow. The key message is sometimes called 'the hook' in the exhibition and museum sector, indicating that it is a way to capture the audience's attention, a means to enable the visitor to navigate and rationalise their experience as they move through the space but also a point from which all other aspects of the content can hang in the development and design of the experience.

When she started at the Tower, Polly Richards discovered, by chance, that her predecessor, Rebecca Richards, and curator, Sally Dixon Smith, shared a short-hand way of explaining the Tower, but had not actioned it as a content and communication strategy. Rebecca Richards said, "you do realise the Tower is a Fortress, a Palace and a Prison". Polly Richards realised this was the hook that could be shared with the visitor and that would provide an organising principle for the whole site. She explains that, in terms of the three-part identity, the Prison is the best known, but the Fortress is most important because the security it provided is the reason the Prison and the Crown Jewels are located there. The Fortress underpins the bulk of the history but it is the least dramatic part of the story. The Palace is the hidden aspect of the Tower.

Working with a core team that included curator Sally Dixon Smith, learning producer Megan Gooch and assistant curator Sarah Okpokam, Richards set up an inclusive process running 72 workshops with four to ten people at a time, over the course of a year. The aim, as far as possible, was to engage all stakeholders in a discussion of the key message, 'Fortress, Palace, Prison', and how it could be mapped onto the space, down to the detail of all stories in each location. The process was successful partly because it was not rushed and everyone had a chance to explain their point of view. In the end, consensus was gained through discussion. It is not well known that the Tower houses two museums, The Royal Armouries and The Fusilier Museum, which were engaged as critical friends. The Royal Armouries which is housed in the White Tower has the collection that relates to the Tower as a fortress. The Tower was the nerve centre for England's wars from the thirteenth century until about 1850. Military equipment was made, stored, managed, issued and shipped from there, taking advantage of the Tower's position on the River Thames. Weapons that had been used in wars or captured from the enemy were brought back as trophies. The Royal Armoury collection is the legacy of 400 years of the Tower as a military nerve centre.

The message 'Fortress, Palace, Prison' was also tested with visitors. Research consultancy Morris Hargreaves Macintyre conducted telephone and on-site interviews, and the same culture consultancy conducted accompanied visits and in-depth focus groups around the site with local residents and organisations in Tower Hamlets. The Tower of London wanted to build a more diverse audience profile that was more representative of the changing UK and local population, and specifically to engage more families, young people and visitors with access needs. Feedback showed audiences fully embraced the key message.

In terms of the visitor journey, there was no introductory space, so Richards and her colleagues had to work out how to communicate the top-level message to visitors before they even arrived. This meant foregrounding 'Fortress, Palace, Prison' on the website, on the visitor map and guidebook, on the signage when people arrived at Tower Hill, even in shops surrounding the Tower. 'Fortress, Palace, Prison' had to be right at the heart of all communications. 'Fortress, Palace, Prison' was then broken down into eight subheadings with associated stories (Figure 4.5).

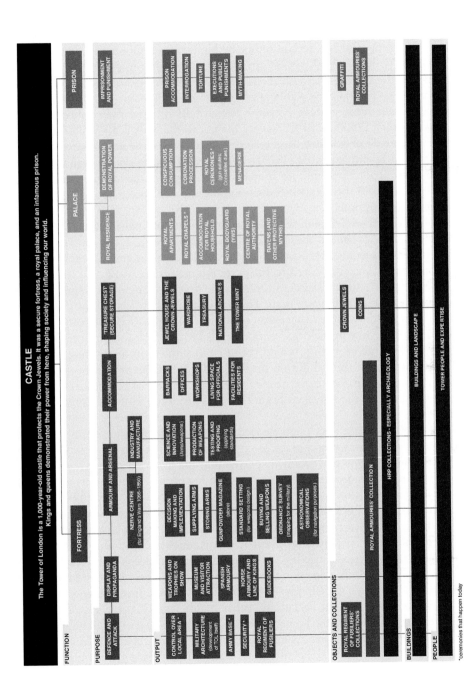

Figure 4.5 Tower of London Core Story Plan, 2016.

It was decided that each space would expand on an aspect of the framework, illustrated through two or three individuals' stories. For example, on entering the medieval palace, visitors learn about two monarchs, King Henry III and Edward I, and at the very least that kings and queens moved around a lot, did not stay at the Tower for very long or very often and what the different Palace spaces were used for. By contrast, in the Bloody Tower, the goal was to communicate high status imprisonment, showing an exhibition about Walter Raleigh on the ground floor and the imprisonment and presumed murder of the Little Princes on the upper floor. The story of the Little Princes is probably best known among the public and gives rise to the name the Bloody Tower. Research shows that most visitors presume Richard III ordered their murder but, as external stakeholders, the Richard III Society maintains that this is a popular myth and in fact there is no proof of his guilt. As a result, this was one of the first projects from the Core Story plan to be implemented. The Tower's Interpretation and Design team commissioned and installed a three-minute animation that explains the mystery and how the rumour mill has worked through time, encouraging the audience to consider the myth and question its assumptions.

The content or interpretive plan was worked and reworked with critical friends and all stakeholders. This produced many documents, for example, a content outline and a content matrix that maps the primary and secondary narratives for each space. A branding consultancy was also hired to integrate the new framework into the Tower's existing brand and to create guidelines to inform the design of any new communication, such as the website, wayfinding and map. This aimed not only to clarify the content but also demonstrate just how much there was to see and give the visitor a better sense of value for money. Everyone in the organisation needed to take the content framework on board because even one exception would cause confusion. From marketing, fundraising, retail and signage to the exhibition display and live interpretation through staged historic re-enactments, the messaging needed to cohere. As part of this process, the Core Story team worked with the Retail team on the redesign of the Tower's shops to reflect the framework.

In each exhibition space, the team needed to decide which moment in history to tell. The Martin Tower was first a place of imprisonment, then accommodation for the keeper of the Crown Jewels and finally displayed that the Crown Jewels were no longer in use. Story priority was decided in terms of telling history where it happened but also needed to consider the visitor journey and experiential sequence. For example, the wall walks are quite linear and suitable for single chronological stories. Research showed that visitors got confused if two periods of time and two parallel stories are featured in one space. The dimensions of the space also impacted on the story. The Bloody Tower is a very tight space, therefore there needed to be a shorter story and a shorter dwell time. As 50% of visitors are not English speaking, the communication needs to be predominantly visual and sensory. Outside the Bloody Tower, for example, the Interpretation team has recently introduced a display of herbal and other plants from Raleigh's garden, which he grew whilst imprisoned at the Tower to concoct his medicinal elixir. The team tried to avoid filling the space with text, using visual, tactile and multimedia means instead.

The framework and proposed narrative was tested on audience groups with positive results. However, the testing also revealed the stories that visitors wanted to hear, such as the story of Anne Boleyn. This was then developed as a live performance showing Anne Boleyn arriving by boat and being tried on the South Lawn, the former site of the Tudor Palace. The testing also revealed another big gap. More than 100 people live on site in the Tower, and one of the most surprising visitor experiences is to look down from the battlements and see washing lines and little children playing outside. Although the Beefeater's tour explains that they live there, most visitors are not aware of this. It is now planned to open one of the empty houses for bespoke tours to tell the story of the Tower Community and how people have lived inside the Fortress walls over the centuries.

Questions also arose throughout this process about stories that the Tower team are now planning to address: how to deal with contentious issues such as imperialism, how to communicate torture without sensationalising the events and how to tell sensitive stories such as enslavement and the history of Jewish people at the Tower without provoking division and hostility. This forms part of the debate on critical heritage discussed in Chapter 8.

Although the two detailed examples, Cisco Hospitality Hubs and the Tower of London, spring from very different territories, motivations and content, they nevertheless share some characteristics. They both involve multiple stakeholders, their developments run over quite extended timelines of two or more years and they both require considerable financial investment. Both are subject to risk of reputational damage if their projects underperform. They both place the same emphasis on the initial content strategy. There is a focus on the importance of consensus to agree content. Content development is managed by designated people. Both have developed systems focused on an overarching message which creates an umbrella in which to nest different stories. They both show how teams need to condense communications to a simple message, theme or metaphor, to construct a visitor invitation and a path into the story. Complex structures of content are diagrammed, which the visitor never sees. The teams developing narrative environments need to attend to all nodes in the tripartite model to synthesise story, space and time with a thorough understanding of audiences' expectations and desires while balancing operational requirements and overall project goals.

The processes of collaboration in project management, content development and exhibition making are well documented in the book *Creating Exhibitions* (McKenna-Cress and Kamien 2013), which focuses mainly on examples of museums in the USA. These processes are under constant review by researchers. The design of narrative environments, as developed at Central Saint Martins and explained in this book, advocates greater integration of spatial design considerations from the beginning of the process and a more iterative exploratory approach. PhD candidate at Central Saint Martins, Julia Pitts, formerly of the Science Museum London and currently an Interpretation Manager at the Victoria and Albert Museum, has undertaken detailed research and, as a result, she proposes changes to the exhibition development process. Pitts (2018) explains that, in the current process, a short exhibition proposal is written by a senior member of the staff. This is reviewed by the audience researchers, who make recommendations, and the interpreters, who explore how to bridge the museum's aspirations and assets with the audiences' interests. These recommendations form the principles for the interpretation strategy. After two to three months of content and interpretation meetings, another written document is produced with the content message hierarchy, audience summative research and what is known about the space and the budget. The designers are then asked to pitch. Pitts argues that spatial considerations are treated as secondary, despite the fact that exhibitions are a spatial medium. From her perspective, the designers should be part of the team from day one. If that were the case, she argues, they could contribute their expertise in the material and spatial dynamics of the visitor experience to create more engaging exhibitions. In this scenario, the whole team could 'play' with the possible inclusion of, and configurations of, objects, lighting, sound and interaction in the actual space. Pitts suggests this process would resolve common conflicts between content and design. All parties would thereby share responsibility for decision-making and audience engagement. Pitts argues for a more even distribution of attention across the tripartite network model of narrative environments.

A similar position is taken by Clare Brown, formerly Chief of Design at the Smithsonian Institution National Museum of American History in Washington DC, who explains that, in her experience, large museums often start the exhibition process with academic messages, typically called key messages, which are developed by the curator and interpretive planners, also known as exhibit developers in the USA. These umbrella messages, designed to be relevant to the museum's target audiences, are often educational or fact based in character, not necessarily formulated as story. This is quite different from starting with an experiential approach expressed through a story arc. By contrast, design-led processes typically start with multidirectional research questioning the 'what, where, how and for whom?' of a project. Design-led teams are therefore likely to aim to envision systemic success as opposed to specifically aiming to evaluate whether they have communicated a particular message. Brown (2019) advocates using the language and methods from service design and Agile software design (Beck et al. 2001). She follows computer scientist Melvin Conway (1968), who suggests the process of development of products effects the final outcome. Brown extrapolates that if the processes of exhibition development are more collaborative, and led by experience design methods such as service design, that the products, or exhibition experiences, will be enhanced. Service design stresses the equal importance of considering the working methods and experience design for back-of-house operations as well as front-of-house experiences. In museums, the exhibition front-of-house is the visitor experience. The back-of-house concerns the resources required and the ways in which people work together. Brown's (2018) research reveals that inbuilt museum hierarchies, lack of face-to-face communication and assumptions about design as technical, rather than creative and strategic, lead to a devaluation of back-of-house processes. In large museums in the USA and elsewhere, the exhibition design team has to follow the curator's lead through a process in which a product is pre-determined and then implemented. This approach closes off opportunities to explore other options. She explains the Agile software development process is different. Using Agile, teams are allocated short periods of time, also known as time-bracketing, to develop specific ideas fully, yet rapidly, and test them. They are then given time to analyse and decide which path to go down. This is a process of discovery as opposed to obligation. Brown advocates for the recognition of the full potential of design as a mode of development work, rather than a technical service, and for design-led, collaborative change in exhibition processes.

Museums and the commercial sector both face obstacles in terms of process but should not lose sight of the crucial difference between narrative environments and other kinds of spaces. Narrative environments have content deliberately embedded in a story form. This is not to suggest that urban realm, architecture and interiors have no meaning. Spaces are replete with multiple meanings. However, narrative environments produce a particular kind of experience, based on communicating specific narrative content to specific audiences. That content is strategically developed to communicate a powerful story that carries particular messages, morals or value systems. Narrative environments can range from reinforcing convention to questioning normative values and they can make poetic or provocative interventions. However, successful narrative environments need content and an exploratory, iterative creative process to unite the content and the space and offer transformational experiences. The tripartite network model ensures this process is tackled by a diverse team and that the designer is not left in isolation.

References

Barthes, R. (1977) Introduction to the structural analysis of narratives. In: Heath, S. ed. *Image-Music-Text*. Glasgow: Fontana, pp. 79–124.

Bass, Andy (2019) Interview with Tricia Austin, 6 August 2019.

Beck, K., et al. (2001) *Manifesto for Agile Software Development*. Online. Available HTTP: http://agilemanifesto.org. Accessed 11 November 2019.

Bedford, L. (2004) Working in the subjunctive mood: Imagination and museums. *Curator: The Museum Journal*, 47(1), 5–11.

Beneker, K. (1958) Exhibits: Firing platforms for the imagination. *Curator: The Museum Journal* 1(4), 76–81.

Brown, C. (2018) DesignThinkers Toronto 2018. Online. Available HTTP: https://www.ico-d.org/connect/events/events/885.php. Accessed 16 November 2019.

Brown, Clare (2019) Interview with Tricia Austin, 14 January 2019.

Campbell, J. (1949) *The Hero with a Thousand Faces*. New York, NY: Pantheon Books.

Chatman, S. (1978) *Story and Discourse: Narrative Structure in Fiction and Film*. Ithaca, NY: Cornell University Press.

Conway, M. (1968) How do committees invent? *Datamation*, 14(4), 28–31.

Greimas, A. J. (1987) Actants, actors, and figures. In: *On Meaning: Selected Writings in Semiotic Theory*. London, UK: Francis Pinter, pp. 106–120.

Heathcote, E. (2014) Tower of London poppies take UK into new age of war commemoration. *Financial Times*, 31 October 2014.

Latour, B. (2005) *Reassembling the Social: An Introduction to Actor-Network-Theory*. Oxford, UK: Oxford University Press.

Massey, D. (2004) *For Space*. London: Sage.

McKee, R. (1997) *Story: Substance, Structure, Style, and the Principles of Screenwriting*. New York, NY: Regan Books.

McKenna-Cress, P. and Kamien, J. (2013) *Creating Exhibitions*. Hoboken, NJ: Wiley.

Murdock, M. (1990) *The Heroine's Journey*. Boston, MA: Shambhala Publications.

Pitts, Julia (2018) Interview with Tricia Austin, 21 December 2018.

Porter Abbott, H. (2002) *The Cambridge Introduction to Narrative*. Cambridge, UK: Cambridge University Press.

Propp, V. (1968) *Morphology of the Folktale*. Austin, TX: University of Texas Press.

Rich, David (2018) Interview with Tricia Austin, 10 August 2018.

Richards, Polly (2018) Interview with Tricia Austin, 13 September 2018.

Ryan, M.-L., (2004) *Narrative across Media: The Languages of Storytelling* (Frontiers of Narrative). Lincoln, NE: University of Nebraska Press.

Shah, G. R. (2014) Ambitious art on display at Mumbai's new airport terminal. *India Ink*. Online. Available HTTP: https://india.blogs.nytimes.com/2014/01/15/ambitious-art-on-display-at-mumbais-new-airport-terminal. Accessed 11 November 2019.

Shklovsky, V. (1917/2012) Art as technique. In: Lemon, L. T. and Reis, M. J., eds. *Russian Formalist Criticism: Four Essays*, 2nd ed., Lincoln, NE: University of Nebraska Press, pp. 3–24.

Vogler, C. (1998) *The Writer's Journey: Mythic Structure for Writers*. Studio City, CA: M. Wiese Productions.

Willis, Sam (2018) Interview with Tricia Austin, 3 September 2018.

Yorke, J. (2013) *Into the Woods: How Stories Work and Why We Tell Them*. London: Penguin Books.

Websites

George P. Johnson Cisco House. https://www.gpj.com/case-study/cisco-house-at-the-london-olympics-2012

JR. https://www.jr-art.net
Rainham Hall. https://www.nationaltrust.org.uk/rainham-hall
Secret Cinema. https://www.secretcinema.org
The Gobbins. https://thegobbinscliffpath.com
The Tower of London. https://www.hrp.org.uk/tower-of-london

5   Story Telling

Having looked, in the previous chapter, at some of the ways content is defined, sourced and structured in narrative environments, this chapter explores how content is *told* in narrative environments, a process of telling in which space acts as a medium of communication. This chapter looks more closely at the relationship between the narrative and environment nodes in the tripartite narrative environments network. The examples below demonstrate that the spatial dimension of narrative environments has often been considered secondary to the content; in other words, the narrative node in the three-node network has often been privileged over the environment node. This is partly because of the higher status afforded to the written word over the visual and the spatial. Language is conventionally seen as anchoring communication and meaning production, despite, as W. J. T. Mitchell (1996 and 2003) argues, word and image being inseparable and all media being multimedia because they open out onto each other. It is also partly because space is so much part of our everyday lives that it is taken for granted (Perec 1997; Massey 2005) and its communicative capability is overlooked and underestimated. Finally, it is also due to a lack of vocabulary for articulating knowledge about space as a medium of communication, outside the specialist discourses of architecture, design and phenomenological research concerning the impacts of space on experience. The intellectual, emotional and physical effects of spatial environments are felt by everyone in their daily lives, but the words, methods and diagrams used to analyse, develop and produce space are not readily available or generally circulated. Space is often considered a technical and functional aspect of the world, but the examples below show its pervasive role in communication, argumentation, the formation of individual and social identity, as well as economic and political narratives.

Following narratology, storytelling, sometimes called narrative discourse (Chatman 1978), involves the organisation and expression of the events and the transformation of characters or entities which result in the rise and fall of dramatic tension. In literature and film, dramatic tension emerges through the causal relationships between one event and the next and this is called the plot. The twists, turns and unfolding of the plot and the changes to the characters keep the reader's or viewer's attention and it is tempting to map the notion of plot onto narrative environments. However, plot is an ambiguous and contested term with at least three different interpretations. Firstly, sometimes plot is used as a synonym for story. Secondly, sometimes it is used to describe the chronological sequence of unfolding events in linear narrative media. Thirdly, it is taken to mean the causal link between one event and another that generates anticipation, ambiguity, surprise or revelation. The third interpretation is of great interest to the inquiry here, which explores how narrative environments generate drama, but due to its ambiguity, the word 'plot' will be avoided. Instead, the phrase 'dramatic arc' will be used.

Dramatic Arcs

Dramatic arcs follow the rising and falling action which move stories forward. Movement is key to the notion of dramatic arcs. Stories follow a pattern; they rise to a peak of tension or climax and then taper off towards resolution. This understanding of dramatic structure was diagrammed and described as a narrative arc by the German novelist and playwright Gustav Freytag (1900) who analysed ancient Greek and Shakespearian drama. The single arc visualises five parts or acts: exposition, rising action, climax, falling action and denouement (Figure 5.1).

According to Freytag, exposition introduces the context and current or normal state of affairs. It is where audiences first encounter characters and their backstories enabling them to envisage the world of the story. In plays and film, this is achieved through the actions and dialogue of actors in designed or selected spaces, although the exposition is occasionally delivered through a live commentator in plays or a voice-over in films. As dramatic conflicts are introduced, rising action is developed through a series of events. Audiences identify with the characters and empathise with their situation as they face growing challenges and dilemmas. This prompts the audience to imagine the consequences of the characters' actions and potential actions. The climax is the most extreme moment, the turning point, which shapes the main character's fate. Falling action charts the steps in the triumph or tragic downfall of the main character and reveals the outcome of the catalysing conflict. As matters are resolved the character returns to normality but is nevertheless transformed by their experience. The audience shares a sense of catharsis or release from tension. The denouement describes the outcomes of the resolution.

Freytag intended his pyramid to be a guide for writers to plan dramatic arcs. To an extent, Freytag follows Aristotle (1996: 13) who defines a play as a single whole with a beginning, middle and end. However, Aristotle described a two-part structure, complication leading to a metaphorical knot followed by the unravelling of that knot. The Roman

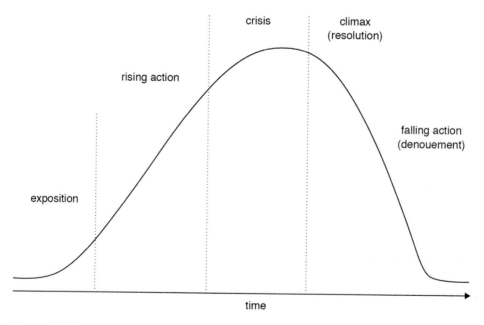

Figure 5.1 The narrative arc.

lyric poet Horace argued there should be five acts in a play. Others have explored three-act, four-act, six-act and eight-act structures. Experiments in modernist and postmodernist playwriting have produced plays with numerous acts. However, no matter how many acts are conceived, there still remains a dramatic arc.

Dramatic arcs unfold in relation to events but increasing the number of events does not necessarily increase the dramatic tension. It is their arrangement and relationships that amplify dramatic tension. There is a debate in literary circles about how many events or changes in state are required even to create a story. Some theorists maintain that just one event can constitute a story (Porter Abbott 2002: 12). Others maintain there should be at least two events (Barthes 1977), and some that events should be causally related (Bal 1997; Bordwell 1985). The view taken in this book is that narrative environments may vary from representing just one event to multiple, strictly sequenced events or multiple non-sequenced events. An example of a narrative environment with one main spatial event is Bunker 599, a national monument in the Netherlands. It takes the form of a single powerful gesture. In 2010, the architects Atelier Lyon and RAAAF 9 (Rosenfield 2013) sliced a passage through a redundant Second World War concrete bunker originally built in 1940. A long wooden boardwalk defines the slice and leads visitors through the bunker and out onto the adjacent water. To those who know the history of the Second World War, the slice evokes the intertwining of landscape and war in a remarkably poetic and concise way, compressing the events of the Second World War into a single resonating experience (Figure 5.2).

By contrast, multiple events can be represented in the chronological strategy taken by the world-renowned Holocaust Museum, Washington. The story is structured as a

Figure 5.2 Bunker 599, RAAAF | Atelier de Lyon, the Netherlands 2012.

three-part unfolding sequence with causal links. The extraordinarily moving exhibition starts on the fourth floor with 'Nazi Assault, 1933 to 1939'. It moves to 'The "Final Solution" 1940 to 1945' on the third floor and then to 'Aftermath – 1945 to present' on the second. It finishes with the Reflection Space that aims to give audiences an opportunity to digest their experiences and transition back to their everyday lives.

Historical examples also reveal a structuring, sequencing and intensification of experiences through particular ceremonial spaces. Rising action can be designed into a space by the careful sequencing of zones, for example, Peng Liu (2018) describes how provincial officials, going to meet the Emperor in Imperial China, would experience rising levels of bodily restraint, physical discomfort and anxiety as they were escorted by eunuchs on the 2-kilometre procession through the multiple courtyards of the Forbidden City in Beijing. The bodies of the officials were disciplined to become docile (Foucault 1991: 138). During the walk, the silenced officials, wearing cumbersome ceremonial clothes, instructed to walk calmly and steadily, became disorientated and exhausted and ever more aware they were exposed to scrutiny as they crossed the vast squares. Their sense of fear gathered momentum as they moved ever more submissively, eventually kneeling in front of the Emperor. Here space and body interact to reinforce powerful political and social hierarchies.

Human Movement through the Story

Human movement through space, engaging with a narrative dramatic arc, is not just a means of getting from 'a' to 'b'. It is a highly symbolic passage. Parades of sacred images or objects and processional performances, structured according to a certain pace and rhythm, are examples of time-based spatial narratives. They have a spatio-temporal start and end. However, many narrative environments are more open to the visitor to decide on the duration of the experience. This is true for visitors to exhibitions, memorials, themed hotels, branded urban quarters and participatory art installations in the public realm. Duration is nevertheless a meaningful design consideration. It is one of the dimensions that links story content, story telling, audience expectations and spatial context. It follows that the framework of visitors' interaction with the space needs to be designed. Visitors may stop, enter installations, touch, listen, take photographs and speak to each other. These opportunities for interaction are often envisaged by using visitor experience storyboards.

World expos and theme parks are interesting, as a genre, in their structuring of the temporal system of visits. Visitors are often pulsed through zones. Some walk-through experiences at Disney, for example, will admit a certain number of visitors and give them a five-minute media introduction before doors open to the next zone. The next group of visitors are then ushered in. In subsequent zones, the exhibits are designed to last no more than 30 seconds to a minute so that the designers can be sure the small crowd will move on rapidly. Regulating crowds can be achieved by putting in spectacular rides as part of the linear journey. At the *Titanic Experience* in Belfast, designed by Event Communications, about half-way through the exhibition, visitors can ride in pods that shuttle them through a three-dimensional, life-size representation of the ship's internal construction, diving up and down, moving towards and away from the giant infrastructure. Visitors then emerge to experience further object displays and media environments. Interactive experiences are also timed to pulse visitors through. For example, at the Playzone at the Millennium Dome in 2000, Land Design Studio, who pioneered interactive narrative environments in the UK, enabled children sitting on a big bed in the centre of the 'bedroom' to transform the bed imaginatively into a boat by pretending to row and, as a result, triggering media on the walls taking them on a virtual journey down the Amazon River. Once they had ventured down the river they moved on to the next experience. Movement and capacity are key design considerations if the experience is expecting thousands of visitors a day. Design can also be used to *increase* visitor dwell time, often desired by the cultural, retail, urban development and tourist sectors. Increased dwell time is achieved by adding a variety of experiences, providing social spaces, designing engaging content, rich activities and, importantly, offering safe and convivial places to rest.

Symbolic bodily movement through space is also present in one strand of modernist building design. The twentieth-century architect Le Corbusier (1995), writing on the architectural promenade, describes incremental points leading up to the threshold or entrance to the building which marks the transition between two realities. He is renowned for designing the pivoting door which serves both to unite and divide the exterior and interior. He calls the space immediately after the threshold the sensitising and reorienting vestibule. This is where people become accustomed to the different atmosphere inside the building. Corbusier envisaged moving from the sensitising vestibule to a large open space which he described as *savoir habiter*, which translates as 'knowing how to live'. Here people can make their own choices about where to go in the space, nevertheless, in his design, Corbusier draws attention to a material focal point, frequently a staircase which takes visitors upwards. This reorients them, literally elevates them and delivers them to the roof as the culmination of the journey. According to architectural academic Flora Samuel (2010: 66), this underlying sequence is a hallmark of Corbusier's buildings and she describes the pattern as "Le Corbusier's narrative path". Corbusier used stories, such as that of Orpheus, Mary Magdelene, Rabelais' Panurge and Theseus as well as the Christian story of Jacob's Ladder, to coordinate the bodily sequence and spiritual progression, often with a redemptive character. As the writers and designers above concur, spatial sequencing is a powerful structural device for the design of meaningful spatial experience.

Considerations of spatial orientation and symbolic sequencing reach beyond functionality. In the design of narrative environments, the triple movement of the body, firstly, over time, secondly, through different spaces and atmospheres and, thirdly, through different representations of content is crucial to shifting visitors emotionally, intellectually and normatively away from the expectations of the everyday and into the world of the story. Sudden changes can disorientate and unsettle audiences. In order to build anticipation, designers need to enable audiences to savour changes. Anticipation is key to audience engagement. Anticipation in narrative environments is created by structuring the communication with audiences. In conventional rituals, such as weddings or funerals, the spatial steps and bodily codes of behaviour, expectations of the sequence of the narrative arc, are passed down through multi-generational cultural practice. Novel narrative environments build on and transform familiar sequences, beginning with invitation to enter and take part, which might take the form of verbal or textual address, print or digital media, or indeed be physical structures such as welcoming or intriguing entrances. Anticipation can be heightened by seeing the entry structures from afar, reinforced by cues at the threshold, such as posters, sculptures, or even glimpses of, or symbolic references to, the forthcoming space. People will not generally venture into a spatial environment unless they recognise what it is offering. Anticipation is sustained through narrative environments partly by the unfolding story but also by having a mental model of the space gleaned from a map and/or, for example, panoramic views offering different clusters of material to look at, touch or listen to.

Making attractive and inviting places is important to the commercial sector, where the notion of experience design has deep resonance. Commercial narrative spaces have been developed all over the world in the form of shopping malls, theme parks, brand visitor experiences, restaurants and hotels. Massive investments of money and thought have been made into how to create successful commercial narrative environments. Christian Mikunda (2004), Austrian experience design writer and consultant, has written several books on the topic, bringing spatial dynamics, cognitive theory and marketing together. Mikunda discusses brand spaces, recommending ways marketers can sequence space and make them coherent, enjoyable visitor experiences and successful commercial spaces. Mikunda argues Baroque castle grounds are the prototype for all staged places because they were designed to delight. He claims their principles translate into shopping malls, hotels, entertainment complexes and theme parks. He cites the gardens of Schonbrunn Castle in Vienna where people would traditionally promenade on Sundays. He suggests visitors relish the view of the central axis between the castle, its flight of steps and the Gloriette, the imperial pavilion on the slope opposite. They stroll down the central axis which is visually reinforced and punctuated by statues set against pruned trees and floral arrangements. The main axis is crossed by several smaller axes, "drawing visitors' attention into the distance" Mikunda (2004:18). The smaller axes lead people to well-remembered or mnemonic locations, such as the old maze or the palm house, that they regularly revisit, not unlike visiting an old friend.

Mikunda (2004: 13) identifies four specific spatial characteristics he believes are needed to create rewarding visitor experiences in commercial environments. They are landmarks, the encouragement of strolling along axes, concept lines and core attractions. He argues landmarks attract our attention and draw us in. Shop windows, views into restaurants, advertising billboards and human activities all vie for people's attention as they move through cities. For landmarks to be effective, they need to be more spectacular than their surroundings. Some may use scale, for example, the London Eye, which reaches high above neighbouring buildings and the River Thames. Large-scale, symbolic architectural form, decorative motifs and courtyard spaces were deployed to produce grand, elaborate nineteenth-century museum entrances, such as the British Museum, fashioned after a Greek temple with a vast forecourt that frames the facade. Twentieth- and twenty-first-century museum architecture has produced dramatically shaped buildings that attract attention through their aesthetics and apparent technical prowess, although many of these are heavily criticised for being unfit for purpose in many other ways. Shops may use what Mikunda calls a 'header' landmark, by which he means a large symbolic object at the entrance or on the facade to attract attention. Another landmark device is a form of dramatic reveal where passers-by can see through facades of shops, restaurants or hotels to glimpse a core attraction inside. These spatial devices parallel visual attention-seeking devices developed in print and digital advertising.

Mikunda writes that once attracted through the entrance, brand spaces such as malls and entertainment centres need to encourage people to stroll through the space and make purchases. To encourage potential customers to circulate, malls need to encourage a searching and finding state of mind, by enabling the customer to develop a cognitive map which aids navigation but also brings the comfort and pleasure of knowing a space. The requirement for the visitor to develop a cognitive map is equally true for museums, theme parks and city centres hoping to attract tourists. Whether as visitors or customers, people need to internalise the main axes and crossings in malls in the same way they might explore a city, by walking down the main street and looking down the side streets. The axes lead to central squares or mnemonic points which, in a city, might be a

Cathedral or a monument but in a shopping mall might take the form of a flagship store or an indoor fountain. As visitors walk, they build up a sense of districts to produce a cognitive map. Districts were traditionally distinguished in cities by clusters of similar shops, for example, bakers, butchers and furniture-makers. In shopping malls and entertainment hubs this typically translates into the café and restaurant area, an entertainment area, a fashion area and a digital technology stores area. Signage is provided in-store to help customers build their cognitive maps. Some visitor attractions, such as large zoos, offer a paper map or an app. Brand experiences, such as Disney, have a hub-and-spokes layout, with the castle in the centre that visitors can see from any point. They are never lost. Others, like Tivoli Gardens in Copenhagen, the first amusement park ever built, are designed as a maze, where you very quickly feel lost. However, Tivoli provides a new surprise around every corner which stimulates a sense of adventure and dérive. The serpentine format also creates the illusion that the space is larger than it actually is.

Mikunda suggests that, since shopping malls and brand experiences are often very large, they need concept lines: an overall story and set of messaging with what might be called leitmotifs or recurrent themes that are repeated every so often to create a sense of a whole. This was embraced as 'theming' in the 1980s and early 1990s, using imagery from popular movies to create the feel of, for example, the Wild West, sci-fi, the circus or the rainforest, conspicuous in themed restaurants such as Planet Hollywood. These fell out of fashion, becoming associated with superficial staging that did not relate to the brand. As a result, visitor experiences were refocused to emphasise characteristics more related to the actual location, the history of the location or the brand, for example, sparkling immersive environments at Swarovski Crystal World in Tyrol, Austria.

Mikunda's final key characteristic is the core attraction. He gives the example of acrobats moving up and down ropes to select bottles for customers from the 17-metre-high wine store in the middle of the Aureole restaurant at the Mandalay Bay Resort in Las Vegas. The wine cellar, normally below ground, has been turned upside down and this unexpected inversion adds to the spatial height effect. Mikunda describes core attractions as mechanisms to create anticipation and internal suspense. He describes them in terms of cognitive dissonance: a pleasant experience that, according to the dramatic arc, needs to be released through a spectacular experience. Other examples are the fountains at the Bellagio Hotel, Las Vegas, fireworks on New Year's Eve and sky laser shows. These light shows are often accompanied by music and attract enormous crowds. Projection mapping technology has provided the means to create such large-scale events to promote brands and cities.

Weaving Story into Space

Some of the most explicit tools and techniques for weaving stories into space have been developed in exhibition design. Duncan McCauley is an award-winning exhibition design company based in Berlin which works predominantly for museums and cultural institutions. It was founded by architects Noel McCauley and Tom Duncan in 2003. They have developed a dynamic process to combine content and space in the development of exhibitions. This process reveals how content is often shaped and inflected by the space it inhabits. Noel McCauley (2018) explains that, in the cultural sector, there is always content at the start of a project. This is mostly gathered by the museum or specific curators who may be cultural historians, art historians or archaeologists. Public bodies, such as national museums, will already have had to get the project signed off by a public funding body before they come to Duncan McCauley, so they normally have a very clear and specific idea about what they want to say and where the exhibition will take place. Sometimes, they have a more generalised idea and ask Duncan McCauley to do more content research in order to turn the material into a format that will engage visitors. In the Brickworks Museum, Zehdenick, Germany, Duncan McCauley gathered information from historical witnesses and complemented this with archive material from public institutions to create a narrative structure that contextualised the industrial and social heritage of the site. The development of content in parallel with the design presented the opportunity for content and design to cross-influence one another to shape the narrative.

Duncan McCauley finds content often comes in the form of raw information, not story. It naturally reflects the professional standpoint of the subject experts; for example, a cultural historian may have a timeline of dense information in text format and multiple objects to back it up. To become a story, the items of information and objects need to be combined by identifying an overarching connection among individual pieces. To do this, all material needs to cohere around an organisational thread or storyline, structured so that the spatialised ambience conveys rising action and dénouement and moves the story forward. There is also the question of the transformation of the visitor as protagonist. Some exhibitions are more like literary narratives, in that they represent characters or entities as protagonists who transform as a result of the story. As in film, theatre and literature, the visitor identifies with that transformation and is transformed in turn. Other exhibitions do not have a literal depiction of an entity's transformation but the physical experience of moving through the space conveys a sense of transformation which is experienced implicitly through the bodily sensations of the visitor. In either case, there is a cumulative effect that initiates transformation in the story and the visitor. Some of Duncan McCauley's projects can be compared to novels or films that have one overarching dramatic arc; others are more like a collection of short stories or episodes in a television series. Sections of exhibitions can be quite different from each other; they may jump centuries, introduce new ideas and use different visuals, materials and spatial layouts in different sections, but all the sections need to add up to a whole when the visitor reflects on the entire experience. For example, in *Botticelli Reimagined* at the V&A, London, designed by Duncan McCauley, the exhibition spaces varied from a dark and elaborate entry to a final white space gallery (see Plates 1 and 2), but the narrative about Botticelli and his influence on others created a coherent whole.

Duncan McCauley often begins a project by running workshops to tease out the key messages and the main elements of the narrative that the client wishes to communicate. McCauley says it is always worth discussing with the client whether a story format is even appropriate. However, using story as a means of communication is often chosen because spatial story can translate information into a temporal, causal and physical experience, distinguishing it from the overload of information already in our environments. Duncan McCauley believes translating information into stories makes the information more accessible, engaging and memorable. McCauley explains that the storyline can be inspired by the space. At Vischering Castle in North Rhine-Westphalia (Münsterland), the existing rooms in the castle were spread over three separate levels with access and vertical circulation across a central courtyard. Not only did the structure and pacing of the spaces influence the narrative but also the atmospheric qualities of the individual spaces themselves. In Vischering Castle, three self-contained storylines were developed to exploit the existing situation, but all used 'mindfulness' as the central tone of voice as a unifying device.

The sheer volume or scarcity of content also needs to be considered against the space available. Long and complex stories can be compressed into video to fit in smaller spaces and short pithy stories can be expanded by adding more contextual information, multiple perspectives or critical commentary. As a result, content always needs to be edited or expanded. This can take lengthy conversations to accommodate the vision of the curatorial team. Specialists from two different backgrounds, curating and design, need expert skills in negotiation and trust building because they are making something neither could do alone.

The division of content into subsections or chapters will also be affected by the nature of the space. A space with five zones, for example, will lend itself to five story segments. McCauley (2018) explains,

> In most museum spaces, particularly historical buildings, there is a strong spatial sequence and the narrative cannot easily break out of that sequence. The story has to be structured to fit the space. A fork in the path with a choice of left and right needs to be reflected in the narrative structure. There needs to be a fork in the story. The story is more malleable than the place you are telling it in. The story and space need to work together as in the three-way fork in the basement of the Jewish Museum in Berlin [for example].

Not only does the story have to align and resonate with the space, it needs to unfold over the particular period of time of a visit and provide a rising and falling emotional journey for the visitor. Some exhibitions are designed to be longer or shorter than others. Duncan McCauley integrates all these factors into diagrams through a process they have developed which they call 'emotional mapping'. Sometimes Duncan McCauley's diagrams are just words, sometimes they are words and images but they are always trying to capture space, content, what the visitor is doing and what the visitor is feeling. In their emotional maps, time lies along the horizontal axis and the other dimensions are on the vertical access as shown in Figures 5.3 and 5.4. Narrative structure is an important part of their planning process and they often reference film in creating a framework for a museum experience (Duncan 2018).

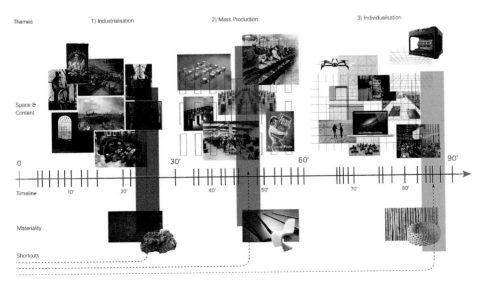

Figure 5.3 Emotional map of the Potsdam Museum, Germany, Duncan McCauley, 2013.

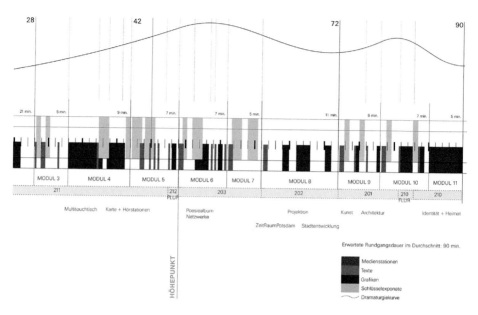

Figure 5.4 Emotional map of the Industriemuseum Oberhausen, Germany, Duncan McCauley, 2018.

In the processes of emotional mapping, Duncan McCauley works together with specialists in spatial communication and specialists in content development to evolve the storyline and envisage the visitor experience. They use a verbal and visual approach, talking through the content, referring to written documents but always alongside architectural plans and images of objects. As they are creating something visual, the discussion needs to be supported by a plethora of visual materials. The exhibition team debate the merits of potential configurations and sequences to judge how particular information or objects would create meaning in a specific room and how this would relate to the next room, creating dramatic tension and moving the story along. They sketch out the dramatic structure, the series of dramatic peaks, through careful placement of objects, using the media that best suit the communication of the content:

> The content and space both play a role in the experience, sometimes the space plays a stronger role and sometimes the content plays a stronger role [...] sometimes the space will force your hand.
>
> (McCauley 2018)

Duncan McCauley thinks through story, object, spaces and media at the same time. The emotional map starts as a rough sketch and evolves in parallel with discussion. It is important to the emotional mapping process at the design stage to be able to envisage the exhibition through the eyes of the visitor. Duncan McCauley often employs role playing activities, which not only bring the design team and the curatorial team closer but help everyone to envisage the expectations and potential experiences of possible individual visitors. At an early stage, they bring in a huge floor plan on a large table at a scale of 1:50 or 1:25. They have figures cut out, for example, groups of three young people, a mother, father and child group and a group of 20 older people. For the role play, they give cards out to the client; they write down names, ages and expectations of the characters they are playing, put the figures into the floor plan and introduce themselves to each other. Everyone feels free to speak because they are no longer in their professional roles. Duncan McCauley also provides a long sheet of paper with areas on it for the comments. This process of role play loosens people up, gets them thinking imaginatively and throws up new ideas.

Duncan McCauley has developed three spatial typologies: linear; radial hub-and-spokes; and dispersed, multidirectional spaces, such as multiple islands in a single exhibition space or the multidirectional urban context. Linear spaces are useful for chronological stories. Hub-and-spokes are useful for stories with a hero object that can be placed in the centre of the space surrounded by contextual information. Multidirectional spatial arrangements with dispersed stories are useful for thematic experiences and complex worlds (Figures 5.5, 5.6 and 5.7).

Tim Gardom Associates Communications (2006: 37), who pioneered interpretive planning in the UK, has worked closely with exhibition designers for many years and developed a comprehensive range of spatial typologies for narrative environments that they call storyshapes. On the prescribed route, visitors cannot turn back and this is fitting for chronological stories where the understanding of each element builds upon what is seen before. Linear visitor experiences can be further articulated in various ways such as 'the inner sanctum', which build on visitors' anticipation, concealing the hero elements until visitors reach the dramatic reveal. Pulsed flow is also prescribed and is commonly used in expos and theme parks, as described above, to control the flow of visitors. In

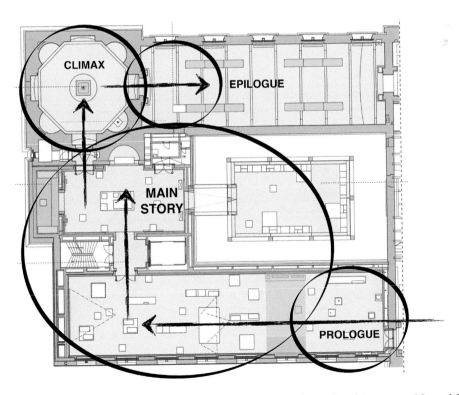

Figure 5.5 Linear narrative format of the exhibition *In the Light of Amarna* at Neues Museum in Berlin, Duncan McCauley, 2012.

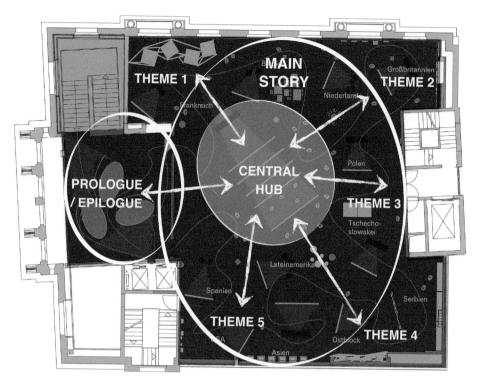

Figure 5.6 Radial format of the exhibition *Conscious Hallucinations: Surrealism in Film* Deutsches Filmmuseum, Frankfurt am Main, Germany, Duncan McCauley, 2014.

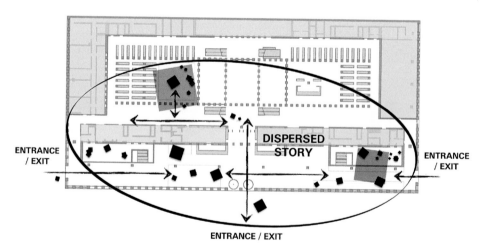

Figure 5.7 Dispersed narrative format of the exhibition *A University Makes History*, Humboldt University Berlin, Duncan McCauley, 2010.

the 'there and back' storyshape, visitors enter and exit through the same door allowing them to see objects twice. This double viewing enables visitors to reflect on how differently they think of the objects once they have learned more about them. Tim Gardom and Alison Grey (2019) give the example of an exhibition about slavery where a block of sugar, seen as a harmless historical item on the way in, would be understood as the cause of greed and untold suffering on the way out.

The MA Narrative Environments has synthesised the Duncan McCauley and the Tim Gardom Associates Communications insights to provide two top-level categories of spatial typologies or storyshapes: linear and non-linear narrative environments, each with subcategories, as shown in Figures 5.8 and 5.9.

Figure 5.8 shows four different subcategories of linear storyshapes: prescribed routes, pulsed flow, there-and-back-again and inner sanctum. Figure 5.9 shows three different subcategories of non-linear storyshapes. 'Hub-and-spokes' are often arranged around a hero item in an exhibition or a central building or space in a city. People can move backwards and forwards as they wish between the centre and the spokes. The 'matrix' arranges content on two axes. The axes might be, for example, themes and chronology allowing visitors to choose between following a theme or following a timeline, or swapping from one to another as they wish. The final subcategory is 'islands', which are typical of science centres and city planning. Visitors can visit the different islands in whatever order they wish.

Storyshapes are useful as they quickly summarise the cumulative and relational logic of the story elements. They allow designers to interrogate that logic and consider amendments. The storyshapes prompt thoughts about how to create transitional experiences between the story sections and the potential effects of the parts on the whole narrative environment. The storyshapes can also be used as a clear and concise means to communicate with clients or an extended design team. Storyshapes are vital in the design of narrative environments, as it is the first step in linking the story to the space and envisioning the visitor experience. Storyshapes also act as a framework for the further layers of content that are added as the project progresses.

The MA Narrative Environments has also developed a design tool called the story matrix. It is a diagram whose sources of influence are Duncan McCauley's emotional map

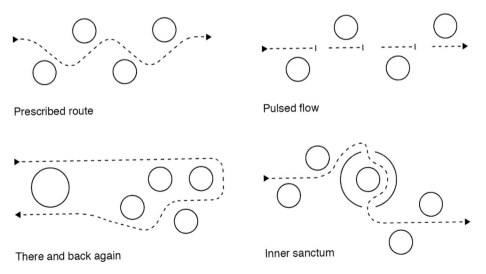

Prescribed route

Pulsed flow

There and back again

Inner sanctum

Figure 5.8 Linear storyshapes.

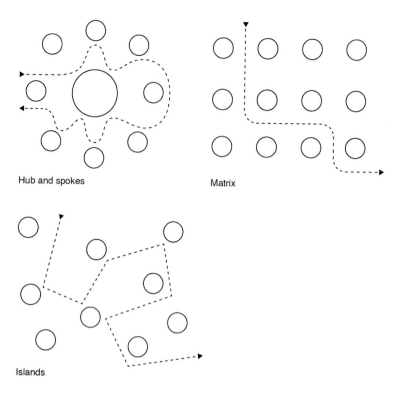

Hub and spokes

Matrix

Islands

Figure 5.9 Non-linear storyshapes.

and Robert McKee's (1997) story units. McKee posits that the smallest units, beats, create scenes; several scenes create a sequence; several sequences form an act; acts cluster to create subplots, which together create a global story. The story matrix uses the principle of identifying smaller elements which are grouped together to create zones, subsequently aggregated to create the overall story experience. However, each zone retains a distinctive feel and the transitions from one zone to another contribute to the dramatic arc and emotional experience of the visitor. The story matrix summarises and aligns a number of different dimensions of a narrative environments experience. For a linear experience, the spaces are named and numbered along the top horizontal bar. The narrative elements, the messages, the tone of voice, the design elements showing the look and feel, the potential visitor interactions and anticipated visitor emotions are arranged on the vertical axis against each space. The cost and delivery dates can also be added for project management purposes. Images can be used if they summarise the factors clearly. For non-linear experiences, the elements on the vertical axis are mapped onto a storyshape of the space. Using the matrix ensures no aspects of the visitor experience are overlooked. However, the story matrix is not a creative device. Rather, it ensures that everything that has been discussed is included and that the client understands what the design team is planning.

Story Telling in Non-Linear Space

As explained above, chronological stories suit linear spaces because audiences encounter events in a predictable order. This allows the design team to plan the cumulative effects of content, spatial design, emotional peaks, dénouement or reflective moments. Part of the skill of designing an impactful narrative environment is the consideration of the anticipation of the visitor before and during the visit, and consequently the step-by-step orchestration and pacing of the experience and encounter with the story elements. This means creating cues for the forthcoming experiences. These are articulated through the design of physical thresholds, movement through different zones that produce a rhythm, effective transitions, pauses in the journey for rest and concluding spaces that allow visitors to digest and reflect on what they have experienced. Linear spaces offer control over the pace of the visitor experience. Large open spaces can also be divided into linear experiences by introducing partitions that snake around the space. Linear spaces offer the design team a great deal of control but visitors can find it quite tiring and restrictive and there is growing interest among designers and clients in softening the linearity in many narrative environments.

In non-linear spaces, narrative works in a different way. Non-linear spaces may be, for example, large open interior spaces, buildings with several routes through them, clusters of buildings or open spaces in the urban fabric. The question arises as to how the design team can tell a story when people can go wherever they want. In this situation, the designer can neither predict what visitors will see nor in what order. These spaces are more suitable for thematic clusters of related or nested stories that can be placed like islands within the whole, enabling visitors to move freely among them. At each island, there may be a linear story that audiences can access and delve into. Nevertheless, the overarching message, the spatial territory and the borders of the narrative experience need to be clear throughout the narrative environment. The design challenge is how to design and then connect the islands of the story. As will be seen below, there are many spatial, audio, graphic and performative ways to do this. Interestingly, both linear and non-linear narrative environments require the designer to think of the space as a continuum. The continuum may be varied and contain dramatic, surprising, even disconcerting contrasts but needs to maintain a distinctive identity as a coherent story space.

Skellon Studio, based in the UK, tackled a non-linear space when they designed the Battle of Britain Bunker visitor centre in Uxbridge, London, in 2017. Exhibition designer Katherine Skellon (2018) explains that the visitor centre is next to the underground bunker which housed the Royal Air Force (RAF) Fighter Command's No.11 Group Operations Room throughout the Second World War. The bunker, 60 feet below ground, is where all information about aircraft movement during the Battle of Britain was represented by coded blocks, denoting enemy and RAF aircraft. The blocks were moved across a large central table-map by women with push sticks. The streams of information coming in were translated into constant updates on the table-map and enabled strategic battle decisions to be made. Hillingdon Council, which owns the site, decided to provide a visitor centre next to the bunker because the site was judged to be of considerable historical importance but the 67 steps down to the operations room made it inaccessible to many people. Skellon explains that the brief was very open. The Council asked her to develop the story content as well as its manifestation.

At the start of the project, Skellon Studio was faced with very complex content about the system of communications, called the Dowding system, which was developed to collect information for the table-map. The system relied on a number of different groups of people making observations or acquiring knowledge of enemy aircraft activity and passing the information through a number of intermediaries until it reached the bunker. For example, there was radar, ground observation, searchlight observation and aircraft-to-aircraft observation of incoming Luftwaffe aeroplanes. The information was sent through a number of intermediary communication hubs to central command in the bunker by telephone. Skellon Studio quickly realised that its main challenge was to find a way to make this complex technical system understandable to visitors of all ages and backgrounds.

Inspiration came from the double-height visitor centre building that had a walkway all the way around on the inside that allowed a view of the ground floor below. This provided an opportunity to create another map, in the spirit of the table-map, that showed the 10 different sources of information, each taking the form of a table station with a display. Each table station was linked to a central table-map by floor graphics. The view that visitors see from the balcony is like a diagram of connections played out in three dimensions. Visitors can go down the steps and walk among the table stations to learn more. Each station had a star object, a small interactive, some peripheral objects and a standard graphic panel. Skellon Studio included very engaging personal effects from women soldiers, for example, their diaries. High above the ground, near the ceiling, she hung two full-size replica aeroplanes, a Spitfire and a Hurricane, apparently flying towards the big glass windows at the far end where there are vinyl graphics of incoming Luftwaffe (Figure 5.10).

The content works on three different levels. The replica aeroplanes and window graphics create an all-encompassing dramatic context that enacts the events of the Battle of Britain. The three-dimensional map on the ground gives an overview of the Dowding system, the core story. Visitors can then find out more about each station by looking at objects explained in the text panel, stepping out of the core story into the personal stories available through the oral testimonies and objects relating to the characters, feeling what it was like to work in the bunker. The visitors can move, as they wish, from the context to the overarching story of the system to the personal, more emotional stories of the people who worked there. They can take in a top-level story or discover numerous details

Figure 5.10 The Battle of Britain Bunker Visitor Centre, UK, Skellon Studios, 2018.

about specific content that may interest them. As a result, different people can experience the visitor centre according to their interests. It is worth noting that the core story for the client, Hillingdon Council, was the operation of the Dowding system and the events depicted in that story are central to moving the story forward, whereas the women's stories add emotional context but are not essential to the Dowding story. In theoretical terms, the events showing the Dowding system were constituent events and the women's stories were supplementary events. However, a visitor with a feminist perspective may well see the actions of the women as constituent events in a bigger story about how women's contribution to the war effort may have been overlooked. The experience is open to both interpretations and, indeed, other interpretations.

The experience literally provides an overview and a mental map of an overarching context with nested stories within it. The overarching context provides orientation and explanation of the relationship of the parts to the whole. There are various layers of information and story available through different media. On a larger scale, these principles can be applied to non-linear city narratives.

Non-Linear City Narratives

The narratives that are embedded in cities play out as non-linear experiences. City narratives are expressed through numerous architectural and urban design characteristics and are sensed through specific materials, scales, temperatures, particular light effects, movements, sounds and smells. Product and graphic cues also orientate and remind you that you are in a specific city. Very recognisable urban features are the dense neon signage of Kowloon, the tree-lined boulevards and vistas of central Paris, the Redstone facades of New York, the hooting of cars and auto rickshaws of Delhi and the fluttering bunting, domes, minarets and bridges of Istanbul. While these features give clues to narrative through the environment node of the tripartite model of narrative environments, the pace and qualities of street life relate the physical environment to the people node of the tripartite model. Lefebvre (1992) uses the word rhythmanalysis to describe methods for analysing urban spaces through the rhythms of social practices. Thus, people moving through the physical and lived characteristics of cities, read or experience narratives that may peacefully co-exist, be contested or be competing for dominance. These different narratives are reinforced by traditional and online media representations, cinematic imagery and literary myths. The multiple, porous layers of cities, their varied authorship and their large geographic scale suggest they have extraordinary potential as complex and intriguing narrative environments. Nested and related stories can be dispersed across city districts. City narratives are sometimes narrated explicitly through audio or GPS-enabled locative media trails or guided walks. Cities are such powerful storytellers that governments invest huge sums of money, not only in enabling the smooth running of the city, but also to ensure they communicate a desired narrative identity.

One example is Skopje, the capital of a relatively new country, the Republic of North Macedonia in the Balkans in Southeast Europe. From 2014 to 2016, the conservative government implemented a scheme, Skopje 2014, to overlay the socialist architecture in the city centre with neoclassical and neo-Baroque facades and to populate the public space with approximately 600 new 'classical' statues. The country was established in 1991 as a result of the break-up of the former Yugoslavia. However, its official name was only agreed in 2018. The delay in agreeing its official name was the result of a long-running dispute with its neighbour, Greece, whose northern province is called Macedonia. As a new country without an agreed name, the Republic of North Macedonia was left in a state of limbo regarding its identity. The government sought to address this lack by evoking a classical Greek history. The Republic of North Macedonia no doubt provoked Greece with its 'Skopje 2014' development project. It not only co-opted neoclassical architectural styles but also renamed the airport and the motorway to Greece after 'Alexander the Great', the legendary Greek king of ancient Macedon, who conquered lands from Greece to northwestern India, but never visited Skopje.

The city centre was 'restyled' by the ruling conservative party, the Internal Macedonian Revolutionary Organization – Democratic Party for Macedonian National Unity (VMRO-DPMNE). While the new facades are all classical in style, the statues range from across the Antique period to include Alexander the Great, his father Philip II and his mother Olympias of Epirus; the saints of early Christianity; famous historical figures who were born or ruled in or around Skopje, such as the Byzantine Emperor Justinian I, the Byzantine Tzar Samuel and Mother Theresa; as well as a more recent group of freedom fighters who fought for Macedonian independence. There is also a Triumphal Arch and a new museum narrating a fictitious history of the Republic of North Macedonia.

Critics of 'Skopje 2014' argue that it is recalling a past that did not exist. The Triumphal Arch on the central square to the city lacks historical veracity. There were no great military victories in Skopje's history. It seems that, from its establishment as an independent country in a period of political and economic upheaval, the Republic of North Macedonia sought a new strategic narrative to 'invent' the idea and history of Macedonia.

In the middle of the central square, the key landmark is a gigantic statue called 'Warrior on a Horse'. The spatial narrative is set out in a loose hub-and-spokes formation. The square and statue is the hero object and the bridges, the Vardar River and roads leading off the square are the spokes. The Eye bridge flanked with numerous stiff, neoclassically styled statues, all men, leads over the Vardar to the archaeological museum with its full set of neoclassical columns and pediment (Figure 5.11).

Figure 5.11 The Eye Bridge, Skopje, the Republic of North Macedonia, 2018.

To the left lie administrative buildings, each sporting rows of similar facades, spot-lit in colour at night (see Plate 3) and dotted with numerous statues to create a flamboyant scenographic vista. On the south side of the river, two boat-themed hotel-restaurants are planted in the river, their artificial feel reminiscent of theme park simulations. The huge Triumphal Arch is located on the southeast side of the square. If people walk south along Macedonia Street, which leads from the central square and other surrounding streets, they see the neoclassical facades of a new theatre, the national archives, the foreign ministry, the constitutional court and the electronic communications agency. No matter which route they take, visitors and inhabitants are confronted by the same monumental neoclassical architectural facades and neoclassical sculptures, the style generally taken to symbolise power. Carved inscriptions on the facades and antiqued metal plaques are also positioned on walls and in squares to provide 'historical' details. Linear sequence is substituted by adjacency, proximity and repetition, so that visitors are surrounded by a specific interpretation of national history. The characters are featured as sculptures and the dramatic arc of the proposed national history is played out in people's minds as they encounter, and are surrounded by, the figures positioned against the strongly symbolic, large-scale, neoclassical facades. The same message is repeated again and again: the Republic of North Macedonia has a powerful and heroic past. Tourists may also have seen the promotional video 'Macedonia Timeless Capital Skopje 2014' (2014). The polished production, set to rousing music, uses the medium of film to lend support to the physical manifestation of the narrative. Tourists will also come across themed wine, marketed using the same story. To find the explicit details of the history, people need to visit the Museum of the Macedonian Struggle, on the north side of the riverbank. The museum opened in 2011. It contains over one hundred life-size wax models of historical figures and several look down from the first floor on visitors as they enter. Entry is by guided tour only. The museum runs scripted tours past large nineteenth-century-style paintings of historical events, populated with male politicians, yet all the paintings were produced in the twenty-first century and it is disputed as to whether some of the events depicted actually happened.

Skopje 2014 has been described as a memorial park of false memories which has produced a neoclassical and Baroque theatre set and laughable kitsch sculpture (Milevska 2014). Milevska suggests the imitation is not intended ironically or as a playful mockery of the obsolete, but rather to send a serious message to the world that North Macedonia is on the map of bourgeois societies. She argues that the city is measuring itself according to the number of monuments, archaeological artefacts and archived documents, worshipping antiquity as 'material content' that guarantees its existence in history according to an accepted chronology of events. She points out that, in fact, the government have partly erased the city's twentieth-century past. Skopje is not like Las Vegas; it lacks a dimension of irony. Nor is it postmodernist, nurturing plural styles (Žižek 1989). It forms a single architectural and socio-cultural code signalling North Macedonia's aspiration to be a super state.

Thomas Sevcik (2019), urban strategist, points out that there are precedents for cities receiving scathing criticism for their urban development. Venice, for example, rose to prominence as the most prosperous city in Europe in the late thirteenth century and at that point many powerful families built grand palaces. As a result, it was criticised at the time for being gaudy and pretentious. Now it has become a European treasure. Other cities, such as London and Washington, D.C., undertook huge urban renewal projects in the nineteenth and twentieth centuries respectively, installing neoclassical buildings, just as much a borrowed style as the Skopje example. This architectural expression of power was accepted in the UK and the USA but the superficial and materially insubstantial facades of Skopje, poorly sculpted figures and the Disneyfication all undermine its intent. The scheme reads as empty rhetoric and fails to convince.

Sevcik (2019) observes that the phenomenon of cities and city quarters adopting narratives is gathering pace. As cities expand and redevelop, new quarters, private and semi-private special zones and edge cities are being built, often feeling very bland. As new city quarters, often driven by functional requirements and investment opportunities, they lack historical, social or cultural substance. Sevcik suggests they need to develop one overarching narrative to be understood in the market, whether that be industrial or touristic. He points out that cities across the world are locked in competition for economic resources, people and prestige. The numerous second- and third-tier cities in China, for example, need to differentiate themselves and discourage their inhabitants from moving to bigger cities. Local government in China is investing heavily in reinforcing the distinctive identities of smaller cities. Cities need to be aware of their unique qualities and build upon their authentic qualities and assets. Narrative city positioning is an important area for the design of narrative environments. The power of narrative is that it can hold together multiple entities and complex layers of meaning.

In summary, the role of environment is essential to storytelling in narrative environments, regardless of whether they are brand spaces, cultural environments or urban realm. The examples show how space is replete with meaning. It is not an empty form onto which story is inscribed but partakes in the story content. The linear or non-linear spatial sequencing reinforces dramatic arcs which shape visitors' physical and emotional journeys. At the scale of the urban, spatial forms and sequences not only narrate city identity but become inseparable from social practices. This reiterates the central methodological principle of the design of narrative environments: people, place and story form a necessary co-dependent coexistence. Spatial environments are effective and affective media that act upon people rationally, emotionally and normatively through telling stories.

References

Aristotle. (1996) *Poetics*. London: Penguin.

Bal, M. (1997) *Narratology: Introduction to the Theory of Narrative*, 2nd ed. Toronto: University of Toronto Press.

Barthes, R. (1977) *Image Music Text*. Glasgow: William Collins.

Bordwell, D. (1985) *Narration in the Fiction Film*. London: Methuen.

Chatman, S. (1978) *Story and Discourse: Narrative Structure in Fiction and Film*. Ithaca, NY: Cornell University Press.

Duncan, T. (2018) Beyond the museum: A comparative study of narrative structures in films and museum design. In: MacLeod, S., Austin, T., Hale, J. and Ho, O., eds. *The Future of Museum and Gallery Design*. London: Routledge, pp. 239–253.

Foucault, M. (1991) *Discipline and Punish: The Birth of the Prison*. London: Penguin.

Freytag, G. (1900) *Freytag's Technique of the Drama, An Exposition of Dramatic Composition and Art by Dr. Gustav Freytag*, 3rd ed. Chicago, IL: Scott, Foresman and Company.

Gardom, Tim and Grey, Alison (2019) Interview with Tricia Austin on 5 March 2019.

Gardom, T., Grey, A. and Booth, C. (2006) *Saying it Differently: A Handbook for Museums Refreshing Their Displays*. London: London Museums Hub.

Le Corbusier. (1995) *Œuvre complète = Complete Works*. Basel: Birkhäuser.

Lefebvre, H. (1992) *Rhythmanalysis: Space, Time and Everyday Life*. London: Continuum.

Liu, P. (2018) Walking in the Forbidden City: Embodied encounters in narrative geography. *Visual Studies*, 33(2), 144–160.

Porter Abbott, H. (2002) *The Cambridge Introduction to Narrative*. Cambridge, UK: Cambridge University Press.

Massey, D. (2005) *For Space*. London: Sage.

McCauley, Noel (2018) Interview with Tricia Austin, 31 August 2018.

McKee, R. (1997) *Story: Substance, Structure, Style and the Principles of Screenwriting*. New York: Reganbooks.

Mikunda, C. (2004) *Brand Lands, Hot Spots & Cool Spaces: Welcome to the Third Place and the Total Marketing Experience*. London: Kogan Page.

Milevska, S. (2014) Ágalma: The "Objet Petit a," Alexander the Great, and Other Excesses of Skopje 2014. *e-flux Journal*, 57, September 2014. Online. Available HTTP: https://www.e-flux.com/journal/57/60425/galma-the-objet-petit-a-alexander-the-great-and-other-excesses-of-skopje-2014/. Accessed 21 August 2019.

Mitchell, W. J. T. (1996) What do pictures "really" want? *October*, 77, 71–82.

Mitchell, W. J. T. (2003) *'Word and Image': Critical Terms for Art History*. Chicago, IL: Chicago University Press.

Perec, G. (1997) *Species of Space and Other Pieces*. London: Penguin.

Rosenfield, K. (2013) Bunker 599 / RAAAF + Atelier de Lyon. *Archdaily*. [video]. Online. Available HTTP: https://www.archdaily.com/462623/video-bunker-599-rietveld-landscape-atelier-de-lyon. Accessed 20 November 2019.

Samuel, F. (2010) *Le Corbusier and the Architectural Promenade*. Basel: Birkhäuser.

Sevcik, Thomas (2019) Interview with Tricia Austin, 20 September 2019.

Skellon, Katherine (2018) Interview with Tricia Austin, 20 August 2018.

Žižek, S. (1989) *The Sublime Object of Ideology*. New York, NY: Verso, 2008.

Websites

Duncan McCauley. http://www.duncanmccauley.com

Holocaust Museum Washington. https://www.ushmm.org

Macedonia Timeless video. http://www.youtube.com/watch?v=iybmt-iLysU

Skellon Studio. http://www.skellonstudio.com

The Battle of Britain Bunker visitor centre. http://battleofbritainbunker.co.uk

Titanic Belfast. https://www.titanicbelfast.com

Plates

Plate 1 The first room of *Botticelli Reimagined*, Duncan McCauley, the Victoria & Albert Museum, London 2016.

Plate 2 The final room of *Botticelli Reimagined*, Duncan McCauley, the Victoria & Albert Museum, London 2016.

Plate 3 The 'antiquitisation' of Skopje, the Republic of North Macedonia 2017.

Plate 4 Mesa Musical Shadows, Phoenix Arizona, USA, Daily Tous les Jours, 2016.

Plate 5 *Amateur Intelligence Radio*, St Paul, Minnesota, USA, Daily Tous les Jours 2014.

Plate 6 The Gobbins cliff pathway suspension bridge, Northern Ireland 2016.

Plate 7 Fair Enough exhibition, Russia pavilion, Venice Architecture Biennale 2014.

Plate 8 Communist architecture tour booth, *Fair Enough* exhibition, Russia pavilion, Venice Architecture Biennale 2014.

Plate 9 Virtual reality encounter with streams of energy in *We Live in an Ocean of Air*, London, Marshmallow Laser Feast 2019.

Plate 10 Virtual reality encounter with a giant Sequoia tree in *We Live in an Ocean of Air*, London, Marshmallow Laser Feast 2019.

Plate 11 Outings Jerusalem, Israel, Julien de Casabianca 2015.

Plate 12 Songboard London, MA Narrative Environments and BA Architecture, Central Saint Martins, UAL 2012.

Plate 13 Digua Community basement library, Beijing 2015.

Plate 14 Digua Community basement view, Beijing 2015.

Plate 15 Chrisp Street On Air, The Decorators, London 2014.

Plate 16 Open Burble, Usman Haque, Singapore, 2006.

Plate 17 VoiceOver Umbrellium, East Durham, UK 2017–2018.

6   Engagement

This chapter examines the impact of the narrative and the environment nodes on the people node of the narrative environments tripartite network, that is to say, how narrative environments *engage* people. Engagement has become a rallying cry in many industries, whether that be a call for greater customer engagement or employee engagement in business sectors, wider audience engagement in the cultural sector or an appeal for more socially-engaged design in activist circles. To understand why engagement has become so significant in recent times, it is useful to consider the change in research paradigms over the past 100 years. Interest has moved away from an ontology that posits an objective reality, with material objects or things identifiable through an empirical, positivist epistemology that points to what everyone can see, while capturing and collating this evidence using quantitative methodologies. While the empirical has remained, research now incorporates subjective ontologies, that is, the *experiential* dimension of reality and the ways that objects are constituted through social practice. Constructivist and interpretivist epistemologies have become necessary because they recognise that not everyone experiences the world in the same way. This shift is evident in the emergence, in the early twentieth century, of phenomenology and hermeneutics and, later in the century, of feminism, postcolonial studies and identity politics. Interpretivist epistemologies continue to shape innovation, to which the design of narrative environments is contributing.

The research of experience uses qualitative methodologies, including, for example, personal testimony and accounts of situated attitudes and feelings. All such qualitative approaches are concerned with the relationship between the subjective and the objective. A relevant architectural and landscape example is Maggie's Centres, which have pioneered new design in support for cancer patients. Maggie's Centres are inspired by the idea that good design could considerably improve the patient's ability to cope with their situation. They focus on changing those aspects of hospital buildings that are demoralising for the patients. Maggie's centres have material properties that mimic domestic settings, such as lightness, airiness, warm colours and they use natural materials creating a porous relationship to the immediate landscape. They also have a clear invitation to enter and feel welcomed plus a range of private and social spaces. They are designed "around the person not the disease" (Maggie's 2014). As a result, they have meaning for a human subject, in providing a breathing space between the two worlds of hospital and normal life and they aim to generate emotional responses such as courage, self-confidence and resourcefulness. The precise meaning may change from person to person, depending on their individual experience, their memories and cultural background. This example shows that while design continues to produce objects and environments with material qualities and practical uses, it has come to incorporate considerations of the meaning production and social impact that accompany the use of objects. Instead of first thinking of the materials and use, many designers now prioritise user experience and interaction. These priorities are manifested in human-centred design, interaction design, user experience (UX) design and participatory design. This emphasis is particularly relevant for narrative environments, which are situations into which people enter, not just artefacts presented to people. The situational quality of narrative environments requires a consideration of these more subjective ontologies. It is in this context that the concept of engagement has assumed a significant role.

The importance of engagement is accompanied by a recognition of the value of narrative. Stories attract and sustain people's attention, both crucial aspects of engagement. In light of this, the chapter describes methods of cognitive and emotional engagement in literary narrative that are transferable to the design of narrative environments, focusing specifically on David Herman's theory that, through narrative, readers conjure up and viscerally inhabit storyworlds in their imaginations. The chapter shows how storyworlds are prompted by multimodal means in the spatial context of narrative environments. It analyses examples of how modes of address in explicit and implicit communications are materialised in space, and shows how cognitive and emotional engagement can be achieved through a synthesis of physical and digital interaction in narrative environments.

Cognitive engagement, explored in the humanities, discusses thought-based absorption in literary stories (Bilandzic and Kinnebrock 2009; Green, Strange and Brock 2002). Such deep mental absorption in narrative occurs when people become so intensely wrapped up in a book that they do not hear someone speaking to them. Such readers are described as captivated by the story, indicating the fascination it holds over their imagination. This is similar to a 'flow state' described by psychologist Mihaly Csíkszentmihályi (1975). The ancient Greeks developed a comparable theory that they called *enargeia* to describe how the world of the story appears so clearly to the reader or listener that they feel like they are actually present at the events in the narrative.

Frank Hakemulder (2011) discusses some narrative devices that may captivate readers. His examples include intense identification with characters. Empathy and affinity with characters prompts absorption in the events of their lives. Authors may allow their readers more information than their characters, which creates a compelling and engaging sense of power among readers. This can also be reversed in situations where the reader is kept in the dark about how much the characters know about their own situation. This encourages readers to engage attentively in order to discover clues (Gerrig, 1996). Readers may be captivated by the desire to know the outcomes, intrigued by the possibilities offered by inconclusive clues. Authors typically introduce uncertainty in the structuring of events, challenging audiences to anticipate and have their expectations confirmed or confounded (Brewer and Lichtenstein, 1982). Readers may be fired up by moral dilemmas if the situation presented resonates with their own. They may be amused by the irony or humour of the work and be carried along by its charm. Readers may feel absorbed by acquiring knowledge. Frank Palmer (1992) also suggests that characters' roles in narrative worlds enable people to learn about social interactions and moral and cultural codes. This is most clearly seen in fairy tales, fables and religious books. Such narratives may guide children in learning acceptable social behaviours and relations. All of these techniques are transferable to the design of narrative environments, as discussed below.

Storyworld and the World of the Story

Readers describe narrative experience as like being 'transported to another place' in their imaginations. In doing so, they transfer their attention away from their immediate surroundings, the 'I-here-now', to the world of the story and, subsequently, to different perspectives or levels within the world of the story. The process indicated by this transportation is mapped in the tripartite network model of narrative environments to develop a more methodical understanding of how the experiential 'I' is addressed by, and drawn into, the narrative to become a fictional 'I' with its own fictional here and now. Linguists, cognitive scientists and literary theorists have studied this phenomenon and describe it as a deictic shift (Galbraith 1995). Deictic shift theory is the departure point for narratologist David Herman (2004), who turns to cognitive science to move attention from the author's structuring of story elements to the recipient's construction of a mental model of the story, the 'storyworld', a notion similar to Rapaport et al.'s (1994) deictic centre: a mental model of spatial, temporal and character information contributed by the reader to understand the narrative. Herman examines and critiques the dominant structuralist approaches, prevalent in twentieth-century narratology (Todorov 1969; Genette 1980; Chatman 1978), arguing that literary stories are not only created through the organisation of story units or story grammar relating events, characters, settings and causality (Prince 1973). He states,

> Interpreters of narrative do not simply construct a sequence of events and existents arranged into a plot but imaginatively, (emotionally and viscerally) inhabit a world in which, besides happening and existing, things matter, agitate, exalt, repulse, provide grounds for laughter and grief [...] storyworlds are mentally and emotionally projected environments in which interpreters are called to live out complex blends of cognitive and imaginative response.
>
> (Herman 2004:16–17)

For Herman, narrative theory is an aspect of cognitive science. He suggests the story recipients construct the storyworld in their minds using inferences from cues provided by the author, who shows the "who did what to and with whom, when, where, why" (Herman 2004:9). The storyworld, as the subjective, imagined mental model of the world of the story, is conjured up slightly differently in the mind of each recipient. Herman suggests that, for each recipient, the storyworld establishes the context and framework of the story. He uses the term 'world' to make the case that audiences do not just create a sequence of events in their minds, as they absorb the story. Rather, they create a multidimensional 'ecology' that integrates past, present and future states, events, actions and spaces. He sees spatialisation as crucially important in stories as it interconnects time, characters, objects and actions. Herman argues a sense of place and context is vital to stimulating people's imaginations. He suggests storyworlds cannot be richly imagined unless the spatial context as well as the historical frame is sufficiently evoked.

Herman's focus on the relationship of imagination, spatialsation and story cues is crucial for the design of narrative environments. The space of a narrative environment is experienced as physically present but it is also used as a cue to evoke a storyworld in the mind of the visitor, providing a double deictic centre. Take, for example, the city of Skopje discussed in the previous chapter. Visitors and inhabitants know they are in the present, but they are encouraged, through associations they make with the neoclassical architecture and statues, to imagine another glorious, heroic, powerful Skopje in the distant past. These acts of imagination are prompted by all manner of cues: spatial, material, object-based, image-based, sound-, smell- and/or text-based. The physical monumentality of the architecture acts on the body to produce a sense of awe which, in turn, persuades the visitor of the actuality of that history. Story recipients are given fragments which do not fully reconstruct the original context but are fundamental in stimulating the narrative imagination. In the design of narrative environments, these fragments and their position, their scale, their look and feel and their sequencing need to be carefully considered if they are to create an engaging experience that transports people in their minds to another place and/or time.

Examples of artists and designers who provide multiple cues and settings include Canadian artist Iris Häussler who reconstructs interiors, peppered with objects, documents and images, such as *The Material Evidence of Obsessive Lives and Works*, to create narratives for visitors to decode. Other artists and designers deliberately give few cues, leaving a great deal to the imagination. French artist JR, for example, in his installation 'Women Are Heroes' shows just the eyes of local women, albeit at an architectural scale. Giving few cues may prompt audiences to imagine more. Narrative imagination is stimulated by gaps (Gerrig 2010) so there is merit in paring back the cues. However, detailed settings with layers of content can offer multiple paths through content and, as a consequence, stimulate choice and imagination. Elaborate settings can also appeal to the senses, creating pleasant feelings of bodily immersion. However, if the setting produces a detailed rendering of the world of the story, without considering the experiential quality the story is trying to evoke, it may be exact but not imaginatively stimulating. In order to evoke storyworlds in people's imaginations, the setting needs to deviate from a literal transposition of the story elements. Carefully chosen materials, text and spatial or sensory cues will allow each individual visitor to imagine their own version of the world of the story, rather than being guided towards one specific vision.

The concept of storyworld, as an individual's spatialised mental model, should not be confused with 'the world of the story' or the 'mise-en-scène'. The world of the story in narrative environments is constructed as a layered, detailed, logical set of interrelating systems and factors that is discussed, sketched, agreed and written about by a multidisciplinary team. The world of the story is the outcome of a great deal of research. The mise-en-scène, a phrase derived from theatre, describes just the elements of that world that are placed on the stage, into the camera shot in film making or, in this case, in the narrative environment. The elements and the characters of the mise-en-scène can be understood as fragments of the world of the story. The world of the story will contain other characters and places which never actually appear in the narrative environment but are implied, for example, the Triumphal Arch in Skopje implies a past victory. The implied world of the story is imagined in the mind of the recipient on the basis of the mise-en-scène. Hence, narrative environments function as sensory or material synecdoches, in other words, tropes where a part represents a whole. In the design of narrative environments, the creative team will develop a comprehensive knowledge of the world of the story in text, image, objects, spaces and sometimes moving image. They will then select key elements to include or emphasise in the narrative environment. In cases such as the exhibition at Vischering Castle, designed by Duncan McCauley Studio and discussed in Chapter 5, visitors' attention is deliberately drawn to the grain of the stone walls, volumes and light in the castle as important clues in the telling of its history.

Multimodality

The advantage of, and the design challenge for, narrative environments is that they combine a broad range of media to engage and stimulate people's imaginations. The question for the design team is when to use which media, in other words, how and when to combine text, image, moving image, object, sound and performance with digital and physical space. Narrative unity is sustained in part through tone of voice, a literary concept explicitly used by interpretation strategists, although not by all designers. It describes the choice of words and the moods and feelings they evoke. The tone could be, for example, formal, informal, technical, authoritative, intimate, humorous, playful or optimistic. The type of textual language used could be interrogative, exclamatory, declarative or imperative; or a mix. As well as being used to shape the text, tone of voice can be applied to multiple modes of communication including font, image, light, sound, form and spaces, which can all establish the atmosphere of the narrative environment. Defining tone of voice enables creative teams to think consciously about how to incorporate multiple voices.

German philosopher Gernot Böhme (2017) describes atmospheres as intangible tinctured interstices, which people sense but cannot attribute precisely. Böhme discusses the aesthetics, feeling and perception of space through, for example, the difference between material and staged materiality and the social character of materials as they are taken to signify particular meanings by particular cultures. He also points to the way spatial atmospheres are commodified to produce deliberately and overtly designed experiences in retail or leisure environments to encourage dwell time, identification with a brand and the purchase of goods and services. Atmospheres are recognised as very powerful communication tools and design researchers such as Valerie Mace (2014) are currently trying to make more explicit the ways in which atmosphere can be applied as part of a critical design process. The architect Peter Zumthor (2006) has spent much time reflecting on atmospheres, claiming that "We perceive atmosphere through our emotional sensibility – a form of perception that works incredibly quickly and which we humans need to help us survive".

Atmosphere is non-tangible but narrative environments, particularly museums and brand experiences, also use tangible objects as ways to engage visitors. Architect and writer Juhani Pallasmaa argues that we live in an image-soaked world and that visuality dominates our other senses and flattens our experience, reducing the multidimensional world to a screen. Pallasmaa (2012: 62) argues for a richer sensorium making a case for the tactile, saying, "The door handle is the handshake of the building". Pallasmaa makes a passionate plea for designers to address all the senses. He stresses designers should consider the eye, the ear and the hand to produce architecture addressed to the intellect and the senses. The tactile is often addressed in narrative environments through the inclusion of objects which, being material, have weight, density and texture, qualities that are typically emphasised through lighting. Light translates the tactile qualities into visual qualities but nevertheless evokes and heightens our sense of materiality.

The scale and materiality of objects, unavailable in books, images and film, can be used in narrative environments to make an argument. For example, Brazilian Néle Azevedo (Burke 2012) uses objects and their materiality to make political statements. Azevedo carved 1000 little ice men as a project for the World Wildlife Fund. The piece has been staged in the urban realm in France, Japan and Italy. The work uses its reduced scale to provoke curiosity and garner attention. As the ice men slowly melt, they make people conjure up the appalling consequences of global warming.

Objects and the narratives they prompt have become the focus of interaction designers (Grimaldi, Fokkinga and Ocnarescu 2013). To understand the emotional importance of objects to people, designers often look to anthropologist Alfred Gell (1998) who argued that artefacts enchant the viewer through technical and stylistic virtuosity which, he suggests, gives works of art an agency on a par with human beings, prompting strong emotional responses, such as love, hate, desire or fear. Research shows objects, including mass produced products, act as complex symbols entangled with, for example, pleasure (Jordon 1999) and/or social status (Harman 2016). Designers of narrative environments need to understand how their audiences are likely to interpret the meanings of any objects used. This knowledge allows them to juggle and juxtapose objects to provoke emotional engagement and deictic shifts in their audiences.

Digital media may appear to stand in direct contrast to material objects but they can be a very powerful narrative addition to object displays. For example, interpretive strategists Tim Gardom and Alison Grey (2019) describe a temporary exhibition they worked on, *Transplant and Life*, at the Hunterian Museum, London, 2016–2017, a medical collection with a permanent display of preserved body parts. The exhibition-making team added screens and sound recordings of doctors' and transplant patients' testimonies. The collection was not touched but the installation transformed the space. Gardom explains the depth and substance of the experience owed much to the 15 years of work by photographer Tim Wainwright and artist John Wayne in collecting the testimonies and images. The power lay in the narrative and the aural and visual tone of voice, not in the technical devices themselves.

Digital media can be used to represent 3D objects using augmented reality (AR). Here, the AR objects are of quite a different order from physical objects. They occupy a place mid-way between representation and spatiality. AR makes use of internet connectivity, location awareness and cameras on smartphones or tablets to allow people to view 3D digital images, text and hear sound through their mobile phones, layered onto the 'real' physical environment. Users can move around the image or sound in three-dimensional space. German design company Art+Com has been researching AR since the mid-1990s. They developed a fixed interface, Timescope (1996), to look at the urban fabric of Berlin that had disappeared due to the dramatic upheavals after reunification, when the wall and border fortifications were demolished. A freeze-frame of the empty border strip was blended with historical edited recordings. Inhabitants and visitors who had never experienced the city divided could see what the wall was like and imagine themselves back in time. Local Projects, one of the leading exhibition design companies in New York, made a 9/11 app. Users could view video of the destruction of the twin towers through their smartphones by standing in the place where the film was originally taken. This was a very powerful geo-located narrative experience that used the actual physical environment to create a palpable deictic shift that would not have been possible in any other way.

In 2018, Chilean artist Sebastian Errazuriz vandalised Jeff Koons' virtual 'Balloon Dog' using virtual graffiti on his own app as part of a "stance against an imminent AR corporate invasion" (Sayer 2018). This opens viewers' imaginations to the remarkable possibilities of AR, which can add facsimile objects, text, sound or moving image to any environment. It is an excellent medium for experimenting with scale. It can produce surprise and wonder, and prompt ideas of new worlds and new situations, transporting people into fantasy worlds, even in their familiar environments. However, AR has also prompted dystopian visions of urban space, such as that of film maker Keiichi Matsuda. In his video, *Hyper-Reality* (Winston 2016), an urban space is saturated with AR, designed as an anonymous backdrop with few material or formal design qualities so that continuously updated media can be projected onto it. In this world, everyone is sealed in their own self-referential system, steered by giant technology companies who have harvested data about each person's preferences.

Joel Lewis (2019), teacher, designer and researcher in sustainable computing and web-based augmented reality, believes AR has enormous potential in narrative environments. This is demonstrated by the worldwide AR phenomenon Pokémon Go, which represents a blend of the digital and the physical world. Lewis adds that the AR technology in itself was not enough to create a compelling proposition, the Pokémon world of characters and stories were needed to bring it alive. Narrative was crucial to its success. Excitement was also created by the opportunity for all to participate, exercise and develop new friendships (Bonas et al. 2017). Lewis explains AR is very versatile in a practical sense. It can be used to prototype experiences at the beginning of the project before anyone has built or encountered the space. It can simulate spaces that are too far away to reach or expensive to get to. It is a cost-effective way of getting past the physical and budgetary limitations of the physical world. Lewis believes AR could also be a social connector. People in different locations could have a three-dimensional experience of eating together or watching a film together. Here AR would be a tool for human empathic engagement. Lewis believes that when the resolution, brightness and refresh rate is developed beyond that of human vision there will be no difference between AR and human experience. Its weakness is that it cannot be touched. Nevertheless, it can enable people to act upon and change the human and physical world around them, so it has an effect on the actual environment.

The relationships among text, image, video, light, objects and AR are among the determinants of our sense of space and place. Space and place, which are major constituents of the environmental node in the tripartite narrative environments network, are both intimately connected to the human body (Casey 2013). The body, the crucial means by which we engage with the world, translates between the people node and the environment node. In infancy, according to phenomenologist Maurice Merleau-Ponty (1962), we develop a body schema as we learn to live space through our bodies in relation to other bodies and objects, using touch, gaze, proximity and sound. Merleau-Ponty envisages the body schema as the physical body plus its sensory extensions into the surrounding world. He argues that, as we move, we exercise a sense of depth, dimensionality, flow, passage, form, colour, tactility, texture and lustre. Our bodies, therefore, extend beyond our skin to include our immediate surroundings and the physical world we perceive at some distance can make us feel disturbed, disrupted, reassured and so on. Merleau-Ponty blurs the boundaries among body, mind, objects and surrounding space arguing for embodied perception, by which he means learning and understanding through our whole body rather than just through cognition. Taking Merleau-Ponty's ideas, it is suggested that we make meaning from our embodied perception of the immediate world around us, through which are woven overt linguistic conceptualisations and that, as moving, perceiving bodies, we are inseparable from space and language. Using Merleau-Ponty as a starting point, spatial forms and rhythms, materials and atmospheres are understood to communicate in an implicit manner. This enables us to move away from the concept of communication as a single channel, two-way transmission model towards a model of communication that is multidimensional and multimodal. Communication is continually unfolding, receiving and sending messages from, and in, multiple directions through multiple senses. It is a model of material semiosis that is reciprocal and responsive, a network of messaging between body and world, with mind arising from and entangled with these ongoing processes, a conceptualisation not unlike Gregory Bateson's (2000) notion of an ecology of mind.

The messaging network and its meanings provoke changes in behaviour. Embodied perception causes people to act. This includes moving, pausing, talking, fighting and so on. One of the modes of acting is making and reshaping our environment, such as our buildings and the spaces around them. Yi-Fu Tuan (1977) discusses the central role of the human body in the conception and design of architectural structures and their orientation. Tuan suggests many buildings echo the upright human body. The fact that we, as a species, have eyes in the front of our heads creates a sense of front and back and orientation to what lies in front of us. This orientation to the front, Tuan suggests, underlies the design of many buildings. Modelled on the human body, many houses, palaces, churches and so on have been designed to have a front and back.

Tuan explores the related meanings of front and back, arguing front represents possibility or future promise and back is regarded as past and is sometimes thought of as tainted. As a result, front is privileged over back. Hence orientation takes on numerous hierarchical and potentially divisive values. This corresponds to expressions in language such as 'going forwards' as a positive metaphor for making progress and 'going backwards' as a negative metaphor. Tuan argues that the standing body, ready for action, is more highly regarded than the prone body. He points out the words status, stature and estate all derive from the word stand. Upwards is privileged over downwards. Tall takes on meanings of importance and short, meanings of powerlessness and servility. Important buildings and monuments are raised on platforms and reach high into the air and command more visual space. This orientation is incorporated into religious belief when heaven is conceived as above and hell below. The body and the values in its orientation are translated into architecture which materialises and expresses values in larger-than-human scale. People then find themselves sensing and reiterating these meanings, consolidating them as cultural codes.

These physical cultural codes evoke emotions and orient our imaginations. In *The Poetics of Space*, Gaston Bachelard (1964) explores our subjective, psychological and emotional investment in the spatial universe of the home. He argues people need houses to dream and imagine. He describes, for example, the house as a dual vertical polarity, the pointed roof averting the rain clouds, the attic being a place where our thoughts are clear, where we can see further. By contrast the cellar is a dark entity which is mysterious, heavy, labyrinthine and conjures up trepidation of a diabolical underground world. In *Body Memory Architecture*, Kent Bloomer and Charles Moore (1978) pursue the argument that architecture is a sensual social art, historically derived from experiences and memories of the human body. Experiential architecture is a phrase that has been used by those interested in how buildings can foster well-being in all its dimensions, beyond the visual.

The presence of the body in the space enables the designers of narrative environments to borrow from "theatre's now moment and feeling machinery" (Lavender 2016: 163), which stimulate affect and a visceral response through intelligible and sensible engagement. Lavender (2016: 163) adds,

> This isn't to relegate it [affect] to a simple register of sensation, sentimentality or consumer satisfaction. It has its own politics to do with invitation, involvement, identity, renunciation, pleasure, community and agency.

In narrative environments, the experience of being in a physical space, in the present and able to move differs from that of literature, film and traditional theatre, where the body is relatively disengaged. The active, embodied dimension of the experience can heighten narrative imagination while the intense feelings are also capable of prompting people to consider the meaning and implications of the narrative. Visitors are often accompanied in narrative environments by friends or surrounded by others and there can be transmission of affect to others nearby which produces, as in theatre, a shared communal involvement. Nigel Thrift (2008: 235) calls this "affective contagion" and suggests that it reinforces emotional and transformative experience. The presence and normative actions of others in narrative environments is another element to consider in the design, as learned behaviours will vary among, for example, commercial, cultural and urban spaces.

To recap, the multimodal and multimedia communication of narrative environments is enacted through embodied perception of cultural encoding in architectural form, spaces, materiality, imagery, sound, sense of atmosphere, text, other people and their actions. Together, they communicate and materialise social norms, hierarchies, values and distinctions, along with the power dynamics enacted through these processes which we learn to read and conform to or resist, consciously or unconsciously. These phenomenologically oriented insights, which establish the intimate relationships among body, space and place, are further grounded in social practice by the thought of the Marxist theorist Henri Lefebvre (1991). Lefebvre, in emphasising that spaces and places are not neutral but sites of struggle over meaning, access and control, enables a more concrete analysis of the expression and contestation of power involving body, space, place and practice. Narrative environments engage with these dimensions in order to raise awareness or bring about material or behavioural change.

Spatial Arrangement as Mode of Address

A key aspect of engagement is mode of address. A useful starting point for examining spatial modes of address is Louis Althusser's (1977) theory of interpellation, in which addressees are called and recruited, as subjects, for specific ideological horizons. Although Althusser's theory of ideology and the state is not pursued here, nevertheless his general insight into how people are drawn into specific worldviews is useful in understanding how narrative environments engage people. It is argued that spatial configurations constitute modes of address which may, for example, be invitational, persuasive or possibly hostile but, in each case, they influence the expectations and behaviour of the subject of address, by calling for a response. Modes of address position the subject in relation to a specific place with its corresponding hierarchical frame of power relations. For example, city promenades invite visitors to stroll towards distant landmarks, positioning them as tourists within both a physical and cultural horizon, registering them in a field of cultural consumption. Museums position visitors as truth seekers through the display of objects which signify authenticity and origin. Luxury retail environments position visitors as belonging to a privileged and exclusive group.

Modes of address call and recruit visitors but this does not necessarily lead to intellectual and emotional engagement. In fact, they can lead to passive consumption. For example, the French critic and activist Guy Debord (2014: 5) argued that spectacle, the product of what Debord calls the dominant mode of production, "is the sun that never sets over the empire of modern passivity". Debord's Situationists were particularly concerned with the dynamics and experience of the city. They saw superficial spectacle, in the form of buildings and events that aimed at increasing touristic entertainment, as obliterating everyday life. Instead, they advocated the deliberate subversion of commercial and mainstream instruments. Whether designers are working with or against its economic and political inferences, the environment 'performs' certain constraints and opportunities. Changes to the mode of address of the urban fabric can have profound effects on inhabitants' responsive behaviour. Erika Fischer-Lichte (2015) maintains that joint action, prompted by physical change to the environment, can transform whole communities. In 2005, for example, during the severe financial crises of the post-communist era, the Mayor of Tirana, Albania, Edi Rama, a former artist, distributed resources to enable residents to paint many of their grey communist buildings in bright colours. Although the change was purely aesthetic, and some said superficial, it immediately provided an uplift in civic pride, prompting an appetite for clearing away piles of rubbish, removing illegal kiosks and installing new street lights (Kramer 2004).

Modes of address can employ a range of communication strategies from predominantly explicit communications to predominantly implicit communications or aim for a more equal mix of both. Explicit communication, such as speech, text and graphics, is taken to mean expression that fully and clearly articulates content, leaving very little implied. Explicit communication is aimed at a cognitive reception. Implicit communication is taken to mean expression where content is not plainly or directly conveyed. It is hinted at, or evoked. Implicit communications can be expressed through three-dimensional forms, such as spatial rhythm, volume, scale, light, colour and atmosphere, often yielding emotional responses.

An example of a multimodal narrative environment that deploys predominantly explicit communications is the Whitney Plantation Visitor Centre, Louisiana, USA. It is a former slave plantation that produced sugar cane. There are numerous small museums in plantations all over the southern United States but the Whitney Plantation is the only one that tells the story of such plantations from the slaves' perspectives. The paucity of museums interpreting history from the slaves' perspectives shows that the slave experience is a neglected narrative in the southern United States and this may be one of the reasons why the communications are so explicit. There is a need to work against a culture in which black people's histories are ignored.

The site's grounds accommodate a car park, the visitor entrance building, a ticketing area, a café and shop, a church, landscape elements such as fields, trees, paths, a pond, a memorial and buildings such as slave cabins, kitchens, workshops and the owner's house. Visitors cannot wander around by themselves; they are required to book and wait to be escorted in a group. The visit takes the form of a two-hour guided tour. There is a fixed spatial sequence and the visitor experience is mediated by the guide or explainer. Spatial barriers or obstacles are used to control the flow and experience of visitors. Guides have standard scripts but they are allowed to improvise and engage in spontaneous conversation with groups. Individual visitors can express their own views.

Once assembled as a group of 10–15 people, visitors are welcomed by the guide, then led into the plantation grounds and invited into the church. The church is an original structure from the neighbourhood which slaves would have used. Visitors are physically inside the same building and can viscerally and psychologically identify with former congregations. There are figurative wooden sculptures of slave children in the church which visitors can choose to photograph (Figure 6.1). The church is a non-negotiable pause on the journey where visitors are requested to sit and view a video giving a visual and verbal overview of the plantation's 262-year history.

In the landscape beyond the church, there is a deliberate physical 'obstacle'. It is the 'Wall of Honour', a long tall slab of black marble. It is a memorial that implicitly communicates its meaning through its scale, material and solidity, firmly asserting the memory of past lives and events and their persistent relevance into the present. The guide stops the tour and asks visitors to read the testimonies inscribed in the stone wall, for example,

When children used to get a whipping they was taught to turn 'round and say. Thank you, ma/am, for whipping me and bow. That was mighty hard to do, but we

Figure 6.1 Wooden sculptures at the Whitney Plantation, Louisiana, USA, 2016.

were never allowed to pout. If we did we got another. And if we just needed being punished, we were put behind a door and had to stand on one foot until we were ready to say we were sorry, and promise not to do it again. If we told a story, our mouths were washed out with a soaped rag.

The direct speech brings the characters alive in the visitors' imaginations and the brief halt on the tour allows time for questions and conversations between guide and visitors.

The tour continues as the guide explains the appalling working conditions and life-threatening hazards of working in the sugar cane fields or being assigned to boiling the sugar cane in the large metal sugar kettles to make molasses. The lives of the slaves are communicated through explicit spoken description but also implicitly brought to life through the physical encounter with the objects and conditions of the plantation regime such as the brutal, cramped holding cells that were used at slave auctions. Visitors are taken to the slave cabins, the kitchens and the workshops, which they can choose to enter and imagine the lives of the slaves through the objects and physical qualities of the spaces (Figure 6.2).

The tour concludes with a visit to the slave-owner's house. The fact that the grand house is the last place to be visited inverts the norm. In many plantation museums and films about slavery, the main focus is centred on the slave-owner's house as luxurious and appealing. In this tour, the slave-owner's house is seen in a different light, as it is explained that some of the architectural features, for example, those that supported the circulation of cool air, were based on African traditions. Slaves with such construction knowledge were highly sought after.

Figure 6.2 Slave cabin at the Whitney Plantation, Louisiana, USA, 2016.

The tour of the space is carefully planned, the overall framework is explicitly scripted, movement and choice are tightly controlled. Invitation is open but punctuated by conceptual and physical obstacles and challenges. The explicit communications are very powerfully complemented by the implicit communications arising from the encounter with spaces, objects and materials. In addition, visitors sense the commitment of the guide. They implicitly feel and share the presence, absorption and reflection of others on the tour and the result is that the multimodal communications challenge conventional plantation narratives. The mode of address is didactic but also radical and activist. Visitors are positioned as respectful listeners who are seeking knowledge. They are required to submit to the regulations of the tour during the visit but the revelations of profound cruelty and exploitation together with discussion about the persistence of racism in the USA suggests that visitors may leave as agents of change after their visit.

In contrast to the explicit narrative and didactic mode of address of the Whitney Plantation, the narratives and modes of address in the work of Daily Tous les Jours are usually implicit and open-ended. Melissa Mongiat and Mouna Andraos co-founded Daily Tous les Jours in Montreal, Canada, in 2009. They create positive, life-enhancing, inclusive interactive installations. Their mission is to enable ordinary citizens to be agents of change in the social and sensory urban landscape. Their work is rooted in designing and producing interactive installations in outdoor public spaces that welcome all passers-by to participate. Their installations demonstrate how participants can transform heavily built urban environments through their human presence and their explicit joy in coordinated, collaborative movement and sound.

Figure 6.3 21 Balançoires, Daily Tous les Jours, Montreal, Canada, 2011–2018.

One of their most well-known pieces is '21 Balançoires', a set of musical swings in Montreal's Quartier des Spectacles (Figure 6.3). As people swing, they play music. The higher they swing the higher the musical tone. Each swing releases its own variation of notes and as people notice the sounds from other swings they adjust their pace to align and harmonise with others. Harmonies emerge through collective cooperation and this stimulates an implicit sense of ownership of the space. A computer system, housed within the physical structure, plays a programmed set of notes that enable people to play freely. The swings are not an open instrument otherwise users would have to be advanced players to make them harmonise. Melissa Mongiat and Mouna Andraos (2019) explain that to facilitate interaction the sound needs to be beautiful the first time anyone uses it. In fact, the sounds are preselected and also progress over time so they do not become repetitive but the preselection is not obvious to the users. Some people will spend two hours on the swings, so the progression has to be quite extensive. Being an interactive installation, the overall narrative, about the potential for people to transform their cities, is activated and played out through people's participation. Each participant brings their own content and interpretation to the overall narrative framework.

At Daily Tous les Jours, they work on the principle that public space installations need to be part of people's everyday lives and habits. When working in public spaces, Daily Tous les Jours does not have a captive audience. Their work has to contend with people's other priorities, such as going to work or shopping. To get attention, outdoor installations need to be big; they need to compete at a city scale. However, they also need to be inviting and appealing on a human scale. There is a great deal of skill in managing these opposing scales. Surprisingly, Daily Tous les Jours tests the scale with cardboard prototypes in situ. They say there is no way to make a fully informed judgement from a computer visualisation. They need to be in the space and work by responding to the surrounding physical environment. They believe the first level of interaction has to be obvious and easy to do. In this case, passers-by recognise and know how to use the swings. Then, as participants, they work out, through trial and error, how to align the sound of their swing with other swings as a second level of interaction. This experience and the other pieces designed and produced by Daily Tous les Jours are more than just fun. They combat urban solitude, they build community fabric, by encouraging people to talk to strangers, and they bring vibrancy to the environment.

Daily Tous les Jours developed a related concept for Mesa, a large suburb of Phoenix, Arizona, that suffers from the same urban problems as many downtown areas in the USA: inhabitants seem to be missing. People do not commune outside and the environment feels lifeless. Mesa Arts Centre is trying to contribute to urban life. It has been looking for reasons for people to spend time outdoors in its locale and commissioned Daily Tous les Jours to develop an installation. Mongiat and Andraos visited to research the space. They ran several days of workshops, meeting and talking with local residents, getting an understanding of the place. They met someone running a community garden who, with others, such as local businesses, wanted to enliven the space. There was an appetite for new initiatives. Mongiat and Andraos found it was very hot in summer, exacerbated by the numerous concrete buildings. Everyone was fighting the sun. As a result, Daily Tous les Jours realised they had to play with the sun and they conceived of Mesa Musical Shadows.

Mesa Musical Shadows (see Plate 4) is a custom-made interactive pavement that enables people's shadows to produce sounds of singing voices performing in musical harmony. As people walk over the pavement, they can join complete strangers in creating complementary melodies. The differing length and intensity of the shadows changes the sounds at different times of the day. For example, the voices are peaceful and ethereal in the early morning and more energetic and staccato in the middle of the day. The technology is hidden and produces a sense of magic and delight among visitors. It not only prompts human to object interaction with the pavement, it also creates a sense of connection and mutual cooperation and affiliation among the many different pedestrians. Mongiat and Andraos say they use music to create a sense of wonder because it is accessible to all, touches the emotions and is less cognitively demanding than screens. People can listen to music and simultaneously interact with each other. It does not prohibit people from speaking to others, fulfilling one of the goals of their studio: they want to create more opportunities for people to communicate with each other and experience the agency they have to transform their environment.

Whilst studying MA Narrative Environments in 2007, Melissa Mongiat and fellow student Kelsey Snook developed a scheme they called 'good participation' as a guide to interactive participatory design to which Daily Tous les Jours still refers. They set out the steps they felt would ensure good participation: send an invitation; provide an incentive; make the rules clear without limiting people's freedom or creativity; provide a feedback loop so that participants can confirm or augment their actions; pay attention to timing, using suspense and surprise; leave traces that can demonstrate the impact of the collective effort; stay authentic and sensitive to your audiences' needs; have fun; deploy technology to support interaction; share authorship; expect the unexpected; use all the senses; engage with narrative fantasy; rely on people's intuition, they know what to do; consider the price.

Daily Tous les Jours also uses a well-established interaction design paradigm to provide different levels of engagement. At their 'Giant Sing Along', part of the Minnesota

State Fair, where hundreds of people attend each day, Daily Tous les Jours provided numerous ways to participate. Giant Sing Along, 2011–2014, is literally a field of microphones where people can do large-scale karaoke. The voices are modulated, adjusting the pitch to achieve the best harmonies. People can listen; they can hum in their heads; they can lip sync the songs; they can sing aloud by themselves; they can go to a mic and start singing to the crowd or they can go online to the website to suggest songs. The multiplicity of possibilities for participation makes a rich environment. All the different levels of participation working at the same time create an air of engagement. The critical mass makes the environment welcoming. Mongiat and Andraos do not judge people by saying advanced users are the best. They believe all means of participation are important (Figure 6.4).

A project by Daily Tous les Jours that tells more explicit stories is Amateur Intelligence Radio (AIR) (see Plate 5). The designers installed a radio station in a building, St. Paul's Union Depot, Minnesota, USA. They undertook interviews with local residents and historians to discover and piece together the building's history. Daily Tous les Jours says people bring a layer of anecdotes while the site itself, the way it has been structured and built, reveals the choices made by planners and architects. In the piece, the building itself appears to be the host. It introduces those who enter or pass by to all kinds of content. This includes the building's history; the stories, apologies and love declarations gathered from visitors; horoscopes; advice for a rainy day; and the real time ambient conditions, for example, the weather forecast. This is a narrative environment that takes the form of a pun on artificial intelligence.

Daily Tous les Jours always works with digital media and its work shows it has a profound understanding of human-to-machine, machine-to-machine and human-to-human interaction. The technology is not viewed as a siloed, non-human sphere. Mongiat and

Figure 6.4 Giant Sing Along, Minnesota State Fair, USA, Daily Tous les Jours, 2011–2014.

Andraos see digital technology as an enabler that can support a seamless integration of space, media, interaction and participation. They see a difference between interaction and participation. They say interaction is the mechanism but participation is more like an active state of being, a readiness. They use digital technology to increase the agency of the audience and address urgent social and spatial issues through the pleasure of the playful and the unexpected.

The mode of address and the balance and combination of implicit and explicit narrative can be scaled up and down. An example of a combination of an explicit and implicit narrative environment is The Gobbins, a remote coastal path in Northern Ireland that invites you to experience the drama of the landscape and the sea but also learn about the local history and flora and fauna (see Plate 6). The Gobbins claims to be the most dramatic walk in Europe. Two miles long, the narrow path hugs the enormous cliff-face along the rugged coastline. Walkers are suspended above the crashing waves of the North Channel by newly engineered bridges that lead to tunnels and staircases carved into the rock. It is an arduous but exhilarating experience, with 50 flights of stairs and a walk up a very steep 1-in-5 gradient. Overall, it takes 2.5 hours to complete the walk (Figure 6.5).

The path first came into being in the early 1900s. It was conceived and constructed by Berkeley Deane Wise, Chief Engineer of the Belfast and Northern Counties Railway Company. He wanted to increase railway use and therefore devised new destinations at the end of railway lines. He applied the engineering that he had developed elsewhere to build the path bridges at The Gobbins. The path was a popular ticketed tourist attraction for many years but was abandoned in the 1960s, until new investment was found in 2013. From 2013 to 2015, UK-based Creative Director Sam Willis oversaw the development of a new pathway commissioned by Larne Borough

Figure 6.5 The Gobbins cliff pathway viewing platform, Northern Ireland, 2018.

Council. It was a restoration project, described as a reimagined project, with completely new, specially engineered bridges, tunnels and staircases to make the coastal path accessible again. Only 30 visitors can take the cliff-face path at any one time, led by a trained guide.

On arrival at the nearby visitor centre, they are put into groups of 15 people, introduced to their guide and shown a safety video. Their footwear and outer garments are checked. They are given a helmet and taken by their guide to the path. Some visitors embark on the walk but get vertigo and need to be brought back. On the walk, there are two kinds of narrative experience that are interwoven. The guide offers an explicit spoken dialogical narration while the visitors are implicitly, bodily and emotionally immersed in the vast scale and proximity to the dramatic landscape and the sea. The guide's script provides three kinds of content: some background history about the path's origins; stories about the geology, flora and fauna and myths related to particular locations on the walk as visitors pass through them; and the stories of the engineering and of the people who worked on the original installation. As visitors walk along the new path, they can see the remains of the original Victorian bridges and pathway and learn about bridge engineering. Being outdoors is very different from the controlled environment inside a building. The physical space acts implicitly on the bodily senses of the visitor to induce a sense of wonder through the dramatic proximity to the forces of nature and their continual transformation. This is complemented by experiencing feats of human ingenuity in engineering. The stories the guide offers explicitly contextualise the main experience, the landscape and seascape which play out in front of the visitor. It is worth noting that here the space, rather than being the backdrop for stories or an actantial relay for them, *acts* as the main character in the story to which the other stories are subordinate.

The examples above demonstrate the priority given to engagement in the design of narrative environments. This reflects a general shift in research paradigms from positivism to interpretivism, resulting in an increasing focus, in narrative terms, on the experience of human action and participation. This has led to multiple creative approaches to visitor interaction in many spheres of design but particularly in the design of narrative environments. Discourse on engagement in literary narrative has a great deal to offer the design of narrative environments but skill and judgement are required to translate these insights into multimodal and multimedia formats. Current thinking on the importance of spatialisation, as a path to imagination in the audiences' construction of mental models or storyworlds, reinforces the need for designers of narrative environments to consider and experiment with a full range of sensory and scalar spatial cues, to develop an awareness of how they position visitors through their chosen modes of address. While pure spectacle creates passive audiences, narrative environments stimulate intellectual, emotional and moral engagement. They do so through implicit and explicit means, interweaving the narrative, or word- and image-based symbolic node in the tripartite model, with the artefactual and place elements of the environment node, while addressing both the psychodynamic self and the body in the people node. Theory and practice flow into one another, demonstrating the value of the tripartite model as a practical working methodology which is non-prescriptive, open and flexible. It is a way to think through common sense notions of narrative imagining to develop and deliver absorbing and moving human experiences. The resulting narrative environments can still be modulated. If the qualities of encounter and being surrounded by the world of the story are intensified, narrative environments produce immersive experiences, as discussed in the next chapter.

References

Althusser, L. (1977) Ideology and ideological state apparatuses (notes towards and investigation). In: *Lenin and Philosophy and other Essays*, 2nd ed. London: New Left Books.

ART+COM (1996) *Timescope* [Exhibition]. Online. Available at HTTP: https://artcom.de/en/project/timescope/. Accessed 8 February 2020.

Bachelard, G. (1964) *The Poetics of Space*. New York, NY: Orion.

Bateson, G. (2000) *The Ecology of Mind*. Chicago, IL: University of Chicago.

Bloomer, K. and Moore, C. (1978) *Body, Memory, Architecture*. New Haven, CT: Yale University Press.

Bilandzic, R. and Kinnebrock, H. (2009) Measuring narrative engagement. *Media Psychology*, 12(4), 321–347.

Bonas, J. A. et al. (2017) Look on the bright side (of Media Effects): Pokémon go as a catalyst for positive life. *Media Psychology*, 21(2), 263–287.

Brewer, W. and Lichtenstein, E. (1982) Stories are to entertain: A structural-affect theory of stories. *Journal of Pragmatics*, 6, 473–486.

Burke, F. (2012) *Interview with Nele Azevedo: All Art Is Quite Useful Environment Art and Social Change*. Online. Available HTTP: https://allartisquiteuseful.wordpress.com/2012/09/12/nele-azevedo/. Accessed 8 July 2019.

Böhme, G. (2017) *Critique of Aesthetic Capitalism: Atmospheric Spaces*. Milan: Mimesis International.

Casey, E. (2013) *The Fate of Place*. Berkeley, CA: University of California Press.

Chatman, S. (1978) *Story and Discourse: Narrative Structure in Fiction and Film*. Ithaca, NY: Cornell University Press.

Csíkszentmihályi, M. (1975) *Beyond Boredom and Anxiety: Experiencing Flow in Work and Play*. San Francisco, CA: Jossey-Bass.

Debord, G. (2014) *Society of the Spectacle*. Berkeley, CA: Bureau of Public Secrets.

Fischer-Lichte, E. (2015) *Performance and the Politics of Space: Theatre and Topology*. New York, NY: Routledge.

Galbraith, M. (1995) Deictic shift theory and the poetics of involvement in narrative. In: Ducken, J., Bruder, G. and Hewitt, L., eds. *Deixis in Narrative: A Cognitive Science Perspective*. Hillsdale, NJ: Lawrence Erlbaum, pp. 19–59.

Gardom, Tim and Grey, Alison (2019) Interview with Tricia Austin, 5 March 2019.

Gell, A. (1998) *Art and Agency: An Anthropological Theory*. Oxford, UK: Clarendon Press.

Genette, G. (1980) *Narrative Discourse: An Essay in Method*. Ithaca, NY: Cornell University Press.

Gerrig, R. (1996) Participatory aspects of narrative understanding. In: Kreuz, R. and MacNealy, M., eds. *Empirical Approaches to Literature and Aesthetics*. Norwood, NJ: Ablex, pp. 127–142.

Gerrig, R. (2010) Readers' experiences of narrative gaps. *Storyworlds: A Journal of Narrative Studies*, 2, 19–37.

Green, M., Strange, J. and Brock, T. (2002) *Narrative Impact: Social and Cognitive Foundations*. Mahwah, NJ: Lawrence Erlbaum Associates.

Grimaldi, S., Fokkinga, S. and Ocnarescu, I. (2013) Narratives in design: A study of the types, applications and functions of narratives in design practice. *Proceedings of the 6th International Conference on Designing Pleasurable Products and Interfaces*, DPPI '13. New York, NY: ACM, pp. 201–210.

Hakemulder, Frank (2011) Ways to engage readers: Relevance in the scientific study of literature. *Scientific Study of Literature*, 1, 143–151.

Harman, G. (2016) *Immaterialism: Objects and Social Theory*. Cambridge: Polity Press.

Herman, D. (2004) *Story Logic: Problems and Possibilities of Narrative*. Lincoln, NE: University of Nebraska Press.

Jordon, P. (1999) Pleasure with products: Human factors for body, mind and soul. In: Green, W. and Jordon, Patrick, eds. *Human Factors in Product Design: Current Practice and Future Trends*. London: Taylor and Francis, pp. 206–217.

Kramer, J. (2004) Painting the town: How Edi Rama reinvented Albanian politics. *New Yorker*, December 2004.

Lavender, A. (2016) *Performance in the Twenty-First Century, Theatres of Engagement*. Abingdon: Routledge.

Lefebvre, H. (1991) *The Construction of Space*. Oxford: Blackwell.

Lewis, Joel (2019) Interview with Tricia Austin, 15 February 2019.

Mace, V. (2014) Sensing the urban interior. *[in]arch conference, Universtitas Indonesia in Depok*, Jakarta, Indonesia, 10–12 September 2014.

Maggies (2014) Maggie's architecture and landscape brief. Online. Available HTTP: https://www.maggiescentres.org/media/uploads/publications/other-publications/Maggies_architecturalbrief_2015.pdf. Accessed 24 November 2019.

Merleau-Ponty, M. (1962) *Phenomenology of Perception*. London: Routledge.

Mongiat, Melissa and Andraos, Mouna (2019) Interview with Tricia Austin, 25 February 2019.

Pallasmaa, J. (2012) *The Eyes of the Skin: Architecture and the Senses*. Chichester: Wiley.

Palmer, F. (1992) *Literature and Moral Understanding: A Philosophical Essay on Ethics, Aesthetics, Education and Culture*. Oxford, UK: Clarendon Press.

Prince, G. (1973) *A Grammar of Stories*. The Hague: Mouton.

Rapaport, W. J. et al. (1994) *Deictic Centers and the Cognitive Structure of Narrative Comprehension*. Buffalo, NY: SUNY Buffalo, Department of Cognitive Science.

Sayer, J. (2018) Who's in charge of the augmented city? *Citylab*. Online. Available HTTP: https://www.citylab.com/design/2018/03/whos-in-charge-of-the-augmented-city/554324/. Accessed 9 August 2018.

Thrift, N. (2008) *Non-representational Theory Space, Politics, Affect*. London: Routledge.

Todorov, T. (1969) Structural analysis of narrative. *A Forum on Fiction*, 3(1), 70–76.

Tuan, Y.-F. (1977) *Space and Place: The Perspective of Experience*. Minneapolis, MN: University of Minnesota Press.

Winston, A. (2016) Keiichi Matsuda's hyper-reality film blurs real and virtual worlds. *Dezeen*. Online. Available HTTP: https://www.dezeen.com/2016/05/23/keiichi-matsuda-hyper-reality-film-dystopian-future-digital-interfaces-augmented-reality/. Accessed 9 August 2018.

Zumthor, P. (2006) *Atmospheres*. Basel: Birkhauser.

Websites

Art+Com. https://artcom.de

Daily Tous Les Jours. http://www.dailytouslesjours.com

Iris Haussler. http://haeussler.ca

Local Projects. https://localprojects.com

The Gobbins. https://www.thegobbinscliffpath.com

Whitney Plantation. https://www.whitneyplantation.com

7 Immersion

Worlds and actions can be evoked so powerfully by literature that people conjure up the scenes in their imaginations. In bringing all bodily senses to bear, narrative environments ignite people's narrative imaginations and the construction of storyworlds in a different way. This chapter explores the notion of immersion in narrative environments as an extension of the term engagement. Engagement, as discussed in the last chapter, involves absorption, which is taken to relate to intense, conscious, cognitive attention and the maintenance of interest, often through physical interaction in combination with the heightening of emotions elicited by implicit communications in the environment. Immersion is taken to refer to the often non-conscious, persistent, ambient sensory experiences, which create a sense of being surrounded by, or wrapped in, a space which fosters people's bonds to that place as a seemingly self-contained world.

Although the term 'immersion' has become overused, it is worth exploring its significance, while identifying the particular qualities of immersion that can produce critical and transformative experiences. In some circumstances, immersive experiences can amount to little more than cheap thrills, for example, a roller coaster ride. The design of narrative environments, however, conceives of more profound kinds of immersion, in particular, critical immersion designed to combine surrounding visceral world-like experiences, emotional engagement, cognitive absorption and insightful reflection to make powerful, meaningful and memorable experiences. Following the logic of deictic shift, narrative environments can lead people away from everyday mundane narratives by using sensory stimulation to interweave fact and fiction, enabling them to be inside, yet also reflecting upon, their everyday reality. The paradox, and the attraction for designers, is that heightened physical awareness, which emphasises the present and current place of being, can also transport people to imaginary places.

The word immersion is derived from a Latin term *immergere*, meaning to dip into a fluid. When fully immersed in the ocean, for example, sound is reduced, every part of your skin is in physical contact with water and you are suspended in its voluminous body. Gravity seems to be overcome, suggesting some of the physical rules of the world are in abeyance. Visual horizons become distorted and the world, like an ocean, seems infinitely extendable. In the 1990s, these kinds of qualities evoked by the word immersion gradually became synonymous with digital experiences and a certain euphoria about the possibilities of VR. Artist Char Davies (1998) describes digital immersion as the transformation of the physical self when enveloped by an artificial media environment. She uses the scuba diver as a metaphor for digital immersion in her *Osmose* in 1995, in which visitors put on VR headsets and motion-tracking equipment. Visitors found they could glide through, or hover between, zones of layered textures and flowing, abstract representations of plants and water. In the last 25 years, VR has advanced, notably in the computer games industry and military training, and is being used by artists and designers. The notion of immersion has seeped from the digital sphere into the physical sphere to describe experiences which may or may not involve digital technologies. Immersion is no longer used solely to refer to VR.

Immersive Experience

How does immersive experience differ from our everyday experience, given that people are already immersed in their familiar surroundings and engaged with the stories unfolding within and around them? Peter Sloterdijk (2006) offers one way of understanding different senses of immersion. Starting from a discussion of technological synthetic immersion, he argues that people are always immersed in an envelope of some kind in their daily lives. He interprets Heidegger's (1996) idea of being thrown into the world as being thrown into a particular envelope with particular material, spatial and narrative qualities. He argues that we cannot exist without being in an envelope: "Being-in designed spaces constitutes our fundamental condition" (Sloterdijk 2006: 109). He uses house building, city building and empire building as examples of different scales of spatial and narrative envelopes. He argues that people take on the founding narrative, for example of empire, to make sense of their immersion in the envelope and in that way, take part in its history, with history itself understood as an immersive environment. Sloterdijk (2006) reflects on the experiences of Soviet and Nazi totalitarianism as experiments in the construction of large-scale envelopes or immersive worlds. These envelopes are spatial, structural, narrative and political at the same time, which he calls, "an architectonics of grand political forms, in whose construction military, diplomatic and psycho-semantic (or religious) functions all participate" (Sloterdijk 2006: 105). People may be aware of their immediate surrounding but only partially conscious of the larger-scale envelopes and the narratives they infer. They may take a deliberate decision to immerse themselves in different envelopes to gain critical distance on their position. Sloterdijk's thought expands the notion of immersion beyond the physical to include the social and the political.

Critical narrative environments aim to heighten awareness of being both in a narrative and in an environment simultaneously. They do not aspire to total immersion. According to academic Mark Wigley (2016), in a discussion of immersion in museums, if we are totally immersed, like a fish in water, we would not perceive the environment, we would just take it for granted. We only become aware of the environmental conditions in which we are immersed when they become problematic. Bruno Latour (1993) makes a similar point when discussing what modernism takes for granted, particularly the environmental dependencies it fails to acknowledge. Hence, designers of narrative environments need to withhold or skew elements of immersion to make people aware of the particular medium in which they are immersed. For example, in Conical Intersect, Paris 1975, Gordon Matta-Clark cuts away sections of a building which undoes the envelope of the walls in a radical way, placing the viewer in a completely different relationship to the room, to the building and to the city. This reaffirms Sloterdijk who says total immersion, as a method, unframes images and vistas, dissolving the boundaries between pictoriality and environment (Parsons 2016). By contrast, in narrative environments, people physically enter and take an active part in a specific world as an immersive experience, while aware of their conditional dependencies, rather than being a disembodied viewer. The environment calls for situated awareness (Endsley 1995) or consciousness of the environment, comprehended through the whole body and all of the senses, as a dynamic relation to the environmental context. By being corporeally present in a specific place, people are implicated or entangled in a narrative environment.

If bodily immersion can lead to imagining, such imagining can become a revealing, transformative experience that enables people to uncover hitherto veiled or contradictory dimensions of their worlds. An example is a mischievous installation called 'Musings on a Glass Box' at the Fondation Cartier in Paris in 2015 by American architects Diller Scofidio + Renfro (Rosenfield 2014). Their intervention was a comment on the iconic glass and steel Fondation building commissioned from world-renowned architect Jean Nouvel in the 1990s. Nouvel's building expressed a key principle of modernism: to dissolve walls and link the exterior to the interior. However, that proved problematic to artists and curators because of the resulting lack of wall space on which to hang artwork. In order to bring this limitation to attention and to exploit it playfully, Diller Scofidio + Renfro staged an apparent leak from the ceiling, which was a visual symbol of the building's dysfunctionality as a museum space. The droplets of water from the leak fell into a robotic red bucket scuttling around in one gallery to collect the drops. In a second adjacent gallery, Diller Scofidio + Renfro designed and installed a large LED screen that hung horizontally, about a metre above the floor. The screen showed a grid that visually echoed the structural grid of the building's ceiling. Viewers on movable flat beds slid underneath the LED screen, as if they were lying in the bucket, under the surface of the water looking up at the ceiling. As each drop of water fell into the bucket, the grid on the screen rippled, magnifying and multiplying the effect of the drop and dissolving the solidity and certainty of the modernist ceiling structure as it swayed back and forth on the screen. Sensors engaged further ethereal surround sound, a choral piece accompanied by musical instruments composed for the installation. Video simultaneously appeared on the glazed walls. The banal event of the water dropping, as a symbol of the building as flawed, was dramatised, turning the familiar into monstrous, provoking questions about the meaning and value of the space and how it is perceived. This brings a new resonance to the Lefebvrian notion of the social production of space through resistance to the building's assumptions about its own magnitude and significance and its power to determine what the space means. Diller Scofidio + Renfro made explicit the clash between any exhibit that appears in the space and the architecture itself. This installation is an example that illustrates the way space is replete with struggle over meaning. In this case, an immersive narrative environment can be seen to use the physical qualities of the real world to create storyworlds in people's minds that, in turn, produce a critical relationship to the everyday world.

Like humour, critical positioning, such as described above, places the audience doubly: as museum visitors becoming aware for themselves that the museum is flawed and as sensors in the bucket registering the flaw, inducing a comic contrast. Feeling simultaneously *inside* the museum and the bucket, *surrounded* by the building and the exhibit and *present* at the moment of the drop are all key to the experience. Immersion seems to promise a sense of undifferentiated wholly being there, following an aesthetic of the sublime where visitors are awed by a wonderful world to which they are fully subjected and have no option but to surrender. However, the design of narrative environments examines and exploits the recognition that such experiences are woven together through careful multimodal and multisensory layering. Narrative environments are not aiming to produce either pure spectacle or exaltation. They are deliberately designed spaces that offer an experience of being inside, surrounded by, close to and present to particular content while enabling or provoking a standing apart from that content, to reflect on how the sense of immersion is constructed. This means that in critical narrative environments people are never fully present, in the sense of being totally submerged in a preconceived world in the form of a complete, enclosed, mesmeric environment-experience.

A sense of immersion is developed not only through being in a wrapped-around physical or digital environment but also by being with other people, for example, being immersed within a crowd or in a conversation. This sense of immersion is discussed through the phenomenological concept of the intercorporeal which grounds subject-to-subject relations, or intersubjectivity, and subject–object relations. These ideas are elaborated in both the literature of phenomenology, for example in the work of Thomas Csordas (2008), and psychoanalysis, as for example in the work of Jacques Lacan (1977) who interprets the research of Melanie Klein and Donald Winnicott.

In the everyday, immersion in the intercorporeal is taken for granted. The everyday implies an undifferentiated state, the unquestioned and unquestionable familiar. In critical narrative environments, people consciously choose to be immersed and can surrender or distance themselves, questioning what they see and feel. In this way, audiences come to their own thoughts that are not fully determined by the narrative. Critical distance is advocated by Berthold Brecht (1978) in his epic theatre, in which dramatic illusion, or suspension of disbelief, is established only to be disrupted by various techniques, for example, when the characters break with the dramatic construct to address and acknowledge the audience directly. This breaks the fourth wall, the imaginary screen across the front of the stage which separates the world of the audience from the world of the actors. Rather than presenting an entertaining, self-contained fictional world, the Brechtian didactic points out to the audience that the action on stage has direct implications for their lived world, forcing them to reflect on the meaning of the action on stage for their own actions. In these situations, audiences pivot back and forth between immersion in illusion and conscious critical reflection on their immersion in their own 'reality'. In critical narrative environments, audiences have already penetrated the fourth wall. They do not abandon themselves wholly to whatever level of illusion is being presented, partly because they are always perceiving as a body in motion and partly because critical narrative environments ask people to reflect on their perceptions.

A sense of presence is also important in discussing immersion. Rhetorical techniques in such media as language, sound, photography, painting and spatial design can produce a vivid and palpable sense of being present. Indeed, the choice of media is crucial to how quickly a sense of presence is conveyed. For example, Perelman and Olbrechts-Tyteca (1969: 117) note that certain masters of rhetoric, with a liking for quick results, advocate the use of concrete objects to move an audience. The example they cite is the bloody tunic of Caesar that Anthony waves in front of the Roman populace to add a strong sense of presence to his argument. Presence is used not just as a display but is part of a persuasive practice making a case for what is real or true. As Perelman and Olbrechts-Tyteca (1969: 118) say, "Presence, and efforts to increase the feeling of presence, must hence not be confused with fidelity to reality".

Professor of theatre and performance Andy Lavender describes how a sense of presence in a fictional world has been pioneered over the years by theme park designers. They offer mass market immersion in scenic 'scapes', consumer-centred experiences that evoke pleasurable sensation, stirring memories and stimulating sentimentality. In contrast to critical narrative environments, the purpose is not to promote critical thinking but rather to enter the fictional world more fully through rides, exhibitions and performances, stunts and technological wizardry. Lavender (2016) argues that, above all, theme parks provide experiences of encounter. Members of the public are put on stage.

As people stroll around the theme park, they expect characters to pop up and provide magic moments to record. The photos act as tangible proof of co-existence in the fictional world. The spectator is incorporated and becomes the subject around which the theme park is choreographed.

The relationship between presence, non-critical and critical immersion can usefully be understood from the point of view of the design of narrative environments in the following three ways. First is the empirical and positivistic understanding of being in the presence of an object, as in daily life, where the object is simply there. It can be observed and contemplated for its aesthetics, valued for its utility or taken as evidence or data. This is immersion in a presumed universal reality where context and environment are taken for granted. Second is non-critical immersion where people perceive objects to be part of an argument about the nature of reality, for example, an object on display in a museum where the context and environment cannot be taken for granted. Museum goers are aware that the museum is designed to encourage them to go on a quest for meaning. This forms part of the social practice of museum going. Third is critical immersion where people are not only interpreting objects but also questioning the context and environment, for example, questioning the narrative of a city redevelopment and asking themselves how that impacts on their own responsibilities and ambitions with their related ethical, legal or political dilemmas.

The Museum of the Future, Dubai

Critical immersive spaces have been developed for educational narrative environments in, for example, the Museum of the Future, Dubai. Noah Raford, Futurist in Chief for the Dubai government and Acting Executive Director of Museum of the Future, firmly believes that immersive storytelling captures people's imaginations in a far more compelling way than the traditional display of objects and labels. This has been proven by his experience of the development of the Museum of the Future. The first iteration of what was to become the Museum of the Future came about when Raford was working in the foresight and innovation team in the UAE Prime Minister's Office. The UAE Minister of Cabinet Affairs, now Minister of Cabinet Affairs and the Future, asked him to develop an exhibition on the future of government services including education, healthcare and security. The idea was for it to be a relatively traditional showcase of new technologies that could be important in the future. However, through his background in design and his PhD at MIT, Raford was part of an emerging group of practitioners who were fusing experiential design with foresight and scenario planning. The traditional discipline of foresight involves researching possible futures and developing a range of future scenarios. The discipline originated in the 1960s from a variety of sources, but was most often practised in either quantitative, analytical, operations research and military planning environments or in more corporate strategy fields. At best, these exercises would result in PowerPoint presentations or long text-based documents. Working with his contemporaries, Raford envisaged a far better way to engage the public in the future.

To create the first Museum of the Future, Raford invited two colleagues to help him envision the approach: Dan Hill, who, at the time, was CEO of Fabrica, Benetton's design research think tank in Italy and Matt Cottom, co-founder of the international experience design firm Tellart. He then assembled a team of the most interesting practitioners working at the time, including Stuart Candy and Jake Dunagan, two leaders in the technique of experiential futures (Candy and Dunagan 2016), Anab Jain and Jon Ardern from Superflux, among others.

Experiential futures aim to use design to create, iterate and explore future worlds and communicate them through tangible and emotional experiences. Instead of reports, the approach produces graphics, videos, scenography, set design and speculative industrial design, building full-scale, walk-in narrative experiences of possible future worlds. The goal is to enable those people who encounter the multisensory environment to develop insights about the worlds created and to imagine further objects, diverse situations, related systems or experiences that the future world may bring.

Raford was inspired by artist and technologist Julian Bleeker, of Near Future Laboratory, who developed and advocates the concept of design fiction, a term first coined by Bruce Stirling in 2005 when he was developing the concept of diegetic prototypes, objects that notionally have fallen from a future world and which suggest systems and experiences in that world. Bleeker (2009) argues that by combining design, science fact and science fiction, future worlds can be envisaged and partially materialised. He noticed *Star Trek* fans were already creating objects based on future worlds. He suggested design fictions developed by multidisciplinary teams could quite quickly and cheaply combine science trajectories, foresight, design thinking and speculation to visualise 'what if' scenarios that encompass the impact of new technologies on the everyday. Raford found he was in the fortunate position of being able to bring these cutting edge creative practitioners together for the first time and to explore this approach at a scale never before possible.

The result was a three-day pop-up exhibition at a Davos-style event in Dubai in 2014 called the Government Summit. It became hugely successful and set the template for an annual event, which has now run for seven years in a row, establishing the case for a permanent Museum of the Future, scheduled to open in 2020. Delegates at the Summit were ushered through a little black door in a big white wall, with no explanatory signage, where they moved through a series of rooms about the future of border control, education, healthcare and other services. For example, after entering through the door to the experience, visitors found themselves in a dark corridor being welcomed by someone with a tray of hand towels. Each guest was given a cool, moist towel, which is a traditional Arabic gesture of welcome. Looking down the corridor, visitors could see a psychedelic tunnel of lights and a scanned representation of themselves at the very end. As they walked down the corridor, the lights and the sound responded to them, suggesting they were being scanned. Signage on the floor also indicated that their travel history and baggage were being tracked and monitored and that this was a border control experience. At the end of the corridor visitors were met by a friendly smiling person who took the hand towel and dropped it into a scanner clearly scanning visitors for infectious diseases. The goal was to reimagine the experience of arriving in a new country, using contemporary technologies to transform it from an intimidating, bureaucratic interrogation to a warm and welcoming experience. It was only at the end that it was revealed to the visitors that they were experiencing a vision of the future of travel arrivals.

The ritualistic border experience was also intended to slightly disorientate people. This disorientation borrows from immersive theatre and the work of anthropologist Victor Turner (1969), who says disorientation takes participants into a liminal space which causes them to question what is real and what is not. From this border experience, visitors were led to an even more puzzling space, a large bathroom where the only clue was a sign that said 'Healthcare of the Future'. Instead of a hospital or a clinic, visitors discovered four mirrors, each with sinks and no instructions about what they should do. The visitors had to work out what to do next, which was part of the principle of the design. The approach prompted them to build a sense of their own narrative and interpretation of what was happening around them, increasing 'buy-in' and emotional resonance. Those arriving later in the space saw others interacting with the mirrors and sinks and followed suit. Although the mirrors looked like regular bathroom mirrors, they were actually 'magic mirrors' that were activated when approached. They provided a short interactive experience which both welcomed visitors while offering a check-up from an AI doctor. Although interactive, the mirror was not actually scanning people's health in any way. Instead, it acted as a convincing simulation to demonstrate how AI personal assistants, sensors and ubiquitous computing could transform healthcare, performing many of the tasks of a doctor or clinic invisibly and effortlessly in your own home. One narrative loop of the mirrors, for example, observed that, "you've been travelling quite a lot, two of your colleagues had colds at the office and so your chance of getting a flu is 15% higher today. Should I put more vitamin C in your breakfast?" After engaging with the mirrors, visitors could interact with other objects around the bathroom, showing how such an integrated, home health care system might become a part of daily life.

The first Museum of the Future experience was quite successful. Not only did people say they enjoyed it, but the design team did not have to provide laborious explanations of policy on AI and how preventative medicine in the public health care system might be implemented. People understood both the opportunities and challenges instantly and viscerally by interacting in the world of the story. One of the more surprising but powerful lessons was the importance of small design details, such as the small mirror plate which, when touched, glowed blue. The glow was a narrative device to help communicate the fact that the plate was not only a mirror but also a health-check device, demonstrating that in the future people would get a daily diagnosis from their AI doctor as they were going about their morning routines. This simple, physical act dramatised the concept of giving permission to share such sensitive data, prompting a deep dialogue among visitors about healthcare policy and data privacy. Numerous visitors asked whether their data was actually being scanned and, if so, where this information was going. Even though they were told it was not real, many visitors reported a sense of anxiety related to scanning and data gathering. This reaction highlights the power of an immersive approach which, in this case, helped Raford and his team to provoke an intense conversation among visitors about the positive potentials of such approaches and also the crucial social concerns they raise.

Raford thinks that the immersive futures approach is even more important in the present media communications climate. He observes that we are constantly assaulted by imagery and advertising in today's media-saturated age and it is often impossible to tell what is authentic or what is trying to influence us. Much of our experience is mediated by our mobile phones. As a result, a direct physical immersive experience, where important questions are implicit in the narrative, is a rare treat. This kind of fulfilling experience creates an exceptional opportunity to open a dialogue that people might otherwise be too cynical or anxious to engage with. He thinks that using the visitor's body in an exhibition in this way, calling on real-world experience to get people to interact, is quite uncommon. He sees it as a form of constructivist learning. For Raford, these environments are ways of interacting and creating our narrative of the world together through experience and discussion.

> The future is unmade. It is first a conversation about ourselves, today; what's possible, what we fear, what we desire, but we only can make the future by engaging with it.
>
> (Raford 2018)

The goal of the new, permanent Museum of the Future is to scale up the approach developed by Raford and his team to a full-time, constantly changing, massively immersive experience, in order to create a global conversation about the future and develop means to envision and test aspirational technologies and policies for the UAE Government.

Although clearly profoundly effective, there are some obstacles to using an immersive, experiential strategy, Raford observes. The scale has to be large enough that people can enter and move around it, which requires considerable resources to execute properly. The number of people you can reach is also smaller than the audience size of a movie release, for example. He and his team are currently experimenting with how they might use broadcast formats like film, virtual reality or games engines to offer a version of the Museum of the Future to a larger audience without them having to be physically present.

He suggests the current isolating quality of the virtual reality experience will soon be overcome in the transition towards social virtual reality. However, he suspects virtual reality will not replace immersive physical experiences. He thinks more experiences, such as escape rooms and other story-like games, will be developed. These games provide cognitive absorption and emotional and physical immersion, prompting participants to act and interact.

Overall, Raford believes immersive narrative environments are not only an effective way of creating remarkable experiences, but also activate visitors. He sees this as potent and timely given today's political context where so many of us, he says, feel anxious and disengaged, cut out of the halls of power, without agency to shape the unfolding of the world around us. He explains that the Museum of the Future aims to produce an environment where people can reacquire a sense of agency in their lives and become actively involved in affecting the future. They are not just learning about the future, as if it was already set in stone, but will be actively developing the potential to change the future through their behaviour. This message is supported by the larger activities of the Dubai Future Foundation, which is the parent company for the Museum of the Future and an important part of the Dubai government's policy and investment apparatus. The Dubai government is investing not just in an entertainment centre but also prototyping a more effective way of drawing people into vital conversations about their future in order to create better policy. Raford says the entire Future Foundation is therefore a kind of armature, taking conversations out of the museum and making them real in the world. This combination of powerful immersive experiences and action-oriented policy-making is unusual and Dubai is a key leader in this area.

Worldbuilding

This initiative in Dubai could be seen as an example of 'worldbuilding' (von Stackelberg and McDowell 2015). Worldbuilding, in this context, is understood as part of the process of writing novels, video-game development, role playing games and creating design fictions. It is also used in foresight scenario-building. The author or authorial team research and synthesise numerous factors to develop an imaginary world, sometimes a whole fictional universe. A coherent logic is developed encompassing spatial relationships and geographies; histories and social conventions; materials and technologies; economic, political and legal systems; and cultural conventions and metaphors. The logic is partly constructed through a collaborative sense-making process (Raltonen and Barth, 2005), whereby imaginary future worlds are developed by multidisciplinary teams examining, discussing and aligning past, present and future circumstances. Teams may consist of designers, storytellers, scientists and technologists and experts in the humanities. The envisioned world is then populated by particular people or personas, that is, invented characters who are given individual traits that shape their needs, desires and behaviours. Personas are used as agents who further develop the constructed world through their behavioural repertoires. Worldbuilding can produce multiple layers of backstories that can be fleshed out and revised while developing specific characters, events and messages. The process provides a contextual framework that is rich in possibilities.

One of the pioneers in this field is Alex McDowell of the USC School of Cinematic Arts in Los Angeles who, in 2008, founded the World Building Institute. McDowell is renowned for the production design of films such as *The Crow* (1994), *Fight Club* (1999) and *Minority Report* (2002). McDowell (2016) explains that for *Minority Report*, Stephen Spielberg asked him to develop a fictional world without a script. This world needed to be a feasible future reality not a science fiction. It needed to be a world that people could recognise but that was clearly in the future. Linear narratives then emerged from the dramatic conflicts in that world. "World building is understanding the world deeply enough so that stories spring almost effortlessly from that base world" (McDowell 2016). He sees the base world as a horizontal slice into which storytellers can delve to query problems and create new stories. He emphasises that base worlds are highly volatile and complex and they can produce multiple narratives. For example, at the 2014 Science of Fiction Festival, run by the World Building Institute, 300 participants wrote 1,000 stories in 2.5 hours derived from a city called Rilao, set on a fictional archipelago in the Pacific Ocean, with aspects of both Los Angeles and Rio de Janeiro. It was used to imagine the impacts of a nation-wide plague and also new architectural approaches to the challenges of overpopulation. As well as narratives, Rilao was used to create future foods and to prototype future objects.

McDowell makes the point that worldbuilding can be used for developing linear film. However, it is also very appropriate for mixed reality and virtual reality worlds. In addition, it can be used for interactive games where multiple players take different trajectories, generating or experiencing different stories that emerge from the logic of the world. The important innovation is that these worlds can offer multiple non-linear story experiences and fully digital virtual worlds, such as McDowell's *Leviathan* project.

Films can impact the real world, for example, *Minority Report* generated more than 100 patents for new technologies based on those imagined in the film, such as gesture controls for computers and self-driving cars. However, McDowell thinks that worldbuilding may have more potential than film to impact the world directly, addressing such challenges as climate change and urbanisation. To substantiate this contention, he worked with the Al-Baydha Foundation to assist an impoverished Bedouin village in Saudi Arabia which was seeking to reverse desertification. Together with local residents, he and his team built a scenario of a possible future village. They developed a VR model of how they imagined sustainable architecture, sustainable agriculture and new irrigation systems would work. The government was persuaded to grant the land use by the arguments conveyed through the VR model. Observations derived from worldbuilding can identify problems and opportunities that might be missed by traditional top-down government-led or aid organisation-led initiatives. Immersive narrative environments, as well as being tangible places, can also be a powerful mode of argumentation. The tripartite model of the design of narrative environments can be seen as a rudimentary frame from which such worldbuilding can begin, gradually becoming more complex as the nodal points themselves become more detailed network models and new deictic centres for understanding the emerging worlds are established.

Fair Enough: The Russian Pavilion for the Venice Architecture Biennale 2014

International writer, curator and designer Brendan McGetrick has explored how irony can be deployed through immersive narrative environments, specifically in *Fair Enough*, an exhibition held in the Russian pavilion for the Venice Architecture Biennale 2014 which he co-curated with Anton Kalgaev and Dasha Paramonova. That year, architect Rem Koolhaas, the overall Biennale Director, challenged all the national pavilions to respond to a single concept. He argued that, over the course of the past century, 1914–2014, nationally distinct and recognisable architectural styles had turned into a generic, universal modernism, as demonstrated by, for example, the near indistinguishable character of the new business districts of London, New York, Shanghai and Moscow. Koolhaas sought responses to this premise by inviting each participating nation to tell the story of the last century of their architecture. McGetrick and his co-curators reflected that, although there was some truth to the assertion, distinct national architectural styles nevertheless persisted in Russia and elsewhere. Rather than using the exhibition to prove or disprove Koolhaas's claim, they decided to engage the architect's theory through the show's form. In order to provide a context for the past century of globalised modern architecture, McGetrick and his collaborators transformed the Russian national pavilion into a simulated trade fair where Russian architectural styles and concepts from the last 100 years were packaged, branded and sold as viable responses to contemporary desires and needs. Through its form as much as its content, the exhibition argued that the universal modern aesthetic that Koolhaas identified is enabled and disseminated through global commercial gatherings, especially expos and trade fairs (see Plates 7 and 8). It is at these events that the architectural standardisation in style, materials, business plans and engineering techniques is established and spread. The most influential architecture and engineering firms are now vast, multinational corporations so, for example, when a certain kind of curtain wall or technological break-through is developed, it is quickly disseminated across the world (Figure 7.1).

The curators designed their trade fair to be entirely believable. They took an earlier twentieth-century Venetian pavilion and put a drop ceiling into it and filled it with anonymous mass produced booths. They took 20 Russian architectural ideas from the last 100 years, updated them to show how they would be relevant to contemporary problems and then presented them as if they were for sale as products and services. Each idea had its own booth and corporate identity, making the exhibition also a commentary on the commercial language in which architecture and design are now most often expressed and advocated. The show was ironic or tongue-in-cheek but it was also sincere in that the curators selected the projects they thought had genuine value and identified problems that really mattered.

> Humour is a tool for delivering uncomfortable truths in an entertaining way and, especially at the event like an architecture biennale, a little bit of humour goes a very long way. So, I think you can and should be funny, but that only works if you're dead serious about your message and why it matters.
>
> (McGetrick 2018)

The show was not postmodernist cynicism. The curators believed that many Soviet architectural ideas remain valuable, even though they have been discarded. The initial architectural projects may have failed or been abandoned in the Soviet Union, but the

Figure 7.1 Russian pavilion opening, Venice Architecture Biennale, 2014.

curators wanted to show that the central impulse behind them remains valid and that they could have a new life. For example, communal apartments, designed right after the revolution by some of the most radical architects of the day, created prototypes of communal living, liberating women from having to cook, rethinking how family and interpersonal relationships could work. The curators took as their example the avant-garde, constructivist Narkomfin Building in Moscow, a revered project among modern architects that is now in a state of ruin. They proposed that it is still a radical design that can provide a model for some of the defining typologies of our time, including co-working and co-living spaces, experimental schools and even prisons.

The curators created original companies for all of these ideas. They invented names, slogans, merchandise and pamphlets, in order to deliver real architectural information. They gave the architecture a corporate language, making a comment on the commercial dimensions of architecture but also critiquing the Venice Biennale itself which puts on a veneer of sophistication but is, for many, a self-promotional event. McGetrick and his co-curators undertook a huge amount of research including numerous interviews with experts in order to develop the project concept and translate it into a corporate format. All the 'corporate' materials were distributed in the trade fair cubicles. At the opening, each cubicle was occupied by academics masquerading as sales people. They pretended, for example, to sell services such as El Lissitzky enterprises. They were, in fact, experts on those architectural styles who could answer visitors' questions in impressive depth. This was just one way of communicating the content. The curators installed multiple layers of communication. There were large signs for the most superficial engagement, slogans for one level lower, handouts and materials in the booths for next level down and finally the 'sales person' to facilitate conversation and debate at a deeper level. Many visitors

Figure 7.2 Communist architecture training booth, Russian pavilion, Venice Architecture Biennale, 2014.

took it to be a real trade fair. This may suggest that people, especially at that time, during the height of the Crimea invasion, had such an ungenerous opinion of Russia that they assumed the Russians had sold their pavilion to a commercial trade fair organisation. The fact that visitors believed that *Fair Enough* was a straight trade fair was borne out by, for example, the overwhelming, non-ironic response to one booth which masqueraded as a tourist agency, called Archipelago Tours. It appeared to offer world tours solely based on the works that Soviet architects built in places like Mongolia, Vietnam and Cuba. During the first week of the Biennale alone, the booth's 'sales rep' collected over 100 email addresses from people who wanted to go on these tours (Figure 7.2).

McGetrick describes *Fair Enough* as a totally immersive experience that delivered much more than a book or a website could, because it provided a fourth dimension in which visitors could actually enter and cultivate social interactions in the world of the story. It was a parallel universe, a complete, designed environment that was entirely geared towards communicating content and establishing a specific atmosphere in order to make a larger point about the state of Russian architecture and capitalism. "The project was played completely straight, never winking" (McGetrick 2018). Controversially, the curators even added hostesses in short skirts which offended some visitors but women dressed like this are typical of the Russian environment and the curators decided that they were needed for the complete veracity of their narrative environment. Some people were annoyed but McGetrick believes it is acceptable to be misunderstood as long as you are sure you have fulfilled your intentions. In this case, the curators' intention was to provoke and to destabilise the narrative sustaining the Biennale's flattering self-image. In pursuit of this, they willingly accepted that visitors come with different needs and aspirations and they would not be able to please them all with the proposed deictic shift.

Edible Stories

Immersive narratives can also take the form of sensory leisure experiences, such as the dining events designed by Chloe Morris who founded Edible Stories in 2012 when she graduated from MA Narrative Environments at Central Saint Martins. Morris was interested in food, interiors and stories. She had a background in interior and product design and wanted to combine all her skills and interests. Over the years she has developed her design process but her starting points have remained the same. She either begins with a story and chooses an appropriate space or she finds an extraordinary space that evokes a story. She launched Edible Stories by developing self-generated projects. Then she found herself being commissioned by private clients who have personal stories or favourite childhood memories they wanted her to communicate through an event. She also went on to work with corporate clients to tell brand stories.

Morris (2019) lets the food do the telling. She says it is the way guests interact with the food, the way that it is served and the way they consume it that tells the story. As a creative director, her first step is to research and develop a conceptual framework for the menu. The menu then acts as the structure for the storytelling, the design of the space, the timing and choreography of the unfolding experience. Each dish evokes a story section. As part of her development process she maps the dishes and the anticipated guests' actions against the story content. She makes mood boards and sketches of the environment and, based on those, she identifies exactly what elements need to go into the space.

Sometimes she needs to do a significant amount of research to develop the story. In 2014, she was commissioned to design and produce a brand experience to promote a Guatemalan rum for the Ron Zacapa brand. The rum is particularly fragrant because it is infused with herbs. She researched the rum production process, the environment, the history of the area and the local culture. She discovered the production included infusing the rum with 23 different herbs and the stages of the rum production were undertaken at different elevations in the landscape. The different elevations provided the story structure and logic for the menu. She found a dish that related, for example, to the sugar cane fields 350 metres above sea level and another that related to the oak barrels 2,300 metres above sea level. She also discovered a local tradition in which people tell stories in the dark and that the stories were said to bring light. All these factors inspired her design.

For the event, each of the 30 guests was picked up in taxis from their workplace. They listened to Guatemalan music as they were driven to the event venue and were offered a small rum taster en route to relax them and orientate them to the evening. On arrival, they were blindfolded and led into a darkened, fresh smelling space infused with Guatemalan herbs. They did not know where they were, whether they were above ground or underground. The space was very raw with a simple curved brick ceiling and brick walls. It evoked a house in the clouds, a setting from a traditional Guatemalan story. There was one big dining table constructed from plain wood fencing with a massive centrepiece made of herbs, earth and beeswax candles from Guatemala. All the materials were natural and produced an earthy smell. On arrival, guests took off their blindfold and lit a beeswax candle. The lights turned on and the story began. Morris invented a ritual that would emphasise the herbs which were an important differentiating factor for that particular rum. The client was cautious about any negative connotations associated with the idea of a ritual but Morris explained that if the guests performed an action they would have a heightened memory of the evening as part of a shared experience. So, before the first dish was served, a brand ambassador explained that this rum was unique because of the infusion process and the guests were each invited to pick up a different herb and simultaneously clap with the herbs in their hands. They filled the space with the smell of the herbs. Being natural smells, they did not linger but worked together and created a warming atmosphere. Morris also got guests to light hay on their plate to connect the story, the location, the smell, the action, the taste and the sight of the food. The brand ambassador came in at the end with a summary and closed the evening by taking the guests out to reveal where they were: in an arch under Putney Bridge, London (Figure 7.3).

For Morris, the setting can be very minimal. It is the taste, smell, sound, interaction and the sequence of the food that carries the story and can be more evocative than a complex visual stage set. In fact, she thinks the set can get in the way of people's imaginations. She pays careful attention to selecting the style and material of the cutlery and crockery appropriate to the story. She has experimented with cutlery. For example, she has served a cocktail in a plate rather than in a glass and provided paint brushes as cutlery in her '50 Shades of Grey' experience because paint brushes suggested experimenting and this was relevant to the story. She never makes it awkward for people by designing too many unexpected or unusual elements that can disorient and confuse them. She occasionally uses text clues, for example, in her 'Alice in Wonderland' experience guests were served edible white roses and red syrup. On the syrup bottle it said, "painting the roses red". She says people will talk to each other naturally throughout the evening, or after one or two glasses of wine, so there is little need to set up artificial prompts to

Figure 7.3 Guests being blindfolded, the Ron Zacapa Reserva Limitada dining experience, London, Chloe Morris, 2014.

interaction. She only uses games when they are appropriate to the story so, for example, when she produced a 'Matilda' experience, which was all about magic and a school environment, she provided chalk boards, scrabble letters, paper and crayons. The guests loved it; they made drawings of the characters, competed in making the longest possible word with the letters given and used the elements of décor such as ribbons in their hair, men and women alike. They became performers. She had not planned for this but she was pleased people had so much fun. She wants people to completely let go of their outside cares. She finds people want to learn all about the details of the back story and this creates added meaning to the experience and becomes part of the draw. Morris's work is sensory and celebratory. Although it does not appear to be overtly critical, it could be taken as a critique of the limited ocularcentric sensuality and narrow functionalism of many aspects of everyday life.

Virtual Reality and Immersion

In the early 1990s, transmedial narratologist Marie-Laure Ryan (2015) introduced the concept of immersion into literary studies by describing mental engagement in experiential virtual worlds, such as digital games, as equivalent to mental engagement in the actual world. Since the 1990s, VR has been gathering pace, driven by the games industry, which is striving to overcome the flatness of the screen and enable players to enter and inhabit virtual three-dimensional worlds. While some postmodern theorists, such as Jay Bolter (2001), critiqued the development of fictional VR worlds, arguing that naive visitors are reduced to passive consumers, nevertheless artists and designers have found ways to use VR to develop critical consciousness.

'We Live in an Ocean of Air' at the Saatchi Gallery, London, December 2018–May 2019, is an exemplary use of VR and narrative. It aims to raise consciousness about forms of reciprocity between human and plant life. It was designed by Marshmallow Laser Feast in collaboration with artists Natan Sinigaglia and Mileece I'Anson. Visitors wore VR headsets, clip-on heart-rate monitors, breath sensors and body tracking technology. The experience followed a narrative arc. Firstly, the visitors' breath was manifested as tiny, moving, coloured bubbles. Using data from the heart monitors, visitors appeared to see blood pumping through their hands. As a consequence, visitors could see others in the experience as a mass of moving dots so that they did not bump into each other. As they stepped forward, they were confronted by a giant life-size Sequoia tree which was also releasing bubbles, drawing a parallel between human and plant life (see Plate 9). Visitors, despite possibly experiencing a momentary hesitation, could walk through the bark into the tree's trunk. Rain then appeared to fall, which released upward energy streams, represented as rippling and intertwining coloured lines (see Plate 10). As people moved through the tree, they could interact with the energy streams, by making hand and body gestures, causing them to undulate and temporarily alter direction. As the experience continued, visitors appeared to float up the 30-storey-high tree.

There were ambient sounds and smells released into the space to increase the sense of total physical immersion. 'We Live in an Ocean of Air' combined photographic representations of the tree with graphic illustrations of the breath and energy streams. Marshmallow Laser Feast tends to apply a simple convention of first having a one-to-one familiar environment and then abstracting it. They have found, through iterative user tests and internal tests, that this sequence makes it easier for people to engage with the unfamiliar aspects of the experience (Figure 7.4).

Figure 7.4 Immersed in foliage, virtual reality encounter, *We Live in an Ocean of Air*, London, Marshmallow Laser Feast, 2019.

Robin McNicholas, one of the founders and the Director of Marshmallow Laser Feast, describes their work as XR, which, he explains, is variously interpreted as extended reality, experiential reality or expanded reality. They install their VR experiences in civic spaces, at festivals, such as the Sundance Festival, USA, and in art galleries and museums across the world. McNicholas (2019) thinks the emerging experiential sector is a convergent medium that uses multiple tools and skills. His background is in film, TV, live music and animation. The company has designers and technologists who share similar interests but they also invite collaboration from experts from such diverse fields as neuroscience to pastry cuisine.

Shared sensibilities within Marshmallow Laser Feast inspire their ongoing research and development through which they are seeking ways to redress the predominant gender bias towards male tech users. They repurpose tools, rebalance and apply ideas that they think are important, such as the wonderment of the natural world. They believe it is important to take a positive and celebratory angle and that overt political messaging about climate change does not get any traction. They want to embrace technology that attracts people who are curious, that engages young people and uncorks wonderment. They are exploring volumetric capture in virtual environments; they re-appropriate architectural tools to scan trees, forests and different foliage, working with developers to make quite sterile scans come to life in virtual space. In their project Sweet Dreams, designed for Sundance, they used live, processional theatre, food, drink, sensory floors and kinetic sets. They say they are mindful of narrative and see it as a huge challenge in the experiential context where dialogue, for example, can conflict with experiential sensory elements. McNicholas explains that much of the time visitors are slightly disoriented. They need time to understand the novel bodily experience of VR. He says the human ability to adapt to other forms of experience is underexplored and the possibilities are very exciting.

Marshmallow Laser Feast describes their pieces as embodied learning. Their research revealed that visitors found 'We Live in an Ocean of Air' an enchanting and calming experience. McNicholas says everything they make aspires to induce a sense of genuine empathy for the environment in which people are immersed. He emphasises the importance of 'on-boarding', in other words, setting visitor expectations before they enter the VR environment. He says people can then explore for themselves, with comfort, confidence and curiosity. This empowers and encourages them to discover more. He reflects that,

> In the age of distraction, it's slightly ironic that you have to put VR goggles on to focus the audience's undivided attention.
>
> (McNicholas 2019)

In other words, people need to be completely removed from the world in order to attend fully to the world (Figure 7.5). The danger with VR, of which Marshmallow Laser Feast is fully aware, may be that it seeks to replace people's imaginary storyworlds, over-writing them with highly sophisticated and compelling technological scripts. The overwhelming novelty may also leave little room for users to reflect on the relationship between this technological construct and the world in which they live. VR can trigger a sense of the sublime or awe which is beyond words and at the limit of experience, a situation that people go in to and come out of without learning anything. At worst, VR can be a packaging of the sublime and, as such, a technological equivalent to a certain kind of unreflective tourism.

Figure 7.5 Virtual reality encounter with streams of energy, *We Live in an Ocean of Air*, London, Marshmallow Laser Feast, 2019.

The examples above show narrative environments are about the lifeworld, even if they appear to immerse people in an illusory world. Immersive narrative environments highlight aspects of the lifeworld which are often overlooked or unseen. Immersive narrative environments may be humorous, entertaining and pleasurable but they are not seeking to distract people from the lifeworld, as a kind of escapism, but to engage with the lifeworld more fully. Narrative environments set out to encourage people to think relationally not discretely or positivistically. In recognising the double directedness of narrative environments, realised through the deictic shift that relates an illusory world to the lifeworld, the oscillatory or in-between status of narrative environments becomes apparent. They are tangible places, part of the world around us, and simultaneously symbolic constructs which make arguments about the world around us. A narrative environment is materially constructed, physically there, which people accept, but it is also presenting a hypothesis with which people may or may not choose to engage. If they do engage, people may accept or reject the hypothesis. In engaging with the argument, people are drawn into critical reflection about their lifeworld. The examples above exhibit the relational thinking needed to understand narrative environments as networks. Networks, as Latour argues, are simultaneously real, narrated and collective (Latour 2005: 6). In the tripartite narrative environments model, the real maps onto the environment node, the narrated maps onto narrative node and the collective maps onto the people node. The advantage of the tripartite network is that it allows people gradually to become aware of the densely interwoven contextual relationships in which they are embedded and, as the example of 'We Live in an Ocean of Air' shows, this may be especially important as people re-configure their understanding of their inter-relationships with other species and their environmental dependencies.

References

Bleeker, J. (2009) Design fiction: A short essay on design, science, fact and fiction. Near Future Laboratory. Online. Available HTTP: http://blog.nearfuturelaboratory.com/2009/03/17/design-fiction-a-short-essay-on-design-science-fact-and-fiction/. Accessed 17 September 2019.

Bolter, J. (2001) *Writing Space: Computers, Hypertext, and the Remediation of Print*, 2nd ed. Mahwah, NJ: Lawrence Erlbaum Associates.

Brecht, B. (1978) The street scene: A basis model for an epic theatre. In: Willett, J. ed. *Brecht on Theatre*. London: Methuen Drama, pp. 121–129.

Candy, S. and Dunagan, J. (2016) The experiential turn. *Human Futures*, 1, 26–28. Online. Available HTTP: https://wfsf.org/communications/wfsf-magazines. Accessed on 15 September 2019.

Csordas, T. J. (2008) Intersubjectivity and intercorporeality. *Subjectivity*, 22(1), 110–121.

Davies, C. (1998) Osmose: Notes on being in immersive virtual space. *Digital Creativity*, 9(2), 65–74.

Endsley, M. R. (1995) Toward a theory of situation awareness in dynamic systems. *Human Factors Journal*, 37(1), 32–64.

Heidegger, M. (1996) *Being and Time*. Albany, NY: State University of New York Press.

Lacan, J. (1977) *Ecrits: A Selection*. London: Tavistock Publications.

Latour, B. (1993) *We Have never Been Modern*. Cambridge, MA: Harvard University Press.

Latour, B. (2005) *Reassembling the Social: An Introduction to Actor-Network-Theory*. Oxford, UK: Oxford University Press.

Lavender, A. (2016) *Performance in the Twenty-First Century, Theatres of Engagement*. Abingdon: Routledge.

McDowell, A. (2016) World building. *Future of Storytelling Summit*. [video]. Online. Available HTTP: https://futureofstorytelling.org/video/alex-mcdowell-world-building. Accessed 17 September 2019.

McGetrick, Brendan (2018) Interview with Tricia Austin, 11 December 2018.

McNicholas, Robin (2019) Interview with Tricia Austin, 10 April 2019.

Morris, Chloe (2019) Interview with Tricia Austin, 23 January 2019.

Parsons, A. (2016) Sloterdijk and narrative environments. *Poiesis and Prolepsis*. Online. Available HTTP: http://prolepsis-ap.blogspot.com/2016/02/sloterdijk-and-narrative-environments.html. Accessed 7 September 2019.

Perelman, C. and Olbrechts-Tyteca, L. (1969) *The New Rhetoric. A Treatise on Argumentation*. Notre Dame, IN: University of Notre Dame Press.

Raford, Noah (2018) Interview with Tricia Austin, 14 December 2018.

Raltonen, M. and Barth, T. (2005) How do we make sense of the future? *Journal of Futures Studies*, 9(4), 45–60.

Rosenfield, K. (2014) Diller Scofidio + Renfro's "musings on a glass box" opens in Paris, *ArchDaily*. Online. Available HTTP: https://www.archdaily.com/563587/diller-scofidio-renfro-s-musings-on-a-glass-box-opens-in-paris. Accessed 2 February 2019.

Ryan, M. L. (2015) *Narrative as Virtual Reality: Immersion and Interactivity in Literature and Electronic Media*. Baltimore, MD: Johns Hopkins University Press.

Sloterdijk, P. (2006) Architectures an art of immersion. *Interstices: Journal of Architecture and Related Art*, 12, 105–109.

Turner, V. (1969) *The Ritual Process*. Chicago, IL: Aldine.

von Stackelberg, P. and McDowell, A. (2015) What in the world? Storyworlds, science fiction, and futures studies. *Journal of Futures Studies*, 20(2), 25–46.

Wigley, M. (2016) Discursive versus immersive. *Stedelijk Studies*, (4). Online. Available HTTP: https://stedelijkstudies.com/issue-4-between-discursive-and-immersive. Accessed 14 September 2019.

Websites

Marshmallow Laser Feast. https://www.marshmallowlaserfeast.com

Edible Stories. http://www.ediblestoriesevents.com

Diller and Scofidio. https://dsrny.com/project/musings-on-a-glass-box

Fair Enough, Venice Biennale. https://vimeo.com/97795897

Museum of the Future Dubai. http://www.museumofthefuture.ae

The Rilao project. http://worldbuilding.usc.edu/projects/rilao/

8   Framing and Reframing

Having looked at immersion in the last chapter, as what is conspicuous to experience, we now turn to what is, from the perspective of immersion, inconspicuous, that is, the framing apparatus of narrative environments that contextualises immersive experience. In narrative environments, the physical, tangible frame that literally surrounds a space is a primary vehicle through which the more intangible cultural, social and political frames are enacted. Together, the tangible and the intangible frames provide a lens through which visitors or inhabitants perceive and interpret narrative environments. However, over time, framings may become so conventional that they grow unresponsive to the dynamics of larger contexts in which they exist. They can harden and become fixed, appearing to be the *only* context. Fixed contexts in dynamic networks create tensions which lead to frame disputes, reframing and frame breaks. The examples below discuss the processes of framing and the transformative effects of changing the lens through which narrative environments are experienced. The chapter argues that for the design of narrative environments, the value of attending to framing as a topic is that it provides a method for realising poetic, critical and speculative narrative environments which result from a play of multiple contextualisations, experienced as co-existent centres for deixis or orientation to the world and to others.

Abundant physical frames are found in the urban environment. Lewis Mumford (1965) talks about the utopian city as a frame that respects the human scale. Kevin Lynch discusses the perception of edges in the city that enables people to imagine the boundaries of the area they are in. Urban planning theorist Mark Childs, discussing urban framing and reframing, writes. "Buildings, landscapes, public works, and other built forms embody aspects of narrative. ... They are, at least, settings that frame and evoke stories" (Childs, 2013, 50). One very particular type of urban space is the town square, plaza or piazza. City squares assume an urban system that bestows upon them the role of hosting civic events, bolstering civic pride, providing a place for social expression and sometimes commercial exchange. They are necessarily bounded by buildings and openings that, through their scale, design and materiality, symbolise the status and meaning of the square. The edges of the square are both physical and cultural frames that shape the narratives played out in them. Granary Square in North London is one such square. It is part of an enormous regeneration project that has been crafted with care from the abandoned Victorian buildings and erstwhile commercial transport hub of Kings Cross, with its canal, railway lines and arches, into a fashionable 'heritage' quarter (Figure 8.1).

The huge space of Granary Square is framed by Regents Canal on the south side with a backdrop of new buildings beyond. The renovated nineteenth-century Granary building on the north side houses Central Saint Martins, University of the Arts London as

Figure 8.1 Aerial view of the Kings Cross development, London, 2019.

well as new restaurants and offices. On the east and west sides, the nineteenth-century architecture has been modernised and new buildings added. Pedestrians can flow in from all sides. The Square has fountains that attract crowds, especially in summer, but is also heavily programmed with events, most of which are free. The events bring people together to create an atmosphere of conviviality. The large crowds give a sense of significance to the place. The physical frame of the Square creates a focus for actions. Images of the Square appear as promotional material online, on television and in the printed press, serving to reinforce its narrative in the public sphere (Habermas 2010). Individuals and groups of visitors take photographs from their own position or point of view. Many of these images appear on Facebook or Instagram producing a set of vistas and mnemonic points, for example, images of groups of friends, sitting on the Granary steps leading to the Regents Canal, show it is a relaxed and sociable space. Through its physical characteristics and media representations, Granary Square implicitly communicates its top-line narrative: industrial heritage has met contemporary design and created a spectacular new leisure destination for London. It plays upon people's imaginary sense of London's Victorian past and its current status as a world-leading centre of creativity and design. This narrative is explicitly communicated through the developer's website (KX 2019) where the tagline "The Story So Far" is used to describe the whole development in the area of Kings Cross which includes new homes, shops, restaurants, bars, offices, galleries, parks and schools. Granary Square has established its narrative, consolidated its physical presence and attracted hundreds of thousands of people to the area since it was opened 2012 and, as such, is a clear enactment of the tripartite network model at the top level of the design of narrative environments (Figure 8.2).

Further understanding of the networked nature of narrative environments can be pursued by looking at the theories of sociologist Erving Goffman. In his book *Frame Analysis: An Essay on the Organization of Experience*, Goffman (1974) examined

Figure 8.2 Granary Square, London, 2015.

everyday behaviour by studying face-to-face interaction. He developed a 'dramaturgical approach' to human interaction, suggesting that frames bring certain information to the fore, consciously or unconsciously and, as a result, shape values and assumptions that lead people to interpret situations in particular ways. Such frames can be thought of as a central organising idea in communication. He theorised that frames operate in four key ways: they define problems, diagnose causes, make moral judgements and suggest remedies. Applying these concepts to Granary Square generates some interesting insights. The space needs to be considered as part of the ambitious urban development undertaken by the developers, Argent PLC, in the Kings Cross area. A 67-acre site, the Kings Cross development is, at present, the largest brownfield development site in Europe. During the Victorian era, the Kings Cross area was a thriving industrial transport hub, with loading stations and warehouses connected by road, rail and canal to the rest of the UK. However, by the mid- to late-twentieth century the transportation of freight had largely moved onto the roads, leaving many of the warehouses at Kings Cross empty. The district became run down, dirty and unsafe, although some alternative music clubs set up there in the 1990s. The problem, the beleaguered abandonment of the area, was defined in the public imagination by reports of crime in the press. Poverty in the neighbouring communities was pictured in films, such as *High Hopes*, made by Mike Leigh in 1988, which used the area as a backdrop. Passers-by could see the urban decay for themselves. The causes included long-running and complex negotiations among local government, commercial and community stakeholders about how the area should be developed. Argent PLC created a vision, or remedy in Goffman's terms. The company followed *The Ten Principles for a Human City* (Argent 2001), in some ways taking a moral stance, envisioning an accessible, mixed-use city quarter that harnessed the value of heritage and promoted environmentally sustainable construction techniques.

In the masterplanning process, Argent focused on the public realm first. They defined the streets, squares and parks that connect different areas to produce a sense of unity and an infrastructure that would persist. They take the view that the streets will stay forever while the plots will come and go. Argent also responded to residents nearby who wanted to see the area become safe and clean. Anna Strongman (2019), Managing Partner at Argent, says the company mantra was to make Kings Cross part of the city, in contrast to being a gated community, as were many other urban developments at the time. The water fountains in particular have attracted local families. They are much more accessible than the fountains in Trafalgar Square, for example. Chairs and tables are set out for people to use for picnics. This approach recognises the preference for diversity and inclusivity among many Londoners and aspires to social equality but it has also brought commercial benefits. As a new slice of the city, the open and active narrative of Granary Square provides a sense of vitality. It has become a desirable, and consequently expensive, place to live or work (Figure 8.3).

The cost dimension brings a tension to the narrative. The social diversity is quite narrow in the fashionable restaurants and upmarket retail in the streets that lead off the Square. This flags up the dilemma of the remedy: How does a private corporation develop a public realm that encourages social inclusivity but at the same time make a financial profit? After all, corporations, unlike local governments, do not have the same duties and obligations to all members of the society (Garrett 2017). Businesses seek profit. The private development of areas designated as public spaces is a very contentious issue. Many people, such as Jack Shenker (2017), argue that private companies are increasingly creating zones of privilege in the city, exacerbating the divisions between

Figure 8.3 Granary Square Fountains, London, 2014.

rich and poor. Argent, to its credit, has engaged with community groups from the beginning of the project and sees them as partners in producing a better quality of urban space.

There is also a question of control. Argent has been criticised for keeping the Square overly clean so that, although the development appears boundaryless, the thresholds are defined by a certain cleanliness and the background presence of security guards. The danger is that Granary Square is scrubbed bare of any surprises, that there is little room left for unscripted actions and unplanned functions, the qualities identified as porosity by Richard Sennett in his vision of an ideal of urbanity where history is made. Sennett makes a case for open and plural narratives. In this context, Argent's curatorial policy can be seen to dictate to a large extent the sorts of events held in the Square and the surrounding spaces. Therefore, the narrative remains quite closed. For some, Granary Square could be thought of as a place of cultural consumption, rather than a place of cultural debate (Habermas 2010). Although it is a hugely successful project, Argent runs the risk of being perceived as instigating a sort of soft regime, in other words, subjecting people to a particular way of being rather than offering a space where people can be themselves (Pimlott 2018). Faced with this question, Argent maintains that it is looking for ways to make the curation of the space more open.

The success of projects such as Kings Cross is measured in financial terms and footfall but also in terms of public perception. Urban redevelopment depends more and more on visitors' and inhabitants' experience of the place and its interpretation, in other words, its narrative. The narrative of Granary Square and its location, Kings Cross, has been 'woven in' (Filep, Thompson-Fawcett & Rae 2014) and reinforced through formal and tacit alliances between the developers, the exhibitors, architectural organisations and the press. Edwin Heathcote of the *Financial Times* wrote, "The King's Cross site is the perfect mix of grittiness and shininess, simultaneously a symbol of London's industrial and engineering past and the creative present" (Heathcote 2013). People are so used to this process of urban regeneration they see it as natural, in other words, unguided and inevitable, a category of primary framing theorised by Goffman (1974: 22), who points out that motive and intent are not included in the frame. The way the visual, the material, the physical, the cultural and the economic are intertwined is sometimes described as place branding. Indeed, the words narrative, story and experience have been widely appropriated by city redevelopment and branding consortia, for example, "the narrative of the masterplan" (Buro Happold 2017) or "experience masterplanning" (Allan, Hobkinson and Hanna 2017) which combines commercial placemaking with place branding. The tools used are urban design, property management, marketing and value propositions that tell stories. The critique is that this commodifies heritage (Davies 2011) and uses narrative as a sales device that transforms local culture into a commercial asset (Pimlott 2018; Minton et al. 2018) limiting the possible uses of urban spaces (Parker 2017). If all experiences are subsumed to business, the narratives are hollowed of meaning, places become bland and, ironically, lose financial value. Rich and engaging city narratives stimulate political, social and environmental debate and action, as well as economic outcomes.

Reframing

Framing and reframing in urban development are mirrored in other sectors. For example, there is an intense debate in the cultural sector about how museums and heritage sites frame knowledge. This debate is unfolding at three levels which question the institutional character of, for example, the museum or the theatre; the kind of narrative content of, for example, the exhibition or the play; and the conventions of representation adopted in, for example, the exhibition making or the style of performance. In recent years, the intangible frame of the single authoritative voice in cultural heritage has been challenged by initiatives that aim to represent multiple, diverse voices and also embrace visitors' perspectives. A current example is 'HumanKind', a series of installations from 2019 to 2021 at Calke Abbey in Derbyshire, England. Calke Abbey was home to the Harpur-Crewe family, who joined the English aristocracy in the seventeenth century. In 1985, the National Trust took over the management of the property, which had become dilapidated. It was decided to repair, not restore, the site because the poor state of the building encapsulated the story of the decline of the English country house, symbolising the decline of the landed gentry across the UK. Slanderous myths had also grown up about the family's social ineptitude and reclusiveness. As late as the 1960s, reprints of diaries demonising the family were still in circulation. Although such scurrilous stories drew crowds to Calke Abbey over the years, their discriminatory nature has been recently criticised and the National Trust has sought to revise those compromising narratives.

The creative lead on 'HumanKind' was Julie Howell, an experience designer and spatial artist. Howell works inclusively with large groups of people in a co-creative process to reinterpret existing stories and bring hidden stories to light. She brought her repertoire to the project of transforming not just the story content but the story frame, repositioning the visitor experience around contemporary social issues. Taking themes that were thought to affect the Harpur-Crewe family as a starting point, such as isolation and the stigma of loneliness, Howell raises questions about the contemporary manifestation of related issues such as growing depression and suicide rates, bereavement, disability, slander and shame. These themes were generated through design development workshops run by Howell as a core member of the team of 40 academics, researchers, National Trust staff and volunteers involved in the project. The aim was not to restore the reputation of the family and the status of the aristocracy but to encourage visitors to consider the relationships between the context in which the Harpur-Crewe family were living and the current context through the lens of socio-political issues, inspired by, for example, the Jo Cox Foundation and the Campaign Against Living Miserably.

Howell (2019) explains that the process of developing HumanKind involved lengthy research into the family and estate archive in Matlock. This revealed stories of love, compassion, kindness and engagement with the world at large. The new archival research showed that Henry Harpur, the so-called 'Isolated Baronet', was far from isolated. He was a leading figure of the Enlightenment. He travelled widely, had eight children in a successful marriage and founded the Library at Calke. Prior to the project, there were no women's stories in the guidebook. The women and servants had been overlooked and removed from its history in favour of the dominant aristocratic male line. In HumanKind, four of the six people featured at Calke Abbey are women, including one of the servants and Winifred Harpur-Crewe, who returned to Calke to grieve for her husband whom she lost in the First World War after only one year of marriage.

Howell was responsible for turning the research into inviting, multimodal visitor experiences that would not only counteract the prevailing myths about the family but transform the narrative frame and prompt visitors to social action. Through the design, she wanted to emphasise the importance of social structure, family and a sense of belonging. She conducted a site survey and developed a map charting the visitors' anticipated spatial and emotional journeys. She decided elements of the exhibition needed to go into the landscape, to reach the visitors who only walk the grounds and never enter the house.

She subcontracted other designers: Anna Lincoln, who designed the graphics, and Lea Nagano, who designed the motion graphics.

Howell created several key moments in terms of the narrative arc to challenge and excite visitors, starting from their arrival. Walking the grounds, people can now see and enter three large, room-like interventions in the landscape. The life-size structures are made of mild steel and are built to the exact dimensions of the favourite rooms of the members of the family they represent. The open-air rooms include interpretations of key objects important to the occupants and each structure is completely powder coated with a colour relating to that specific family member. Howell aimed to strike an empathetic tone. In the meadow, for example, there is Winifred's Boudoir, a monument to her husband. On the lawn, the Library installation shows drawings by the 13-year-old Henry, scribbled in his school books. Far from being someone with a 'disease of the mind', the installation shows he had notable skills as an inventor (Figure 8.4).

Once inside the house, visitors see smaller, more intimate installations made with sound, light, animation and objects that convey the new material discovered by the researchers. There are no traditional text panels. The content is communicated through emotional and sensory experiences. For example, in the family sitting room, atmospheric projections roll across the walls showing the content of letters between Sir Vauncey and his mother, who was a well-known traveller and horticulturalist (Figure 8.5).

Howell designed numerous additional structures, such as bespoke seesaws to encourage people to interact, reading benches to encourage moments of reflection and 'Hopper tables' – named after the painter Edward Hopper, whose work often depicts isolated individuals staring through restaurant or hotel windows, these desks are divided by a Perspex barrier. The Perspex hinders conversation across the table but makes it fun, especially for children, to find new ways to communicate and overcome the obstacle.

Figure 8.4 Outdoor installation, *HumanKind*, Calke Abbey, UK, 2019.

Figure 8.5 Media installation, *HumanKind*, Calke Abbey, UK, 2019.

Howell's 'Pledge Walls' are located in the restaurant and gardens. They invite visitors to promise to donate to food banks or call up an old friend, for example. The aim is to encourage visitors to make human connections through such small acts of kindness in their own lives, to stem growing isolation in the UK today.

Howell's contribution to HumanKind follows her principles. She chooses to work in the physical spaces where the events she is recounting took place because she believes this gives visitors an authentic experience. She takes a strong feminist position on socio-political issues. In her work, she also aims to leave a legacy. In the case of HumanKind, several new initiatives have been fostered, including a volunteer research team at Calke, which continues to look for further evidence for future interpretation, and a kinder, more inclusive attitude amongst the staff and volunteers, which extends to include the visitors. In her approach to storytelling, in the context of the heritage industry, she recognises the need to deliver multiple perspectives to acknowledge that, as Bennett (2009) argues, the voice telling a singular, unquestionable truth is no longer acceptable. This has been exacerbated in the age of the internet, as all stories enter into a realm of debate and contestation.

The overall transformation of Calke Abbey, which also represents a significant change in the National Trust's previous approaches to site and heritage, can be understood in terms of a series of shifts: from ungrounded legends to contemporary issues; from aristocracy to ordinary people; from men to women; from acts of slander to acts of kindness; from neutral description to purposeful social action; from a single voice to multiple voices; and from exclusivity to inclusivity.

Reframing heritage is also underway in narrative environments at the scale of countries or nations. In the following example, Iceland, known for its remarkable landscape, is reinterpreted through a lesbian, gay, bisexual, transgender plus (LGBT+) lens. The company Pink Iceland was founded by lesbian couple Eva Maria Lange and Birna Hrönn Björnsdóttir in 2011. While studying for an MA in Tourism and managing the only gay café in Reykjavik, Eva met lots of LGBT+ tourists looking for something to do, not least finding a space where they might meet and interact with their fellow LGBT+ community. She conceived the idea of Pink Iceland as a business that would cater to this community and its allies. Its strength was that it had a well-defined market segment. In 2012, Eva invited Hannes Palsson, who was managing the gay bar above her café, to join them. Eva knew Hannes as someone who did a lot of pro bono design work for the LGBT+ community. Hannes loved the way the company promised to reframe both tourism and Iceland. He was happy to risk leaving a steady well-paid job for a concept he really believed in. Eight years later, the company has 12 core staff; nobody has ever left.

Palsson, having worked for large Icelandic companies who had stakes in numerous international, high-end retail businesses, had noticed those brands did not sustain a consistent tone of voice across their online services, their interaction in stores or how the staff communicated across the company or with contractors. In contrast, Pink Iceland worked very hard to develop a consistent tone of voice that expresses its core values and the experiences it offers across all the company's touch points. Although they are a 'for profit' company, they place their values above profits. As Palsson (2019) says, they are edgy and political, they can be humble or triumphant depending on the occasion. Their core value is honesty. As a queer company, they have a whole set of issues that many other companies do not have to contend with. They are dealing with vulnerable minorities and have important social responsibilities because they work in a world that assumes, and is designed for, heteronormativity. This means they have to anticipate and avert situations which could potentially be awkward for their clients, for example, at the hotel check-in, where same-sex couples might be given a room with two single beds; when a trans person who is not comfortable with either changing room at a hotel or a local pool needs their own space; where wedding photographers are taken aback or offended when shooting a same-sex kiss on a wedding day; and that LGBT+-friendly suppliers' policy follows through to floor staff. Pink Iceland is aware of 'gay-washing', where companies target an LGBT+ clientele but only to be perceived as progressive, modern and tolerant. The owners and staff of Pink Iceland are almost all queer and their principle is that to make their business successful they believe they have to give a genuine service addressing the community's needs.

The landscape of Iceland is their master storyteller. It is natural and unspoilt, humbling and inspiring. It changes with the unpredictable weather, with huge storms that can easily block the roads. The drama of the landscape and the weather are core to Nordic culture and Pink Iceland's organisation and services. Pink Iceland reinforces its connection to the locale by using pagan Nordic chieftains to conduct marriages. The chieftains call upon the ancient Norse Gods Odin, Thor, Freya and Frigg. Icelandic pagan religion is very welcoming to all denominations. Earth is the most important figure in their preaching. Conventional limitations on marriage thereby are dismissed. People are permitted to be who they want to be when they get married. Pink Iceland had a wealthy LGBT+ couple from Dubai and India. Despite their wealth, they had never felt safe to hold hands in public before they were married in Iceland.

Pink Iceland considers itself somewhat archaic in one way, since travel agents are practically unheard of in 2019, but they believe in the importance of curating an authentic experience. It has now started selling merchandise, sweaters and bags, not for profit but for ambassadorship. The company works on face-to-face recommendations, with

Figure 8.6 Tess and Alice's wedding, Pink Iceland, 2019.

their clients as their ambassadors. Following their principles of inclusivity, they do not exclude heterosexual customers. The LGBT+ identity filters out bigots, and the volatility of the weather means clients have to be sure they want an event whose choreography is open to an element of the unexpected or improvisation (Figure 8.6).

The workspace of Pink Iceland reflects its values. It has a large shop-front location on a main street in Reykjavik that allows passers-by to see in. The space is designed to reflect visually who they are and ensure LGBT+ clients are comfortable. There is an upside-down map of Iceland in the window, which signals that the company is queer. Inside, a rainbow is displayed; products are sold for Pride fundraising; the slogan 'keep calm and stay queer' is displayed on the wall; there are images of unicorns, an LGBT+ symbol, on the wall; and, following their principles of honesty and transparency, they display their tax returns and their carbon neutral certificate. The communal office has a huge 'Thankyou' wall covered in thank you notes (Figure 8.7).

The example of Pink Iceland clearly demonstrates the validity of the tripartite model in understanding how a narrative environment is designed and works. Pink Iceland links a specific group of people, the LGBT+ community, to a specific place, Iceland's landscape, and a specific narrative tradition, Icelandic pagan sagas. In doing so, they have reframed the narrative and the environmental resource that Iceland offers by redirecting it away from a potential for nationalist conservatism towards more liberal progressive, inclusive values. In other words, they have taken the pride that exists in respecting their long-running cultural traditions and their awe-inspiring landscape and translated them into a respect for the pride of being part of an LGBT+ intersubjectivity. The second reframing in which Pink Iceland engages is commercial in character. By adhering to the network inherent in the notion of narrative environments, Pink Iceland's business model

Figure 8.7 The Pink Iceland office, Reykjavik, Iceland, 2019.

remains faithful to the given narrative, environmental and human inter-connectedness. It does not assume that resources can be endlessly exploited. It recognises that they have to nourish each other, thereby promoting an understanding of sustainability.

These two examples, HumanKind and Pink Iceland, bring to attention framing issues that concern differences among conservatism, as the maintenance of the status quo in terms of power relations; conservation, as the prolongation of traditional cultural forms; and sustainability, as the continual maintenance of an open, inclusive and democratic society. This is one area of framing issues that concerns the design of narrative environments.

Reframing can take the form of subversion and surprise in order to bring issues to attention. Détournement is a French word meaning rerouting or hijacking and was adopted to describe one of the tactics of the Situationist International in the 1960s. Détournement, which inspired the culture jamming movement in the late 1980s, entails taking a well-known symbol that evokes an associated narrative into another context to subvert its meaning. Culture jamming aims to expose the commercial motivations underlying some cultural institutions and corporate advertising. It uses the language and rhetoric of the mainstream to critique that culture. One of the most well-known proponents of culture jamming is Adbusters, a global collective of anti-consumerist, pro-environment artists, designers and activists, founded in 1989 in Vancouver, Canada. It has created publications that critique corporate communications by generating spoof ads and placed products and poster campaigns in the urban environment. Notably, it initiated Occupy Wall Street, a protest that supports direct action to highlight economic systems that perpetuate uneven wealth distribution. One example of reframing that takes the form of a narrative environment was the intervention *Subverting the City with Adbusting* (Fuhrmann 2017). A group of artists and designers replaced adverts with their own printed artwork in Berlin's Kreuzberg district. The billboard hackers were making the case for citizens to have greater control over communications in their city streets, emphasising the tension between the city as a civic space and the city as a commercial space.

In her article *F(r)ictions: Design as Cultural Form of Dissent*, Mònica Gaspar Mallol (2010) turns to Michel de Certeau's (1984) notions of dissent through the unspectacular and the everyday. She also discusses the writing of philosopher, Jacques Rancière, who expands upon de Certeau's theories of laying bare the politics of daily actions. Rancière (2004) argues that fiction should not be seen as utopian tales but as a critique exposing everyday power relations concealed in the banal. He maintains that this prevents people becoming normalised and their actions and outputs being commodified. Strands of art practice follow this approach, for example, *Fake Estates* by Gordon Matta-Clark, a critical intervention in the New York real estate world. Starting in 1973, Matta-Clark purchased tiny lots in the city of New York, Queens and Staten Island through public auctions. Some of the lots were inaccessible and others were too small to enter. He documented, mapped and catalogued the lots in order to question the meaning and value of urban property and to reveal its contradictions. More so than the general intervention in Berlin, this is a more precise dispute in which Matta-Clark mocks the relentless logic of real estate valuation. By taking it to its logical conclusion, he demonstrates its inadequacy as a way of valuing the city.

An example of a critical narrative environment is *The Shed in Dulwich*, a restaurant that reached number one in London on TripAdvisor. The only problem for guests was that it did not exist. It was a hoax by journalist Oobah Butler for *Vice* magazine (2018), who sought to challenge TripAdvisor's hegemony in dispensing travel advice. This project disputes the validity of the online rating system as a valuation frame by questioning the correlation between online phenomena and geo-cultural reality.

The design of narrative environments also has a part to play in design activism and political protest. There has been a growing upsurge in political demonstrations in the West in recent years. This is partly a result of controversial government policies, economic and political turbulence across the world since the financial crash in 2007–2008 and a growing awareness of the worldwide environmental crisis. Street demonstrations are now attracting a wide mix of people and consideration is being given to the design of urban space that can accommodate democratic protest (Ford and Zogran 2017). The design of protest has become an area of research (Hatuka 2011) where activism is seen not as negative but as generative (Thorpe 2014). As well as considering the functional requirements for peaceful demonstrations, such as orientation devices, access, shelter and shade, designers need to consider the content and purpose, the narrative of the protest, which can be communicated through the choreography of the participants and the use of images and objects which are read against the meaning of the surrounding architecture. For example, from 2007 to 2015, Cuvry Brache, in the Kreuzberg neighbourhood of central Berlin, has acted as a narrative environment that questioned the meaning of the space. Threatened with gentrification since 1998, and being in the heart of a leftist community, it became a contested space and developed as a site for protest against profit-driven urban development (Carver 2018). In 2007, artists Blu and JR painted a huge mural showing two enormous figures pulling at each other's hoods. Other graffiti artists also drew images at the base of the wall. As a consequence, the site became an icon for the progressive Berlin scene. However, as can often happen to critical and political initiatives, its renown was appropriated. It was promoted on the city's tourism website and began to attract visitors. Nevertheless, it persisted as an encampment of 150 homes for anti-gentrification protestors until they were cleared in 2014, when the area was fenced off to make way for a mixed-use development. During this period Blu returned more than once and changed the mural. First, he outlined the figures and later blackened the background. Another artist added a large provocative extended middle finger and vulgar messages which were subsequently blacked over. When the site was cleared and the fence erected the mural was blackened out completely to prevent the murals from being used as a marketing tool. In 2015, other graffiti artists in Berlin restored the finger and the aggressive slogans. The whole mural wall is now obscured by new buildings. Despite its ultimate eradication, Carver (2018: 200) argues that the key concepts framing the dispute over the space since 1989 were "reunification, capitalism, gentrification, and the right to the city … [in] a complex and continually changing story", refracting the dynamics of the national and the international political economy. Again, this highlights the frame dispute between place as dwelling and space as an abstract system susceptible to financial capture.

Another example of reframing, manifest through protest design that takes a narrative form, is the urban interventions by Extinction Rebellion in 2019. Extinction Rebellion is a group of activists protesting about what has now become defined as the global climate emergency. They have adopted a strategy of peaceful civil disobedience, setting up camp and appropriating city centres in the UK, blocking movement and bringing business-as-usual to a halt for several days. They are disputing the city framed as a commercial flow. They actively interrupt the rhythm of commercial transactions by creating encampments and deploying large-scale objects as symbols. They bring painted life-size boats as a focus for the protest and a stage from which to speak. The first protest in London, which disrupted Oxford Circus, the heart of retail in London, used a pink boat with the injunction 'Tell the truth' in large capital letters on the side. Boats were chosen to evoke the ocean and rising sea levels. Their bright colours also speak of the energy and good will of the protestors. The destination of these boats has become significant in terms of the ongoing dispute: the pink boat was impounded by the police, while the blue boat has been put on display at the Maritime Museum London. One destination criminalises while the other legitimises the action.

Puncturing Boundaries

Narrative frames, as explained above, differ from frame stories. Narrative frames provide the perspective on a topic whereas frame stories are the overall story arc within which other stories unfold. Early literary examples of frame stories are the Indian classics, such as *the Ramayana, Seven Wise Masters, Hitopadesha* and *Vikram and the Vampire*. Boccaccio's *Decameron* contains 10 different stories within the overarching framing narrative. Perhaps the most famous framing narratives is *A Thousand and One Nights*. In the book, the Persian ruler Shahryār is outraged by the infidelity of his brother's wife and his own wife whom he has executed. In his anger and pain, he decides all women are deceitful and therefore proceeds to marry a succession of virgins and execute them the day after the wedding, before they have the opportunity to betray him. Eventually, the supply of virgins found by the vizier runs dry and the vizier's own daughter, Scheherazade, volunteers to be the next bride. On the night of her wedding Scheherazade starts to recount a story but withholds the ending. As a result, Shahryār postpones her execution. The following night she finishes the story but begins another. Readers hear her numerous tales of love, war, tragedy and comedy. After a thousand and one nights, Shahryār spares her.

Frame stories can also be observed in narrative environments. The narrative of a city quarter is expressed through its built form, use and reputation, nested within the overall narrative of the city in which it is located. For example, the historical narrative of Paris, as the pinnacle of artistic endeavour in the late nineteenth and early twentieth centuries, framed the more specific narrative of the Left Bank as a centre for the bohemian avant-garde. Interestingly, the Left Bank, as a legendary destination in the twentieth century, served to reinforce the narrative of Paris as a dynamic city. The narrative of the city quarter may frame the narrative of museums located within it. For example, the Mall in Washington leading to Capitol Hill implicitly expresses its identity and story as the centre of governmental power in the United States through its formal layout and grand architecture. The Mall houses the Smithsonian Institution with its 17 museums, 21 libraries and 9 research centres which, while addressing different topics such as science, history, art and so on, together form the largest museum cluster in the world. The narrative of the Smithsonian reciprocally substantiates the narrative of the USA as the most powerful nation in the world. Museums project overarching frame stories for the different narratives they host. For example, the science museum, Parque Explora in Medellin, Columbia, houses three subdomains with different narrative emphases: a science and technology park, an aquarium and a planetarium. Individual exhibitions provide an overarching frame story for specific objects, each with its own sub-story. The same principles apply in the digital world, where interactive interfaces can open up further nested sub-narratives. For example, Art+Com, the pioneering creative digital agency in Berlin, has developed numerous museum interactives that enable visitors to delve ever more deeply into specific stories. In 2012, at the Clock Harbour gallery of the Hamburg Museum, Art+Com designed and made a large, interactive media table called *The Emergence of Hamburg*. The installation is touch-sensitive and provides an interactive time travel experience of the city's evolution through 11 epochs from the Middle Ages to the present using pictures, film and text.

These nested narratives also exist in commercial narrative environments, for example, department stores that communicate their stories through their buildings, window displays, shop floors, scenographic installations around escalators, brands, goods and online information. The identity and stories of department stores are nested within the stories of particular shopping streets. Brand narratives are nested within department stores. Within the brand spaces, individual products with their own narratives compete for attention.

As mentioned above, while the overarching frame shapes and defines the scope of the nested stories within it, the nested stories can also impact the meaning of the overarching frame. This is used in culture-led city development through deliberately situating cultural buildings, such as museums, in run-down areas that are scheduled for regeneration. New cultural institutions can bring media attention to the area. They can attract new, well-to-do audiences and further investment. Critics argue that this is the instrumentalisation of culture, history or science for long-term profit in the urban development sector. It is an instance of the cultural sector being exploited or appropriated by market forces or in some cases, cynically aligned with profit-oriented businesses. Suzanne MacLeod (2017: 175) argues that museums can too easily become tools of commercial business or self-promoting local government:

> implicit in this colonisation of culture by market is the concomitant devaluation of civil society and of cultural engagement as a necessary investment in people and that side of their human being that is not about work or consumption.

Spatialised narratives can actively subvert such dominant market-driven forces. They can take the form of, for example, artists' walks that emerge from psychogeography (Debord 1956). Psychogeography involves dérive or wandering, usually in an urban context, taking non-official routes leading to surprise encounters and registering how the environment affects the emotions. A dérive might use playful rules to rid the walker of unconscious patterns of decision-making. While psychogeographers reject the status quo and surrender to chance, they also pay close attention to their feelings and their observations, using these to interrogate their surroundings. Recent years have seen a rise in activist walking, for example, Stalker/Osservatorio Nomade, first established in Rome in the 1990s. Stalker explained that they carry out their walks in 'void' spaces of the city, which have long been abandoned or considered problematic. They interact with inhabitants, gathering stories using walking as a form of discovery. They then apply knowledge and experience to address urban planning and territorial issues. Urban Interaction Design (UrbanIxD) (Waal and Lang 2014–) is a multidisciplinary practice that develops platforms to enable citizens to input into the governance of their own cities and, as such, is an activist practice that aligns with critical and participatory dimensions of the design of narrative environments. In Goffman's terms, they are provoking a frame transformation.

Metalepsis and Heterotopias

Metalepsis is a vital concept for the design of narrative environments. Stories usually have different diegetic levels which are conceived in narratology as perspectives given by different narrators who speak from different positions in relation to the story (Genette 1980; Ryan 2004). Narrators should not be confused with authors. Narrators are the invention of the author. In literature or film, there may be events told by an unseen narrator positioned outside the story and who describes the characters' actions using the third person, he, she, it and they. In movies, the narrator can be conceived as the unseen camera witnessing a scene (Bordwell 2008) in as much as the camera shot is experienced by the viewer as external to the story, telling you about the story. These are called extradiegetic narrators in narratology (Hühn 2019). They do not appear as characters in the story. Events may also be told from the perspective of the characters in stories in the form 'I' and, in film, the camera may switch from being a so-called neutral witness to showing the view of the protagonist. Here the narrator becomes intradiegetic, telling the story as a character from within the world of the story. Characters may also tell stories about another character in the narrative which becomes a third diegetic level. While these perspectives are not frames in the sense of being overall positioning contexts, as discussed above, they are nevertheless domains of interpretation with distinctive characteristics and boundaries. In the case of narrative environments in museums, for example, the extradiegetic narrator is constituted by the curator as a voice evident in the panel text which explains the causal logic of the selection and the relationships among the different elements in the exhibition. Intradiegetic narrators appear as witness testimony in video interviews, hand-written letters, personal photographs or artefacts collected or created by characters in the story. Visitor-generated content, which often takes the form of Post-it note comments at the end of the exhibit or a selfie taken by a visitor next to an exhibit and posted on Instagram for a different audience, are extradiegetic to the content of the exhibition but intradiegetic in terms of the visitor's own story of visiting the exhibition.

These different narrative levels usually remain distinct diegetic universes. However, elements from one diegetic universe can sometimes cross into another. This is called metalepsis. Ryan (2004) explains that, in literature, metalepsis occurs when the narrator interrupts the story with side remarks and as a result crosses the border from the outside to the inside of the world of the story. Characters or objects may also stray from one story into other stories. Examples in narrative environments would be the inclusion of modern television characters in traditional parades; art interventions in traditional museums (Putnam 2001) and the juxtaposition of different historical architectural styles in amusement parks. For recipients, this causes surprise and disruption, to humorous, fantastical or ironic effect. Metalepsis is one of the ways artists and designers make things strange and sometimes wonderful. This is a process akin to the artistic tactic of defamiliarisation (Shklovsky 1965) and to Brechtian epic theatre, which disrupts audience expectations about the nature of drama, and to the strategies used in culture jamming.

Metalepsis in narrative environments relates to literary and film practice but it takes a different character in narrative environments because narrative environments are multimodal. In narrative environments, the scope for metalepsis is extended because story in narrative environments is communicated through a variety of materials, objects or events. An example is the Walled Off Hotel designed by Banksy, a mile from the centre of Bethlehem, directly adjacent to the wall separating Israel from Palestine. The Walled Off Hotel takes a narrative about exclusivity and turns it into a narrative about exclusion. This translation is achieved, in part, through a pun which makes it seem as if the Walled Off Hotel is related to the Waldorf hotel chain. This shift turns what seems to be a simple narrative about luxury into a more complex narrative about the relationship between commercial exclusivity, since it is still an exclusive boutique hotel for art tourists, and political exclusion. The story medium is the hotel building with all its styling and performance. The hotel moves from one city narrative to another and in doing so gives rise to incongruity whereby a story of luxury and possession collides with a story of oppression and dispossession. It problematises the agency of tourists who have to confront their own position as commercial and political actors, as well as highlighting the double commercial and political status of the Waldorf and Walled Off hotels.

Both Marie-Laure Ryan (2004) and Alice Bell and Jan Alber (2012) have developed the concept of metalepsis discussed by Gerard Genette (1980). Bell and Alber modify Genette's model in order to define two modes of ontological metalepsis. The first category is vertical interactions between the lifeworld and the world of the story or between nested or hierarchised worlds of the story. The second is horizontal two-way migrations across worlds of stories. Bell and Alber discuss metalepsis in terms of interactions between ontologically distinct worlds rather than narrative levels as in Genette. The design of narrative environments takes ontological metalepsis to occur when characters or objects from the world of the story stray into the lifeworld or real figures or objects appear in the world of a story. This device has been used by artists such as Julien de Casabianca (2013–) in his ongoing 'Outings' project. He 'releases' characters from artworks into the urban environment and encourages others to follow his lead. He uses his mobile phone to photograph a figure in a painting in a museum. He then reproduces this, typically without specific permission, quite cheaply and quickly, as a large-scale print and pastes it to the walls of backstreets, car parks, hoardings and similar environments (see Plate 11). The contrast between the sumptuous historical images and dilapidated settings is extraordinarily striking. As part of the process, Casabianca shows interested passers-by and local residents, usually low income, non-museum-visiting members of the public, how they too can use his techniques to create their own 'Outing'. They create poignant narrative environments and they can often make poetic or political points about the circumstances of the places where they are located.

Performance artists Improv Everywhere (2014) also use metalepsis. Improv Everywhere, initiated in 2001, is a New York City-based collective that stages performances in unexpected public places. For example, on a very hot day in the summer of 2014, they set up a one-hour, unauthorised, luxury spa on the New York subway at 34th Street station. The performers rode the subway dressed only in towels. On arrival, they altered the station signage to read 34th Street Spa. They unfolded sauna tables and set up a welcome station, with lemon- and mint-infused water. They provided towels, hot stone massage and a misting station to cool passengers. The unexpected intervention played on the stifling heat of the New York subway. It transplanted the conventions of the sauna, as a calming therapeutic private experience, into the harried space of the public transportation system. This kind of place-based experiential contrast, taking one embodied situation and embedding it in another flow of events, turns the emergent situation into a narrative environment.

Augmented reality (AR) can also enact metalepsis. Pokémon Go is an example where Pokémon monsters appear in the everyday environment, albeit viewed through players' phones. Players said it gave them and their friends a kind of 'licence' to be in various places that they would not normally go, like parks and residential streets late at night. However, some Pokémon Go players have invaded government offices, hospitals and intruded into people's homes. Players were accused of treating the whole city as an urban playground without taking into account social, racial and legal barriers. This highlights that public spaces are not equally accessible to everyone. Geoff Manaugh (2016) writes about how some players caused physical damage which led to the consideration of new zoning laws, 'geofencing' augmented reality. This kind of thinking has prompted debate on who governs the augmented city and the politics and etiquette of gamified spatial narratives. AR is a new medium with unknown potential but there are numerous legal questions about where anyone can legitimately intervene and in what way: Can someone install something inflammatory over government buildings? How will people be protected from commercial interests flooding AR with advertising?

Metalepsis enables objects to take on two meanings simultaneously, which is why it is an intriguing device. In a further development of metalepsis, the concept of heterotopia, as discussed by Michel Foucault (1967), is being used to refer to the insertion of a narrative environment as a whole into the lifeworld. The transposition is not just of an object or character from the world of a story to the lifeworld or vice versa but the transposition of a whole environment. This is one way of defining a narrative environment. Narrative environments have a double meaning. They are both lifeworlds and worlds of a story at the same time. Visitors enter a narrative environment which is a storied world that nevertheless talks about or reflects upon their lifeworlds in the same media as the lifeworld is lived, while also incorporating discrete nested media frames. This characteristic undoes the separation of the notion of medium of communication, conventionally understood as representational print, broadcast, cinematic and digital formats, and the notion of environment, conventionally understood as that which enables, underlies or sustains life. The first is assumed to enclose a message and the second to enclose living organisms. It creates space and place as media of communication. An example is the Dau project, a narrative environment enacted in Ukraine from 2009 to 2011, and reiterated in Paris in 2019. The project was initially conceived by the Russian film director Ilya Khrzhanovsky in Moscow in 2005 as a setting for a film about the Soviet physicist Lev Landau. The constructed environment both reproduced and reflected on life in the Soviet era. People could enter the Dau project and live there in character for extended periods of time. James Meek (2015) explains,

> For more than two years, between 2009 and 2011, hundreds of volunteers, few of them professional actors, were filmed living, sleeping, eating, gossiping, working, loving, betraying each other and being punished in character, in costume, with nothing by way of a script.

Teodor Currentzis was cast as the lead actor, playing the part of the real-life Russian scientist Lev Landau. He lived, slept and ate there 24 hours a day for weeks at a time.

When interviewed, he stated that he participated in order to explore how to be himself and not to be himself at the same time: this situation would not work if you were not yourself, even though you also know it is a fiction. So effective was this 'immersion' in role and in situation, this double articulation of one's participant self and one's 'real' self, that when leaving the world of Dau and re-entering the outside world, some participants felt it was like visiting another time: the real world became like a stage or film set to them.

Michel Foucault's (1986) concept of heterotopia is useful for grasping the implications of the status of narrative environments as commonplace yet exceptional places. From Foucault's discussion of heterotopias his third principle is particularly useful. He focuses on the juxtaposition of several incompatible spaces in a single real place, the oldest example of which is the garden. He discusses the Persian garden as a microcosm which brings together all the elements of the world into one place. In this way, heterotopias compress space and time. For example, modern botanical gardens and zoological gardens both compress incompatible regions of the planet, one through the medium of plants and the other through animal life. Like gardens understood in this sense, narrative environments can gather together disparate elements in one place shaped by narrative to form a lens on the world. Foucault also discusses those heterotopias which can be understood to be "indefinitely accumulating time" (Foucault 1986: 26). His examples are museums and libraries as they took shape in the nineteenth century, when the collecting was based not on individual choice but on the idea of accumulating everything and establishing a universal archive which enclosed in one place, "all times, all epochs, all forms, all tastes, the idea of constituting a place of all times that is itself outside of time" (Foucault 1986: 26). Rather than assembling a collection which aspires to an eternal universality, narrative environments remain with historicity, compressing time using narrative, in order to create places for reflection on, and questioning the historical constitution of cultures. Foucault also discusses the way in which heterotopias open and close with specific rules of access, both isolating them and making them accessible. This corresponds to the looping and twisting dynamic of narrative environments which are both open to the everyday but distinct from the everyday. Narrative environments, like heterotopias, could be considered as "something like counter-sites, … . In which the real sites, all the other real sites that can be found within the culture are simultaneously represented, contested, and inverted" (Foucault 1986: 24).

As the examples above demonstrate, part of the emergence of narrative environments from the dynamics of the tripartite network is the enaction of frames. If the aim were to design wholly immersive experiences, frames would be invisible. This chapter argues that in the case of narrative environments it is crucial that the visitor or inhabitant becomes aware of the processes of framing, because the goal is to enable reflection on whether the existing frames are adequate and to consider what kind of reframing may be necessary for a sustainable culture. This question is the context for a discussion of authorship in the next chapter.

References

Allan, M. Hobkinson, R. and Hanna, J. (2017) How to integrate placemaking and branding through experience masterplanning. *The Brand Observer*. Online. Available HTTP: https://placebrandobserver.com/experience-masterplanning-how-to-guide/. Accessed 9 August 2018.

Argent PLC. (2001) *Ten Principles for a Human City*. Edition 3. Online. Available HTTP: https://www.kingscross.co.uk/media/Principles_for_a_Human_City.pdf. Accessed 26 October 2019.

Bell, A. and Alber, J. (2012) Ontological metalepsis and unnatural narratology. *Journal of Narrative Theory*, 42(2), 166–192. Online. Available HTTP: http://muse.jhu.edu/journals/jnt/summary/v042/42.2.bell.html. Accessed 18 March 2016.

Bennett, T. (2009) *The Birth of the Museum: History, Theory, Politics*. London: Routledge.

Bordwell, D. (2008) *Narration in the Fiction Film*. London: Routledge.

Buro Happold. (2017) Designing buildings wiki – masterplanning. *Buro Happold Engineering*. Online. Available HTTP: https://www.designingbuildings.co.uk/wiki/Masterplanning. Accessed 9 August 2018.

Carver, E. H. (2018) Graffiti writing as urban narrative. *Literary Geographies*, 4(2), 188–203.

Casabianca, J. (2013–17) *Julian de Casabianca Outings Project*. Online. Available HTTP: http://www.outings-project.org/#!about/c66t. Accessed 5 October 2019.

Certeau, M. D. (1984) *The Practice of Everyday Life*. Berkeley, CA: University of California Press.

Childs, M. C. (2013) *Urban Composition: Developing Community through Design*. New York, NY: Princeton Architectural Press.

Davies, M. L. (2011) *Imprisoned by History: Aspects of Historized Life*. London: Routledge.

Debord, G. (1956) Theory of the Dérive. *Les Lèvres Nues*, 9. Online. Available HTTP: https://www.cddc.vt.edu/sionline/si/theory.html. Accessed 8 February 2020.

Filep, C., Thompson-Fawcett, M and Rae, M. (2014) Built narratives. *Journal of Urban Design*, 19(3), 298–316.

Ford, G. and Zogran, M. (2017) 8 ways we can improve the design of our streets for protest. *Archdaily*. Online. Available HTTP: https://www.archdaily.com/873608/8-ways-we-can-improve-the-design-of-our-streets-for-protest. Accessed 5 October 2019.

Foucault, M. (1986) Of other spaces. *Diacritics*, 16(1), 22–27.

Fuhrmann, P. (2017) Anonymous group adbusting billboards in Berlin. *ParcCitypatory*. Online. Available HTTP: http://parcitypatory.org/2017/12/30/adbusting/. Accessed 9 August 2018.

Garrett, B. (2017) These squares are our squares: Be angry about the privatisation of public space. *Guardian*. [website]. Online. Available HTTP: https://www.theguardian.com/cities/2017/jul/25/squares-angry-privatisation-public-space. Accessed 9 September 2019.

Gaspar Maillol, M. (2010) Displaying F(r)ictions: Design as cultural form of dissent. *Negotiating Futures – Design Fiction, 6th Swiss Design Network Conference*. Basel: FHNW, pp. 106–117. Online. Available HTTP: http://www.historiadeldisseny.org/congres/pdf/38%20Gaspar%20Mallol,%20Monica%20FRICTIONS%20DESIGN%20AS%20CULTURAL%20FORM%20OF%20DISSENT.pdf. Accessed 5 October 2019.

Genette, G. (1980) *Narrative Discourse: An Essay in Method*. Ithaca, NY: Cornell University Press.

Goffman, E. (1974) *Frame Analysis and Essay on the Organisation of Experience*. Boston, MA: Northeastern University Press.

Habermas, J. (2010) *The Structural Transformation of the Public Sphere: An Inquiry Into a Category of Bourgeois Society*. Cambridge, UK: Polity.

Hatuka, T. (2011) Design protests in urban public space. *Metropolitics*. Online. Available HTTP: https://www.metropolitiques.eu/Designing-Protests-in-Urban-Public.html. Accessed 24 November 2019.

Heathcote, E. (2013) A place for cyberspace. *Financial Times*. Online. Available HTTP: https://www.ft.com/content/31ff7e18-661b-11e2-bb67-00144feab49a. Accessed 9 August 2018.

High Hopes. (1988) Directed by Mike Leigh. [DVD] UK. Portman Productions.

Howell, Julie (2019) Interview with Tricia Austin, 12 March 2019.

Hühn, P. et al. (eds.) (2019) *The Living Handbook of Narratology*. Hamburg: Hamburg University. Online. Available HTTP: http://www.lhn.uni-hamburg.de. Accessed 5 October 2019.

Improv Everywhere. (2014) The subway spa. *Improv Everywhere*. Online. Available HTTP: https://improveverywhere.com/2014/08/05/the-subway-spa. Accessed 8 July 2019.

KX. (2019) The story so far. *KX*. Online. Available HTTP: https://www.kingscross.co.uk/the-story-so-far. Accessed 10 September 2019.

Lyotard, J.-F. (1984) *The Postmodern Condition: A Report on Knowledge*. Manchester: Manchester University Press.

MacLeod, S. (2017) Image and life: Museum architecture, social sustainability and design for creative lives. In: Beisiegel, K. and Art Centre Basel, eds. *New Museums: Intentions, Expectations, Challenges.* Munich: Hirmer Verlag, pp. 174–183.

Manaugh, G. (2016) How augmented reality will reshape cities. *Motherboard.* Online. Available HTTP: https://motherboard.vice.com/en_us/article/ezpamw/zoning-forpokemon-go-and-augmented-reality. Accessed 9 August 2018.

Meek, J. (2015) Diary. *London Review of Books*, 37(19), 42–43. Online. Available HTTP: https://www.lrb.co.uk/v37/n19/james-meek/diary. Accessed 2 September 2018.

Minton, A., et al. (2018) *Regeneration Songs: Sounds of Investment and Loss in East London.* London: Penguin Random House.

Mumford, L. (1965) Utopia, the city and the machine. *Daedalus*, 94(2), 271–292. Utopia.

Palsson, Hannes (2019) Interview with Tricia Austin, 2 April 2019.

Parker, G. (2017) How private 'public' space in cities shuts out protest. *Financial Times.* Online. Available HTTP: https://www.ft.com/content/45cd3dbe-34dd-11e7-99bd-13beb0903fa3. Accessed 10 September 2019.

Pimlott, M. (2018) Interiority and the conditions of interior. *Interiority*, 1(1), 5–20. Online. Available HTTP: http://interiority.eng.ui.ac.id/index.php/journal/article/view/5. Accessed 9 August 2018.

Putnam, J. (2001) *Art and the Museum as Medium.* New York, NY: Thames & Hudson.

Rancière, Jacques (2004) *The Politics of Aesthetics: The Distribution of the Sensible.* London: Continuum.

Ryan, M.-L. (2004) Metaleptic machines. *Semiotica*, 150, 439–469.

Shenker, J. (2017) Revealed: The insidious creep of pseudo-public space in London. *The Guardian.* Online. Available HTTP: https://www.theguardian.com/cities/2017/jul/24/revealed-pseudo-public-space-pops-london-investigation-map. Accessed 21 November 2019.

Shklovsky, V. (1965) Art as technique. In: Lemon, L. T. and Reiss, M. J., eds. *Russian Formalist Criticism: Four Essays.* Lincoln, NE: University of Nebraska, pp. 3–24.

Strongman, Anna (2019) Interview with Tricia Austin, 18 October 2019.

Thorpe, A. (2014) Applying protest event analysis to architecture and design. *Social Movement Studies*, 13(2), 275–295.

VICE. (2018) I made my shed the number one restaurant in London. Youtube. [video]. Online. Available HTTP: https://www.youtube.com/watch?v=bqPARIKHbN8. Accessed 17 November 2019.

Waal, M. de and Lang, M. De. (2014–) *The Mobile City.* Online. Available HTTP: http://themobilecity.nl. Accessed 14 April 2018.

Websites

Art+Com. https://artcom.de/en/project/the-formation-of-hamburg

Argent LLP. https://www.argentllp.co.uk

Adbusters. https://www.adbusters.org

Central Saint Martins, University of the Arts London. https://www.arts.ac.uk/colleges/central-saint-martins

Extinction Rebellion. https://rebellion.earth

HumanKind. https://www.nationaltrust.org.uk/calke-abbey/features/humankind-at-calke-abbey

Improv Everywhere. https://improveverywhere.com

Pink Iceland. https://www.pinkiceland.is

Smithsonian Institution. https://www.si.edu/

Stalker/Osservatorio Nomade. http://www.osservatorionomade.net

Parque Explora. https://www.parqueexplora.org

9   From Sole Authorship to Co-creation

Given that narration is a core element of the design of narrative environments, as is creativity, it inevitably draws upon recent discourses and media theories concerning the creative process going back to the invention of the author and the artist, in their modern senses, in the eighteenth and nineteenth centuries. Thus, these two figures from the Western cultural imaginary affect the understanding of design and the designer. Since the early twentieth century, the figure of the visual artist combines creativity with critical intelligence, becoming the avant-garde artist, while the modernist writer breaks with many of the conventions of nineteenth-century realism, to highlight what might be called experiential realism. Given this cultural history, the assumption arises that the designer as creator must aspire to the authority of authorship, on the one hand, and the critical creativity of avant-gardism, on the other. Co-creation, as a principle, challenges the assumptions concerning creativity and authority as inherent in the individual, predominantly the male individual. Co-creation recognises that both authority and creativity are socially constituted and maintained, thus altering the characteristics and roles of the designer. The responsibility for creative practice cannot be given over to the author or artist as the singular creative genius. A rethinking of the creative process and the nature of what is produced is needed. The design of narrative environments enters the arena at a point where creative practice already incorporates an openness to collaborative and collective making, reception and iterative remaking by multiple professional and non-professional actors. The author and the artist are opened up to collectivity and the work is opened to continual revision, breaking the identification of the author and the artist with the work and the authoritative status that they together assume. The responsibility is shared for creation and its consequences. This distinguishes the design of participatory narrative environments from related practices which seek to maintain, for example, the status of the literary author through literary publishing and its prizes, and the status of the artist and the star architect, through international biennales and awards. The shift from sole creator and closed work to co-creation and open-ended participation is examined below through theoretical writings and participatory practices in urban design, art and technology. These points are further elaborated through several examples of participatory narrative environments.

An author has been thought of as the person who invents and crafts the content and intent of a story. The word author stems from the Latin '*auctor*', which meant father or founder and which also implied a notion of 'authority'. Author and authority both suggest taking the dominant role in decision-making. In this model, it is assumed that authors independently produce and control content, while readers or audiences consume their stories in an attempt to understand the authors' intentions. This was the norm in literary studies until the mid-twentieth century when the authority of the literary author was challenged by reception theory and reader response theory. These theories emphasised the role of the reader in constructing the meaning of a text. For example, in *The Open Work*, Umberto Eco (1989: 3) discusses the relationship of musical scores to their performances. He argues the performers refashion the piece according to their own sensibilities and their interpretation is part of the appeal of listening to the music. He says artists leave elements open to performers or publics to interpret "the form of the work of art gains its aesthetic validity precisely in proportion to the number of different perspectives from which it can be viewed and understood". Eco traces the question of audience interpretation, allegory, suggestiveness and ambiguity from Plato through the writing of Dante, Augustine and Bede in the Middle Ages, Baroque and Romantic poetry of the nineteenth century to the work of Kafka and James Joyce in the twentieth century.

In *The Death of the Author*, Roland Barthes (1968: 142–148) argues that it is the reader who interprets the text and consequently holds the power over its meaning. Barthes argued there is no secret meaning to be deciphered by the audience: "a text's unity lies not in its origin but in its destination". For Barthes, the author and the reader enter into a dialogue through their shared cultural semiotic resources. Moving the context from print culture to broadcast multimedia, cultural theorist Stuart Hall examines how audiences interpret television according to their own experiences. Hall (1973) discusses the politics of mass communication as a vehicle of the transmission of symbolic value and how different interpretations may arise depending on the ideological frames at play. While initially discussing high culture in the form of art, music and literature Eco, Barthes and Hall extend semiotic analysis to mass media and everyday situations. The figures of the author and the artist, particularly the avant-garde artist, belong to high culture. They have much less relevance for the kind of cultural production that takes place in the late twentieth and early twenty-first centuries, although they still play a huge part in the cultural imaginary. The starting point for the design of narrative environments is the refusal of the hierarchy of high and low culture, instead drawing on them as distinct modes of cultural production which can be cited and critically engaged.

In his essay 'What Is an Author?', Michel Foucault (1979) makes the point that authorship or the 'author function' is a comparatively recent phenomenon associated with the development of the novel in the eighteenth century and the cult of the individual arising from modernity, the Enlightenment and the capitalist system. He argues the author function is different from the author. It is a set of assumptions about the author created by means of legally specifying, reproducing, disseminating, selling and consuming the text, in other words, a set of beliefs constructed by the publishing industry. The author acquires their authority from the production system and the values and profit motives of the publishers who filter authors, legitimising some and not others, reinforcing the readers' role as consumers. The independent authority of the author is illusory.

Literature and mass media continue to provide lenses through which the lifeworld is represented and understood. The design of narrative environments acknowledges the prevalence of these ways of elaborating cultural meaning but recontextualises them by bringing them into relation with the lifeworld in both its experiential dimensions and in its materiality. Heavily pre-scripted narrative from literature and the media world is equivalent to the fixed forms of the material environment. The physical world however offers more scope for individuals and groups to reshape it. While a novel cannot be rewritten by readers or a film reshot by an audience, the built environment is susceptible to change by its inhabitants. They can deliberately re-create aspects of their given environment to emphasise their own interpretations of their circumstances. Stuart Brand (1997) presents a study of how industrial and residential buildings are modified

Figure 9.1 Personalised windows in a residential block, Maribor, Slovenia, 2012.

over time. He shows how buildings are mutable and capable of playing different roles. Wealthy owners pay engineers and architects to change their buildings at a structural level, but sometimes the residents make minor but significant modifications themselves. Figure 9.1 shows a residential block in Maribor, Slovenia, where each resident has customised their own window frame. The apparently finished building is re-opened by the inhabitants to become a part of their active interpretation, showing that the environment is not closed and finality cannot be imposed upon the physical and social environment.

This is an example of multiple authorship, involving multiple actors, each pursuing their own agenda. This kind of authorship comes into being after the formal 'completion' of an environment, as a deliberate act to change that environment. This differs from current practices of collaboration, co-creation, co-design or participatory design, which are based on inclusive strategies knowingly shared among diverse stakeholders to achieve a common goal, not from the moment of *reception* but from a continual process of *inception*.

Collaboration and Co-creation

Co-creation is particularly relevant for the design of narrative environments, as it produces new and dynamic ways to connect the people node to the narrative and environment nodes in the tripartite network. Collaboration among professional designers comes about for many reasons. For example, the complexity of the projects may require a range of expertise. Technical and entrepreneurial collaboration are also necessary business strategies to reduce risk. However conventionally, the practice of professional collaboration is not extended to the inhabitants or future users of spaces. Consultation with local residents or potential visitors does take place but the processes for this, developed in twentieth-century architecture practice and urban development, have been widely criticised as a tick-box system that simply collects opinions to legitimise development strategy and in no way involves any shared decision-making (Sanhoff 1999). This criticism reaches back to Sherry Arnstein's (1969) *Ladder of Citizen Participation*, based on her research on the different levels of citizen involvement in decision-making in urban planning processes in the United States. It has provided a useful model for more recent participatory approaches (Figure 9.2).

Over the past 70 years, two other threads in design have fed into the collaborative and participatory dimensions of the design of narrative environments: human-centred, market-driven design and socially engaged critical design. In the 1980s, industrial designer Bill Moggeridge promoted human-centred design, in which design decisions are informed by empathy with the people for whom you are designing, as opposed to design being solely driven by technology or aesthetics. This approach has helped to embed design research and design strategy as of equal importance to the physical outcome of design, whether it is a logo, a building or a service. The process was refined into 'design thinking' as a method, often described as a human-centred, empathetic approach to problem-shaping and problem-solving. Design thinking advocates working with clients and consumers to achieve collective engagement and support the communication of shared values, to spur transformation. As a business innovation, human-centred design thinking is rooted in an economic principle to make more contextually appropriate products and services and expand the market.

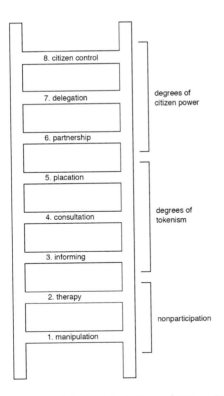

Figure 9.2 Arnstein's Ladder of Citizen Participation.

Alongside human-centred design thinking, socially purposeful design developed as a distinct design paradigm under which there are three strands. First, service design emerged in the 1990s incorporating the inventiveness and creativity among 'ordinary people' to solve everyday issues related to, for example, housing, diet, ageing, transport and work. Like the design of narrative environments, service design envisages customer or visitor journeys and uses personas (Cooper 2004), or imaginary characters constructed from characteristics based on social research. Although there are pros and cons to using personas, they are preferable to pages of written analysis on categories of target audiences that can seem very abstract. Personas offer concrete characters for the development of new narratives. Second, user experience design (UX) typically researches users at the beginning of the design process and then at the end when trialling the proposed solutions. Third, participatory design approaches, which involve recipients or inhabitants at more points in the design process, have gathered pace since 2000, influenced by principles from co-design. The term 'co-design' first appears in the UK in 1971 (Sanders and Stappers 2008). Co-design implies sharing authority in decision-making. The user assumes the role of expert in their area of experience. Co-designers work as mediators among partners, facilitating and designing workshops and communication networks. Co-designers also work as strategists, envisioning the steps and impact of the design, and as ideators generating concepts, visualising and catalysing ideas within transdisciplinary teams that include a mix of professional and non-professional experts. Co-design for social innovation, for example, aims to benefit multiple stakeholders and empower communities. The aspects which are most relevant to the design of narrative environments are those features of service design which engage with the everyday and the expanded role of design in the co-design process.

Another area of practice that has been considering the relationship between design and audience and which is relevant to the design of narrative environments in exhibition making is museums. Pille Runnel, Krista Lepik and Pille Pruulmann-Vengerfeldt (2014) have developed a ladder of engagement from their studies of people's relationships with museums. Starting from the lowest level of engagement, they progress through public, audiences, visitors and users to the highest level whom they suggest are participants. For Runnel, Lepik and Pruulmann-Vengerfeldt, 'public' means everyone with the potential to become engaged with the museum, although they do not form a unified group who can be reached in the same way. For the design of narrative environments, 'public' is a useful concept both because of its generality and inclusivity and for the possibility that it allows of defining specific publics, in terms of their histories and political constitution in civil society, with their implied rights and obligations.

Runnel, Lepik and Pruulmann-Vengerfeldt define the next level, audiences, as more engaged than public. They say the word audiences may describe people who are connected through online means only. The discourse on the word audience, developed in media studies, refers to those who just see, hear and make sense of the story. Nevertheless, they are skilled in audienceship. In other words, they are accustomed to interpreting particular visual and verbal codes and they are familiar with the social contracts that enable audienceship, that is, that being an audience involves work to make meaning. Audienceship in the physical world, however, also includes knowledge of codes of behaviour, for example, when to laugh or not laugh at live standup comedy. Laughing is rewarded by the pleasurable sense of belonging to a group and jointly interacting with a performer (Harbidge 2011). At live events, audiences may stay silent or heckle, sing along, stay seated, stand, clap or shout. As such, they have agency to shape the feel of the performance. As a result, audiences are a specific public that has been addressed and drawn in.

Runnel, Lepik and Pruulmann-Vengerfeldt place visitors at the next level saying that, by choosing to visit, they are more self-determining than audiences. This is not only true of museums but applies in other kinds of narrative environments, such as religious buildings, festivals, parks, heritage sites, art installations, brand experiences, narrativised educational spaces and public realm. However, as visitors, they are thereby invitation only and always have to leave. This signals their outsider status and their lack of involvement in any decision-making processes. Nevertheless, they assemble their own story as self-narrating visitors, as discussed by Tiina Roppola (2012).

While the next level discussed by Runnel, Lepik, and Pruulmann-Vengerfeldt is 'user', this term is not a principal concept guiding the design of narrative environments. The term user originated in human-computer interaction studies (Norman and Draper 1986). It suggests interaction with or use of an entity. For Runnel, Lepik and Pruulmann-Vengerfeldt, a 'user' is more engaged than a visitor. In narrative environments, visitors are considered as having specific demographic or ethnographic profiles, in contrast to the notion of user which implies universality.

The word collaborator is inserted into this hierarchy of engagement to describe people who actively contribute resources, such as objects or comments, to narrative environments. Collaborators are more engaged than visitors, who do not necessarily contribute. The result can be very compelling. For example, *The Gun Violence Memorial Project*, at the Chicago Architecture Biennial 2019, features four houses made of glass bricks (Figure 9.3). Each house represents the average number of lives lost due to gun violence each week in America. Each brick displays the name, year of birth and year of death of the person being honoured. Some of the bricks contain personal objects donated by

Figure 9.3 The Gun Violence Memorial Project, Chicago, USA, MASS Design Group 2019.

people who have lost family members to gun violence. Inside the house, visitors can hear audio recordings of interviews with the families. The presence of the objects and the audio heighten the power of the experience. It is worth noting in passing that the exhibit itself resulted from a different kind of collaboration, one that included MASS Design Group, artist Hank Willis Thomas and two gun violence prevention organisations, Purpose Over Pain and Everytown for Gun Safety. Both kinds of collaboration are relevant for the design of narrative environments.

Public contributions, such as those in *The Gun Violence Memorial Project*, have a profound impact on visitors' experiences because they provide multiple authentic voices sharing personal perspectives and emotions. Such narrative environments can also produce a sense of involvement among the contributors. However, the contributions do not change the format, methods or purpose of the narrative environment. In this situation, 'ordinary people' may collaborate and contribute but they do not participate in the design of strategies or frameworks (Austin 2018).

Runnel, Lepik and Pruulmann-Vengerfeldt use the word participant to describe those most fully involved in project development and realisation. At this, the highest form of engagement, participants share decision-making and, as such, co-create. There is a growing participatory impulse in art and design and the cultural industries as a whole. This is borne out by publications such as *The Art of Participation* (Frieling et al. 2008), *The Participatory Museum* (Simon 2010) and *Practicable: From Participation to Interaction in Contemporary Art* (Bianchini et al. 2016). In the context of the design of narrative environments, the tripartite network model, which incorporates principles of distributed agency, reciprocity and reflexivity, is open to full participatory design and co-creation.

Participatory Art Practice

In order to explore participatory practices in narrative environments, it is worth reflecting on participatory art practice which, since the 1960s, has blurred the distinction between art production and consumption, on the one hand, and art and life, on the other. Claire Bishop (2006) argues that a major figure in this strand of art practice is Joseph Beuys. His social sculpture is interesting because it opens the work of art to participation. However, his belief that every person is an artist is valuable in recognising a certain kind of egalitarianism but problematic in as far as it seems to be confined to being a radical pedagogy within art practice. Bishop describes how conceptual artist Tom Marioni devised the piece *The Act of Drinking Beer with Friends Is the Highest Form of Art*, in 1970 in the Oakland Museum. He called it an interactive installation. He set up a space with yellow light, jazz music, guest bartenders and gave away beer. People drank and socialised, without realising they were taking the stage. Their interactions became the work. In 2012, Martha Rosler, set up a garage sale in the Museum of Modern Art, New York, where visitors could browse and buy second-hand goods. In 1992, Rirkrit Tiravanija transformed the back rooms of a New York gallery into a working kitchen. The piece, part installation, part performance, was called *Untitled (Free)*. Tiravanija cooked Thai cuisine for his audience. Visitors first had to locate the backrooms; then they ate the food and talked to the artist and each other. While all of these artists challenge the production and consumption axis, nevertheless the participation tended to be within the horizon of art practice, and in consequence, the participants took part in the making of someone else's artwork. It was not their joint 'work'. Although still referencing the figure of the artist, art critic, historian and curator Nicolas Bourriaud (2002) coined the term 'relational aesthetics', to describe the development of what seemed like non-artistic everyday situations that artists chose to set up in galleries or stage as interventions. Bourriaud had noticed that artists, such as Rirkrit Tiravanija, instead of imagining utopias, were seeking to explore living in the here and now. For Bourriaud, relational art displaces visuality with intersubjective social relations. Rather than a displacement of visuality in terms of priority, the design of narrative environments conceives of visuality as continuing to be important. However, this is not in a traditional aesthetic sense but rather in the context of its significance for intersubjective and intercorporeal relations, much like Ranciere's (2004) conception of the partition of the sensible, which concerns the dynamic between intellectual sense-making and embodied perception and sensibility.

Bishop (2004) criticises Bourriaud for assuming that looking at art is passive and disengaged and that relational aesthetics are intrinsically democratic. She advocates exposing antagonism as a political act, such as is achieved in Tania Bruguera's '*Tatlin's Whisper #5*' at the Tate Modern, London in 2008. During this piece, visitors encountered two mounted policemen directing them around the space. Participation was compulsory. People were not warned that this was a performance piece and so it caused alarm and anxiety. This is an avant-garde strategy to unsettle the audience. Such confrontations may be used in narrative environments if the theme warrants an extreme or provocative approach to highlight issues of corporeal subjection and overt intersubjective power struggles.

In parallel with these art gallery-based initiatives, a trend called community art developed through the 1980s and 1990s. Critic Tom Finkelpearl (2014) describes how, in the early 1990s, a group of African American artists in Houston, Texas, developed an initiative, Project Row Houses, working with Rice University's architecture programme. The first step provided a space for artists but over time the group developed educational programmes, a laundromat and a ballroom. Community art, which was not initially regarded in high esteem by the art world, has now gained credibility and is currently described as socially engaged practice. It derives its value from a deliberate attempt to address social and political inequity and to shift power dynamics in deprived neighbourhoods. Socially engaged art practice embraces the concept of professionals and nonprofessionals working together. The citizen is seen as knowing more about their own life and circumstances than the professional and is regarded as a citizen expert, in line with the principles of co-design, representing, in some respects, cultural democracy in practice. It is, therefore, closer to the principles of the design of critical narrative environments than the artists mentioned above

An artist who spans both gallery art and direct interventions in the urban realm is Theaster Gates. As part of his oeuvre, Gates initiated a network connecting funders and local residents in low-income African American urban areas, refurbishing run-down buildings to transform them into cultural hubs. He explains that he creates situations, processes and events that are intended to improve the material circumstances of the participants by transferring the resources from large solvent institutions, such as elite universities, charitable foundations and arts organisations, to marginalised populations. Although there is a resemblance to performance art and relational aesthetics, Gates' work acts as a 'parasite' on centres of power and wealth. He diverts the flow of capital to create institutions mainly for black communities. Gates' work allows people to maintain their self-respect, rather than be seen as recipients of welfare services, while making visible the sociability of the black metropolis and creating archives and new buildings that establish a tangible heritage. Although he says the centres are the product of his art practice, they materially benefit local residents. Gates is operating in a sphere very closely related to narrative environments as a design practice, because it is woven into the urban fabric and because his placemaking has such a strong narrative component. However, in the absence of a better term, as he says in an interview (Gates and Marlow 2012), he defines his practice as art.

Gates' strategies resemble those of socially engaged architects aligned to a lineage of participatory, user-centred approaches emanating from urbanists active in the 1960s. One such activist was writer Jane Jacobs (2011), who maintained that urban regeneration should be a response to the human activities and events of the street. Socially engaged architecture and interest in self-organising urban design have produced a substantial body of critical writing and examples of practice (Bundell Jones, Petrescu and Till 2005). Public Lab, USA, is known for its groundbreaking participatory work. Large-scale initiatives in the UK include Participatory City, which is bringing participatory urbanism to Dagenham in East London. Such projects are usually situated within social and community contexts, with multiple partners. Engagements are preferably long term and new propositions may well challenge existing socio-economic and political paradigms, in order to bring about significant positive social change. These projects build upon informal urbanism, where citizens make DIY interventions in their neighbourhoods (Douglas 2018). From the perspective of the design of narrative environments, these urban and architectural approaches often use narrative to engage people and co-create scenarios to envision futures but they do not necessarily use narrative as a central methodological principle for the design of spatial experience.

Participatory Narrative Environments

Socially-engaged participatory narrative environments have embraced the principles of co-design and subscribe to the inclusion of multiple, diverse voices and user-generated content. An example is Songboard London, an interactive installation at Kings Cross, London, commissioned by the Greater London Authority for the London Olympics, 2012 (see Plate 12). It was 15 metres long and 2 metres high and was designed by students from MA Narrative Environments and BA Architecture at Central Saint Martins, University of the Arts London. It consisted of a wall of spheres, half yellow, half black, that were hand-sized and could be turned so that people interacting could spell out words or make simple pictures. In the spirit of the Olympics, it was designed to be accessible for all to interact with, regardless of nationality or language. It was an empty page, a creative invitation, onto which anyone could write or draw what they wanted. Being positioned at one of the busiest train stations in the UK, on the route to the Olympics, it attracted constant interaction from the moment it opened. It was self-regulating. Offensive words were edited out by others. Like every design, it entered into the politics of the existing space. In this case, as well as being an interactive installation, it also served a public relations function in covering an unsightly part of Kings Cross station, part of the promotion of London during the Olympics. Participatory work does not operate in isolation and may, under certain circumstances, become a vehicle for business or government ends (Figure 9.4).

An example of a group who are developing participatory narrative environments is the Digua community, Beijing, China. Designer Zishu Zhou, a graduate of MA Narrative Environments, founded the Digua community in 2015. 'Digua' means sweet potato in Chinese and refers to rhizomic root systems, networks in which each point is neither beginning nor end but a connection to other points (Deleuze and Guattari 2014). Zhou was concerned about the plight of an estimated one million young Chinese people who had moved from the country to the city in search of a better life and found themselves living in cramped and squalid conditions in the basements of tower blocks. The basements

Figure 9.4 Passers-by interacting with *Songboard London*, 2012 Olympics.

had been built originally as bomb shelters during the Mao era but were being rented out illegally. The basement dwellers were literally excluded from the network of opportunities above ground. Many of them were isolated and lacked basic knowledge about how to progress their lives. Zhou lived in one of the basements for two months to get to know the inhabitants and explore ways he might improve their situation. He devised and tested a library and a skill exchange system but neither of these integrated the basement dwellers with the community above ground. Finally, he developed a strategy to bring the people above ground down into the basements (Figure 9.5).

He envisaged folding the vertical functions of the tower block above, which were apartments, restaurants and offices, into the basements to create workspaces and leisure spaces, as an invitation to the people above, while enabling the people below to meet them. In the process, this created a new narrative frame for the basements, away from their Cold War past, weaving them into the entrepreneurial texture of contemporary China. The people above ground paid a minimal charge and the money was used to develop the residential areas of the basement for the benefit of the dwellers (see Plates 13 and 14). The new basements became social and economic places of exchange between the life above ground and the life below ground. They generated funds for material improvements and the employment of a local manager.

Zhou explains that there were two main steps in the process of development. In the first 'Digua' community in Beijing's Anyuanbelli neighbourhood, the basement was empty. Therefore, Zhou engaged the community above ground. He invited four grandmothers to visit the space. Their first reaction was that the space was very small and dark

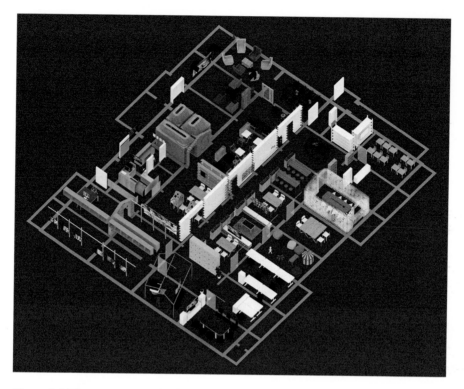

Figure 9.5 The Digua community plan for the conversion of an air defence basement, Beijing, 2015.

but that they would nevertheless like to use it. They said they believed if they came down, others would follow. Zhou realised that the limited size of the space was not an obstacle but the flow of people and the function had to be well managed. The second step was for the Digua team of eight people to involve all the residents living above ground in voting for the functions of the spaces in the basement. The team made various installations to encourage people to discuss the options with each other. Zhou secured initial funding from both private and government sources and the Anyuanbelli site opened in 2015. It had a children's play area, barber shop, library, 3D printing facility, cafe, an exercise area and meeting rooms, plus an open centre area which was used freely by the public (Figure 9.6).

The Digua team also installed a customised air ventilation system in response to major concerns of many of the residents. The day-to-day running of the basement was managed by a local resident. The team has since gone on to make a further four Digua community centres and a fifth was completed by the end of 2019. The Beijing government no longer allows people to occupy air defence basements so the Digua community is applying the same principles to locations above ground in the city of Chengdu with the same goal to enable social and economic exchange among established communities and newcomers.

Instead of simply making the basements more aesthetically pleasing, the Digua community fosters a community network. They work with the residents prior to and in the process of transforming spaces, involving them in decision-making and ensuring that they see the space as a resource designed for them. As Zhou (2019) says, this enables the

Figure 9.6 A new gym in the Digua community, Beijing, 2015.

Digua team to foster a community of 'pro-sumers', producers who are also consumers, who share their own creations and skills with their neighbours, while also benefiting from the skills of others. The project is a platform where communities can build their collective narratives and sharing economy, utilising the skills, interests and relationships that are already present within each community.

The next case study is located in the UK. In November 2014, a multidisciplinary design group, the Decorators, won a tender to research the relationship between public space and well-being at Chrisp Street Market in the Borough of Tower Hamlets, East London. They developed a project that demonstrated the value of the market as a civic and community space in order to help secure its future. The Decorators work with local authorities and public institutions to design, produce and deliver community building interventions, often in areas undergoing change. Chrisp Street Market is located at the centre of the Lansbury Estate, which was built as the 'live architecture' exhibit in the 1951 Festival of Britain. It was a utopian project promoting a new way of city living, with everything people might need on their doorstep, so there was therefore less need to leave the immediate neighbourhood. By 2014, like many twentieth-century utopian public housing schemes, the area had become deprived and the market was financially barely viable. This was all the more ironic since Canary Wharf, one of the main financial centres in London and one of the wealthiest zones in the world, is just five minutes away.

By 2014, due to a rapidly rising population and a lack of housing stock, Tower Hamlets, the local council, needed to build more accommodation and they wanted to explore how the district could be changed. Several government departments and private property developers were involved but controversy over private/public partnerships and experiences of gentrification made the local residents wary of any changes. The Decorators, who are Carolina Caicedo, Xavier Llarch Font, Suzanne O'Connell and

Mariana Pestana, brought a research-led narrative design process to this complex, multilayered environment. It is a good example of a project where the entire content came from the residents. The Decorators knew they would put on a series of events at the end of the project as tactical interventions which aimed to reclaim the civic character of the square, but they were entirely open to what these would be. The Decorators' design principle is first to research the context through 'conversations' with all parties, collecting stories from the widest range of groups and individuals. They go into spaces without assumptions or preconceived design propositions. The Decorators use their process of research and collaboration to evolve and test design proposals. As a result, their design proposals are tailor-made and site-specific. They ask, "What works for this place?" (Llarch Font 2019). They look with fresh eyes at what should be celebrated, what should be improved, creating communication networks among all of the actors, including residents and clients. They prefer not to make one-off spectacular interventions but to create a communication strategy and related events that play out over time. Indeed, their first move was to insist on extending the length of the project from two months to five months to allow time for research and trust building.

The clock tower at the market suggested the idea of broadcasting to the neighbourhood, so the Decorators created a radio station, a new institution in the market. "Everyone understood the idea 'Crisp Street market now has a radio station'" (Llarch Font 2019). Radio was an ideal medium as it is a conversational narrative vehicle and a platform for political opinion. Since the Decorators did not have enough time to go door to door to connect with individual residents, they set up the radio station in an empty shop to give them a physical presence. They were now visible and welcoming but not intrusive. People could come to them. They also designed and built a mobile radio unit that could be pushed into the market and fit in with the other market stalls. They held live shows and discussions, bringing invited experts from outside the area, members of the council and local people to co-curate events. They facilitated discussions about the future of the market, which normally took place in formal settings, bringing them into the public realm, flattening hierarchies and creating connections. They took the mobile structure to local institutions and invited individuals en route to contribute. They tried to find out what would excite and motivate local people rather than imposing their own ideas on the residents. They discovered the Lansbury Amateur Boxing Club. During a radio programme conversation, the idea came up to do a boxing tournament in the market. As it transpired, many local residents had family members who boxed but did not attend tournaments because of the expense. The Decorators and the boxing club worked together to put on a boxing match which was part of an official tournament (see Plate 15) (Figures 9.7 and 9.8).

The Decorators did not force collaborations; participants did what they do best, exercising and demonstrating their skills. The Decorators provided the context and the setting. They created a cohering framework. However, they were well aware that this framework needs to be flexible to allow new collaborations to arise. Llarch Font emphasises that when working on an engagement project with local communities you have to be open. He says when you have multiple participants, the challenges are higher and the risks are higher. You have to be there to steer and agree on the process. However, serendipity keeps the projects fresh and challenging. It is also important to achieve some output or legacy rather than just good conversations. The legacy depends on the project goals, whether that be community cohesion or to inform a regeneration project. Designers may need to insist that the client makes their intentions clear in the brief.

Figure 9.7 The Market Radio, Chrisp Street, London, The Decorators, 2014.

The final example is Umbrellium (2019), an internationally renowned design company whose stated vision is to 'make cities work for everyone'. It was launched by Usman Haque in 2013 as an extension of his design practice, Haque Design, which he initiated in the late 1990s. At Umbrellium, Haque brought together experts from several different sectors to explore the intersection of urban space, technologies and communities. This, he says, is often referred to as the 'smart city'. However, Haque is critical of that label, believing it is not important *what* is smart but *how* meaningfully people are engaged. Umbrellium is focussed on doing projects outside the studio, working with local authorities, local communities, complex contexts and, in most cases, employing technologies to start to "rip apart the question [of] who is the designer, who is governing what this thing does, how local communities can take ownership of the stuff" (Haque 2019).

Haque was trained as an architect but has always believed that space is dynamic, conversant and responsive to people. Questioning the role of the architect has been at the heart of everything he has done. Over the years, he says, digital technology has played a vital part in his process, in so far as it can counter the centralisation of single authorship. He is frustrated by, and sceptical of, the idea of the solitary male architect as an inventive genius and keeper of the knowledge. He says there are two conflicting explanations for his interest in alternative forms of creation. The first is explicitly political. As an architect, he sets out to question the structures of participation and role that architecture, as a durable cultural artefact, plays within the socio-political context, how it changes the way people interact with the world. He says the second explanation is quite personal:

> I don't know at the beginning what's right in terms of the final output [...] I have always deferred to someone else to make the final step. Even at architecture school

Figure 9.8 The Boxing Match, Chrisp Street Market, London, The Decorators, 2014.

there were all the people who were so confident about design, who grabbed a pen and did amazing drawings. The drawings looked beautiful but I didn't know if they were any good.

Haque sets out to share authorship as a method to deliver specific outputs. He sees collaboration as a process of working together on something, but, for him, participation talks more particularly about governance and owning the responsibility for what emerges. Umbrellium explores infrastructures that enable very different kinds of participation. It understands that there are many different flavours of governance systems and hierarchies of participation. Haque believes hierarchies cannot be completely removed. There needs to be a structure, but the question is whether that structure is rigid or whether it can evolve and dynamically respond to a given context.

Haque's thinking on participation evolved over time. In 2002, he developed a project called *Sky Ear*, with balloons that changed colour in response to electromagnetic fields in the sky. He wanted to reveal the invisible topography of electromagnetic space. The physical structure was quite large and every time he did experiments in public spaces, crowds would gather and people would ask if they could inflate or hold onto a section. He could not allow that without specific permission at that time but he was really struck by people wanting to know what he was doing and wanting to be part of it. About three years later, he started wondering how ordinary people could do something so large that it would change the city skyline, even though the structure might be temporary, and might, as a result, prompt in participants the same sense of accomplishment as an architect who has designed a tall building. He harnessed the experience of *Sky Ear* and devised *Open Burble* for the 2006 Singapore Biennale (see Plate 16). The final

Open Burble structure, which was 10 floors high, tapped into people's desire to make, design and do things together. Over the course of a day several hundreds of Biennale visitors became involved. Haque provided the kit of parts but the participants decided how to assemble them through their own internal debate about the aesthetics. The first few people self-organised into clusters of five. Haque and his team gave each person a carbon fibre 'molecule' and instructions on how to snap it together, a bit like Lego. They explained that the goal was to erect the largest possible structure. They made it clear that the design was up to the participants and that, for example, people might choose to make a line or a circle or other forms. When all the molecules were distributed, the next phase was for each group to connect to two other groups. They had to decide what to change and how to minimise or maximise connections. Finally, all groups connected to other groups to complete the structure.

Haque explains that, if this had been a computer screen, it would have been easy to make all the edges a particular colour but, because Burble was made of units connected to balloons inflated as buoyancy devices, the LED lights could not be connected to each other. However, Haque programmed the boards in the balloons following cellular automata principles. Each balloon could communicate only with the balloon next to it and, as a result, they self-configured according to the structure. Once the structure was complete, the team attached interactive handle-bars so that when it was inflated people could hold the handle-bars and wave gently or pull fast to pump in colour of different hues at the lower edge at different rates. The movement mixed colour according to the algorithm designed by Haque. This was an early exploration of artificial intelligence to see if algorithmic behaviour could be generated that would make the structure act like a lifelike entity. Although Haque designed the algorithm, the manifestation also responded to the structure designed by the participants and their interaction with the handle-bars to create moving patterns of light.

Haque says he does not want to be the designer in control of the final output. He realises decisions have to be made and he will own some but he is interested in exploring how many decisions can be taken by others. In Burble, Haque decided on the context, the design of the molecules and the algorithm. In all, he took about 60% of the decisions. The participants took about 40% of the decisions about the design of the structure and the tempo of the movement. More recently, in the project VoiceOver (2017–2018) more of the decision-making was taken by the inhabitant participants. Umbrellium produced VoiceOver three times, firstly in East Durham, secondly in Finsbury Park, London, and thirdly in Brighton, with different communities each time. VoiceOver was originally commissioned by Forma Arts and Media with East Durham Creates and took place across two villages which were ex-mining communities. There was no brief. It took two to three years to develop the project by doing workshops and experiments. What began to emerge was that people, even on the same street, no longer knew each other. This situation was very different for the older generation who had been brought up knowing their neighbours. It also emerged that people felt they did not have a connection to their wider community, particularly in relation to Durham. The project evolved into everyone having a VoiceOver social radio box, not just for listening but also for speaking. What is more, everyone on the network can hear the conversation and join when they want. Each box has a two-way connection with an antenna outside each participant's window. People see a representation of incoming and outgoing conversations in the form of light moving up and down the LED antenna (see Plate 17).

The project was developed without Umbrellium determining what it would be used for. Indeed, there was a whole layer of discussion among the participants about that.

Haque calls it a radically public communication network. Regarding the question of censorship, Haque asked the participants to tell him how they would like to govern the system. The participants in East Durham decided there should be somebody who could use a red button to turn off the system if it was abused.

In the Finsbury Park VoiceOver, Umbrellium worked in collaboration with digital arts group Furtherfield and took more of a back seat. The project was funded by the Museum of London and Thirteen Ways to develop 'An Idea for a future London'. VoiceOver was installed, as a hyper-local social radio network, in a tower block, Park House, selected on the basis on the residents' existing relationship with Furtherfield. Residents decided they wanted to share local news, event updates or general community chit-chat. Umbrellium played a 40% decision-making role. Brighton VoiceOver was commissioned by the Brighton Digital Festival for the trans and non-binary community which was, at the beginning of the project, not actually a community of place in that they did not live next to each other as in Durham and London. Whenever participants at home recorded something on their radio box, a banner embedded with LED lights located outside the Marlborough Pub and Theatre responded in real-time by displaying their chosen colour. As participation grew, the banner filled with coloured lights, signalling the growing number of participants. In Brighton, Umbrellium further reduced their role to technical support taking responsibility for about 20% of the final manifestation. The Umbrellium team gets its sense of achievement from enabling people to get what they want out of projects.

The long location-based, lead-in workshop process, typically two to three years, ensures relevance and specificity. Although individual participants might leave the area before the project is finalised, they will nevertheless have helped shape the project. Some people will become more involved than others. Flexibility on participation needs to be built into the system (Haque 2010). The beginning of a project has no firmly defined edges. There may be some elements agreed such as dates and stakeholders. Umbrellium start by doing workshops with a small group of people to establish the first iteration of the project goal. The participants identify other stakeholders who are invited to the next workshop to discuss, debate and refine or reformulate the goal. This process is repeated, expanding the participant group, until a clear plan is jointly conceived. However, there is no point at which the goal is completely fixed. The goals are questioned throughout. Participants come prepared to work, ready to share their thoughts. They write, draw out connections between ideas and explore each other's perspectives. At each workshop, something tangible is made. Sometimes there are really heated discussions. Disagreements go on record and Umbrellium believes that even if people do not agree they can still work together (Haque 2017). Throughout the workshops, the designers are not acting in a traditional role as decision-makers, arbiters of good taste or functionality. They are facilitators. Their role is to keep the focus and manage the conflicting perspectives through negotiation and to establish and maintain trust. These are all design steps published as an urban innovation toolkit, on Umbrellium's website. The toolkit was commissioned by the Future Cities Catapult.

Haque aims to create ongoing projects that are run by the participants. An example is Cinder, a project for a school in a recent urban development at Trumpington on the outskirts of Cambridge, England. Umbrellium worked with schoolchildren in their new high-tech school building which was filled with sensors to manage environmental sustainability monitoring systems. The outcome was a digital cat called Cinder, which can be seen through an augmented reality app on students' mobile phones. Cinder lives in the network hunting for food and the students have to make a decision about what to feed

Figure 9.9 Cinder Augmented Reality Mirror, Cambridge, UK, Umbrellium, 2016.

it based on reading the sustainability data, for example, how much solar energy has been produced. The cat grows or shrinks depending on its state of health. As the students take on the responsibility for keeping the cat healthy, the project becomes a compelling way to engage them with environmental sustainability. The interface has to be easy enough to use, not by lessening the ambition or simplifying the system, but by making the first step low friction and high reward (Figure 9.9).

Another ongoing Umbrellium project is Pollution Explorers which was set up in London, Paris and Brussels in 2017. Haque has a long-standing interest in environmental issues. In 2008, he developed an internet of things data platform for citizen science to monitor radiation data and air quality data. Pollution Explorers actively involves people in the process of monitoring levels of air pollution. First, Umbrellium ran workshops with 20–30 people in neighbourhoods where there is limited air quality data or where there is no other data, such as traffic noise levels, that can be correlated. Second, two groups of local residents walked the neighbourhood to map pollution through their own perception as well as using digital sensors. The groups were given a gestural vocabulary to perform their perception of, for example, higher levels of pollution near roads. By wearing smart outfits, data about their movements were captured. Interestingly, the data collected through the group's subjective experiences is quite accurate in terms of levels of pollution. The group also attracted attention on the street and encouraged others to become involved. Umbrellium took all the data to produce a much higher resolution map of air quality than the norm. They also asked the people who attended the workshops to commit to some action that would improve air quality and they have had a 90% success rate in participants following their pledges. The project resulted in better data, better informed and empowered citizens and incremental behaviour change (Figure 9.10).

Haque sees digital technology as a condensation of political and socio-cultural practices deriving from and influencing our lives. What concerns him most now is that the decisions about the production of technology are being made behind closed doors in

Figure 9.10 WearAQ, Tower Hamlets, London, Umbrellium, 2017.

Silicon Valley by very powerful, non-diverse groups of people. He says technology is sold to us as convenience and optimisation. As we buy into these ideas, we are letting the algorithms make decisions for us. Haque believes change is coming, no matter what, and the question is: What change do we want and how do we get to it? He says we have seen that our democratic institutions are not producing the best possible outcomes: our environmental systems, our financial systems and even our technological systems are not adequate to deal with the complexity of the world. Whether we use the word participation or not, what has previously been a strict hierarchical structure is not working and is under threat.

Haque says he does not know if Umbrellium is working with narrative. For him, content and framework are the same thing. His interest is that there should be no single narrative. Multiplicity drives Umbrellium's projects and the outcomes cannot be anticipated in advance. The design of narrative environments advocates this kind of narrative openess for example, the Digua community and the Decorators projects are open, episodic narratives. Such open, participatory narratives share some structural similarities with online multiplayer game worlds. Both provide frameworks in which participants negotiate, act and, as a result, events unfold episodically in the present around the themes available in the framework. Espen Aarseth (1997) describes this as ergodic narrative. However, online gaming and the work above differ in terms of purpose. While gaming is part of the entertainment industry, the work above is more politically motivated in setting out to make a tangible difference to people's lives by bringing important decisions back to them.

As argued above, the nineteenth-century concept of the author and the twentieth-century concept of the avant-garde artist persist as part of the modern Western cultural imaginary. This is not the approach to creativity which is advocated through the design of participatory narrative environments. The values of authority and authenticity which are assumed in the figures of the author and the artist arise in the design of participatory narrative environments through negotiation and shared decision-making as collective processes, rather than from individual qualities. Participatory narrative environments actively incorporate diversity. This is not to argue that the designer's aesthetic repertoire is not valuable in the communication process which grounds negotiation. The designer's professional skills should not be dismissed in the co-creation process. This leads to a recognition that the designer has several roles: as an expert in visual and spatial intelligence; as a group facilitator; and as an activist with a socio-political goal. These roles are potentially contradictory and require considerable skill to integrate. Constant vigilance is needed to ensure that they are being appropriately and legitimately deployed at any point in the overall process. This attention to the ethical dimensions in the design of participatory narrative environments can be seen in the examples of the Digua community, the work of the Decorators and the work of Umbrellium. They show how it is possible to combine critical practice and co-creation. The design of participatory narrative environments is not a deterministic or coercive approach. Non-participation must be a choice for the inhabitants or visitors. Adapting Alistair Macintyre's (2007: 216) insight, the starting point for the design of narrative environments is not what story do I want to tell, but rather, "of what story or stories do I find myself a part?" In some ways, this is a reworking of Marx's (2003) contention that people make their own histories but not as they please, and not under circumstances of their own choosing, but under already existing conditions given by and transmitted from the past. It is insights such as these that are incorporated into the tripartite model that guides the design of narrative environments.

References

Aarseth, E. J. (1997) *Cybertext – Perspectives on Ergodic Literature*. Baltimore, MD: Johns Hopkins University Press.

Arnstein, S. (1969) A ladder of citizen participation. *Journal of the American Planning Association*, 35(4), 216–224.

Austin, T. (2018) The designer's role in museums that acta as agents of change. In: McCleod, S., Austin, T., Hale, J, and Ho Hing-Kay, O. eds. *The Future of Museum and Gallery Design: Purpose, Process, Perception*. London: Routledge.

Barthes, R. (1968) The death of the author. In: Heath, S. ed. *Image – Music – Text*. London: Fontana, pp. 142–148.

Bianchini, S. et al. (2016) *Practicable: From Participation to Interaction in Contemporary Art*. Cambridge, MA: MIT Press.

Bishop, C. (2004) Antagonism and relational aesthetics. *October*, 110, 51–79.

Bishop, C. (ed.) (2006) *Participation*. Cambridge, MA: MIT Press.

Blundell Jones, P., Petrescu, D. and Till, J. (eds.) (2005) *Architecture and Participation*. London: Spon Press.

Bourriaud, N. (2002) *Relational Aesthetics*. Dijon: Presses du Réel.

Brand, S. (1997) *How Buildings Learn: What Happens after They're Built*. New York, NY: Penguin.

Bruguera, T. (2008) *Tatlin's Whisper #5* [Art performance] Tate Modern. Online. Available at HTTPS: https://www.tate.org.uk/art/artworks/bruguera-tatlins-whisper-5-t12989. Accessed 8 February 2020.

Cooper, A. (2004) *Inmates Are Running the Asylum*. Indianapolis, IN: Sams.

The Decorators. (2013–14) Chrisp street on air. *The Decorators*. Online. Available HTTP: http://the-decorators.net/Chrisp-Street-on-Air. Accessed 11 April 2018.

Deleuze, G. and Guattari, F. (2014) *A Thousand Plateaus: Capitalism and Schizophrenia*. London: Bloomsbury Academic.

Douglas, G. (2018) *The Help-Yourself City: Legitimacy and Inequality in DIY Urbanism*. New York, NY: Oxford University Press.

Eco, U. (1989) *The Open Work*. Cambridge, UK: Harvard University Press.

Finkelpearl, T. (2014) Participatory art. In: Kelly, M. ed. *Encyclopedia of Aesthetics*. Oxford, UK: Oxford University Press.

Foucault, M. (1979) What is an author. In: Harari, J. V. ed. *Textual Strategies: Perspectives in Post-Structuralist Criticism*. London: Methuen, pp. 141–160.

Frieling, R. et al. (2008) *The Art of Participation: 1950 to Now*. New York, NY: Thames & Hudson.

Gates, T. (2019) *Theaster Gates*. Online. Available HTTP: https://www.theastergates.com/. Accessed 8 July 2019.

Gates, T. and Marlow, T. (2012) Theaster Gates [interview]. *White Cube*. Online. Available HTTP: https://whitecube.com/channel/channel/theaster_gates_in_the_studio_2012.

Hall, S. (1973) Encoding and decoding in the television discourse. *CCCS Stencilled Occasional Papers*, Media Series No. 7. Online. Available HTTP: https://www.birmingham.ac.uk/Documents/college-artslaw/history/cccs/stencilled-occasional-papers/1to8and11to24and38to48/SOP07.pdf. Accessed 08 July 2019.

Haque, U. (2010) On the design of participatory systems – for the city or for the planet. *Haque Design and Research*. Online. Available HTTP: https://www.haque.co.uk/papers.php. Accessed 8 July 2019.

Haque, U. (2017) Mutually assured construction. *Medium*. Online. Available HTTP: https://medium.com/@uah/mutually-assured-construction-6b3f90fd3083. Accessed 8 July 2019.

Haque, Usman (2019) Interview with Tricia Austin, 4 June 2019.

Harbidge, L. (2011) Audienceship and (Non)laughter in the stand-up comedy of Steve Martin. *Participations: Journal of Audience & Reception Studies*, 8(2), 128–144.

Jacobs, J. (2011) *The Death and Life of Great American Cities*. New York, NY: Vintage Books.

Llarch Font, Xavier (2019) Interview with Tricia Austin, 9 May 2019.

Macintyre, A. (2007) *After Virtue: A Study in Moral Theory*, 3rd ed. Notre Dame, IN: University of Notre Dame Press.

Marx, K. (2003) *The Eighteenth Brumaire of Luis Bonaparte*. Mountain View, CA: Socialist Labor Party of America.

Norman, D. and Draper, S. (1986) *User-Centered System Design: New Perspectives on Human-Computer Interaction*. Hillsdale, NJ: Erlbaum.

Ranciere, J. (2004) *The Politics of Aesthetics: The Distribution of the Sensible*. London: Continuum.

Roppola, T. (2012) *Designing for the Museum Visitor Experience*. New York, NY: Routledge.

Runnel, P., Lepik, K. and Pruulmann-Vengerfeldt, P. (2014) Visitors, users, audiences: Conceptualising people in the museum. In: *Democratising the Museum*. Frankfurt: Peter Lang Publishing Group, pp. 219–238.

Sanders, E. and Stappers, P. (2008) Co-creation and the new landscapes of design. *Codesign*, 4(1), 5–18.

Sanhoff, H. (1999) *Community Participation Methods in Design and Planning*. New York, NY: Wiley.

Umbrellium (2019) Umbrellium [Website]. Online. Available at HTTPS: https://umbrellium.co.uk/. Accessed 8 February 2020.

Simon, N. (2010) *The Participatory Museum*. Santa Cruz, CA: Museum 2.0.

Zhou, Spencer (2019) Interview with Tricia Austin, 8 September 2019.

Websites

Participatory city. http://www.participatorycity.org

Epilogue

Design practices are becoming ever more vital to our precarious world. The expanding and increasingly important roles played by design practitioners come with greater socio-political and ecological responsibilities. The design of narrative environments responds to this shift through innovations in design education and design practice. It reimagines the figure of the designer and the processes of designing by adopting an open, systemic, multidisciplinary approach that promotes collaboration, participation and negotiation among disciplines, institutions and publics. It produces a dialogue between practice-led research and research-led practice in iterative cycles of learning.

As a flexible basis from which to proceed, and also as part of its pedagogy, the design of narrative environments has developed a tripartite network model. This model enables designers gradually to deepen their understanding of the complexity of contemporary issues. The aim is to create environments that enable publics to engage critically with those issues through their own experiences. The model posits that human action cannot be understood independently from the cultural narratives and the environmental forms in which that action is embedded and through which it is enacted. The design of narrative environments is an explicit, reflexive focus on the ways in which narrative practices and spatial practices are interwoven to constitute an environmental understanding of the human. As the examples have shown, the tripartite network model has value in the design process, in the formulation of strategy, in the research process and as an organisational guide for collaboration.

The premise for the design of narrative environments is that we are all subject to the stories and the places in which we find ourselves. Our agency as individuals, groups or societies emerges from those specific conditions. The design of narrative environments therefore has developed a methodological framework encompassing a number of principles. The framework interrelates dramatic conflict and agonistic politics; story content and cultural imaginaries; multimodal, embodied spatial storytelling; engagement through interaction, imagination and perception; realising the critical through the immersive; enacting practical, poetic and political dynamics through framing and reframing; and practising co-creation to reconfigure the design process and evolve the roles of the designer. Together, these facilitate the creation of narrative environments that are both in the world and about the world. Such places have a double existence. They both demonstrate and represent human entanglement in the world. They allow us to perceive our actions in a different light and, as a consequence, enable us to decide whether and how we need to act differently.

Index

Italic page numbers indicate figures or photos.

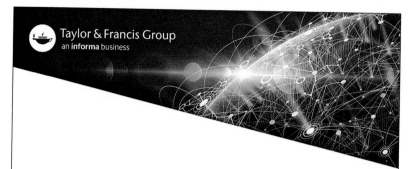